CW00448829

British Studies Series

General Editor JEREMY BLACK

Published

Forthcoming

(List continued overleaf)

Thomas Mayer **Britain, 1450–1603**
Michael Mendle **The English Civil War and Political Thought**
Alexander Murdoch **British History, 1660–1832**
W. Rubinstein **History of Britain in the Twentieth Century**
Howard Temperley **Britain and America**

British Studies Series
Series Standing Order ISBN 0–333–69332–9

You can receive future titles in this series as they are published by placing a standing order. Please contact your bookseller or, in case of difficulty, write to us at the address below with your name and address, the title of the series and the ISBN quoted above.

Customer Services Department, Macmillan Distribution Ltd
Houndmills, Basingstoke, Hampshire RG21 6XS, England

Retreat from New Jerusalem
British Politics, 1951–64

Kevin Jefferys
Senior Lecturer
University of Plymouth

First published 1997 by
MACMILLAN PRESS LTD
Houndmills, Basingstoke, Hampshire RG21 6XS
and London
Companies and representatives
throughout the world

ISBN 0–333–62970–1 hardcover
ISBN 0–333–62971–X paperback

A catalogue record for this book is available
from the British Library.

This book is printed on paper suitable for recycling and
made from fully managed and sustained forest sources.

10   9   8   7   6   5   4   3   2   1
06   05   04   03   02   01   00   99   98   97

Printed in Hong Kong

Typeset by T&A Typesetting Services, Rochdale, England.

Published in the United States of America 1997 by
ST. MARTIN'S PRESS, INC.,
Scholarly and Reference Division
175 Fifth Avenue, New York, N.Y. 10010

ISBN 0–312–16538–2

For Peter and Katie

Contents

List of Illustrations

All cartoons are by 'Vicky' (Victor Weisz) and reproduced with permission of the *Evening Standard* and the *Daily Mirror*.

Acknowledgements

I am grateful to many individuals and institutions for the help they have provided in the preparation of this work. Among those I should particularly like to mention are Harry Bennett, Rodney Lowe, Nick Patch (for his invaluable assistance as Research Assistant on the project), Nick Smart, Richard Williams, Simon Winder and Ina Zweiniger-Bargielowska.

Thanks must go to numerous archivists and archive assistants, especially at the following: Birmingham University Library; Bodleian Library, Oxford; Churchill College, Cambridge; the Centre for the Study of Cartoons and Caricature, University of Kent, Canterbury; Leeds University Library; National Museum of Labour History, Manchester; the National Newspaper Library, Colindale; the Public Record Office, Kew; Trinity College, Cambridge.

For permission to use copyright material I am indebted to: Lady Avon (Sir Anthony Eden papers); Dr Ann Gold (Lord Boyle papers); Conservative Central Office (Conservative Party papers, Bodleian Library, Oxford); *The Economist* (issues dated 3 July 1954, 28 June 1958, 25 July 1959, 14 September 1963); Macmillan General Books (Harold Macmillan, *Tides of Fortune* and *At the End of the Day*); Nigel Nicolson (Harold Nicolson diaries); Peters, Fraser & Dunlop Group Ltd (extracts from Alistair Horne's *Macmillan*, Anthony Sampson's *Anatomy of Britain* and Arthur Koestler's edited volume *Suicide of a Nation?*); the Public Record Office; the Master and Fellows of Trinity College, Cambridge (Lord Butler papers); and the University of Chicago Press (for Figure 1, 'The British Electorate, 1960': which originally appeared in Mark Abrams, 'Social Class and British Politics', *Public Opinion Quarterly*, xxv: 3 (1961).

Introduction

In October 1951 Winston Churchill returned in triumph to Downing Street. After two hard-fought elections in eighteen months, the Conservatives secured a small but workable parliamentary majority, finally dislodging the Labour government under Attlee that swept to power in 1945. It had been no easy ride for Labour ministers. Clement Attlee's Cabinet had been confronted by desperate economic hardships and was forced to devalue sterling in 1949. Labour's large majority all but disappeared at the general election early in 1950, and the outbreak of the Korean War later in the year imposed crippling new defence burdens. It also undermined the unity of the government, culminating in Aneurin Bevan's resignation from high office and the emergence of a disaffected 'Bevanite' left. With Attlee unwilling to prolong the life of his second administration, the way was open for the Conservatives to complete their recovery from the humiliation of 1945. This required exploiting both Churchill's reputation as Britain's wartime saviour and the new-found reputation for progressive Toryism cultivated by loyal lieutenants such as R. A. ('Rab') Butler. At the heart of the Tory campaign in 1951 was a popular pledge to end the continued austerity that was said to have resulted from socialist mismanagement. Yet Labour in defeat remained defiant. Outgoing ministers looked back with pride on what had been achieved. The face of domestic politics had been altered by the introduction of a 'post-war settlement': extensive welfare reform; a mixed economy containing many newly nationalised industries; and the maintenance of high wartime levels of employment. Labour leaders also took comfort from the narrowness of the party's defeat. Some regarded opposition as a welcome respite after several exhausting years in office, confident that the Tories would be exposed as unfit to govern. The onward march of democratic socialism, it was believed, would soon be resumed. Such confidence was seriously misplaced: Churchill and his successors, as we shall see in what follows, were to remain at the helm for thirteen years. The 'onward march' would have to wait.

Historians have debated long and hard about the sort of Britain the Conservatives inherited in 1951. The Attlee governments have no shortage of admirers. The counsel for the defence has included distinguished writers such as Kenneth Morgan, Henry Pelling, Alec Cairncross and Peter Hennessy, who regard the 1945–51 administrations as Labour's 'finest hour'. As well as ensuring economic recovery after the ravages of war, ministers established – with reforms such as Bevan's health service – the framework of a welfare state designed to provide protection 'from the cradle to the grave'. In short, Labour went some way towards satisfying wartime demands for a 'New Jerusalem'.[1] Others have been less impressed. The case for the prosecution has been put firstly by left-wing critics, who see the period as one of wasted opportunity. Instead of using the 1945 victory to introduce wholesale socialist change, Labour stands accused of cautious reformism at home – failing to break down class barriers or to redistribute wealth – and a foreign policy that tied Britain to the militantly capitalist United States.[2] From a second and alternative standpoint, Corelli Barnett has taken the lead in criticising ministers for introducing too much rather than too little socialism. In his concern to explain Britain's relative economic decline, Barnett attacks wartime evangelists of a 'Brave New World', for example Beveridge and Keynes, who were allowed to prevail over those who were bleakly aware of the 'Cruel Real World' of lost exports and vanished overseas investment. The folly of giving priority to welfare reform over economic regeneration was compounded by Labour, with the result that Britain missed a unique opportunity to remake itself industrially while her rivals were crippled by defeat and occupation. In this line of thinking, the state had overstretched itself: full employment was to lead to higher inflation, and the newly imposed 'burden' of social provision was unsustainable in the long term.[3]

Both lines of attack on Attlee have been forcefully rebutted. The weakness of the Labour left in the late 1940s indicated that a more radical agenda was not readily available. Corelli Barnett's critics have also been quick to respond, pointing out the remarkable success of Labour in boosting industrial production, manufacturing output and the volume of exports (the latter up by 73.1 per cent over five years). The priority given to social needs was hardly surprising given the nation's verdict in 1945: voters promised jam tomorrow and homes fit for heroes were adamant that 'never again' should there be a return to the misery associated with inter-war Britain. If there was a failure to modernise industrial infrastructure, then this could not realistically be expected of a government hemmed in by external constraints and harried by the Tory opposition.[4]

Other nations, moreover, demonstrated that it was possible in time to achieve *both* economic regeneration and social reform. Far from imposing crippling costs, the British version of the welfare state has been described as 'an austerity product of an age of austerity'; it consumed quite limited resources, especially when regarded as a positive contributor to the economy rather than simply as a burden upon the taxpayer.[5] Barnett's argument also fails to take account of the 'fair-shares' ethos left by the searing experience of war. 'What got us through the war', Attlee said in 1950, 'was unselfishness.' Recent writers have been keen to stress that – alongside the priority given to regaining lost export markets – Labour ministers sought to put the needs of the community before those of the individual. There was, in short, a desire for moral as well as economic change, an unusual combination of 'hope and public purpose'.[6] Indeed one cause of Labour's demise in 1950–1 has been identified as the party's mistaken view that voters fully shared its ethical vision. Measures to sustain a wartime sense of community, instead of transforming people into 'active citizens', foundered in the face of apathy. But the effort had been made. 'There were many more responsible than the Labour Party', claims one recent study, for ensuring that the high ideals of the 1940s were 'never achieved'.[7]

Controversy about Britain in the 1950s has been less prominent but similarly intense. In the first place, there is little agreement as to which label most accurately describes the years of Conservative government after 1951. The 'affluent society', the 'opportunity state', the 'stagnant society' – these are but a few of the many terms used, either at the time or subsequently, to sum up British society as it gradually left behind the legacy of war. At the level of popular discourse, opinions about the 1950s are polarised. Some, looking back from the 1990s, have tended to see the 1950s as a golden age when family values prospered, the streets were safe to walk and the nation possessed an enviable sense of community. Others, such as the journalist Peter Kellner, challenge nostalgic images of a Britain where gardens were seemingly always tidy and bakers were said to be selling warm, crusty bread on every street corner:

Were the Fifties really that idyllic? My answer is that they were not, and that, in truth, that decade did Britain far more harm than

the Sixties. In 1950, Britain was a stable society whose infrastructure and industrial base had survived the war intact. By 1960 we
were the sick man of Europe. Along the way we nonchalantly
resisted almost every attempt to open British society to new ideas,
new freedoms and new talent. We blew it.[8]

Here we find echoes of the politcal debate carried out in the run up
to the election in 1964 that finally dislodged the Tories from power.
Labour spoke of 'thirteen wasted years', alleging that the competitive
advantages of 1951 had been squandered. Conservatives retorted
that prosperity had replaced the hardships associated with the late
1940s and that unemployment averaged less than 2 per cent since
they came to power, compared with 9 per cent for much of inter-war
period.[9]

These claims and counter-claims have been taken up by contemporary historians, though, in contrast to the Attlee years, detailed
studies of the 1950s remain thin on the ground. Those few accounts
which focus exclusively on the whole of the 1951–64 period were
written over twenty years ago, without the benefit of access to official
papers.[10] More recent work has taken several forms. We have, for
example, several assessments of individual administrations, such as
Anthony Seldon's study of Churchill's 'Indian Summer' and Richard
Lamb's work on the Eden government and Macmillan's premiership
from 1957 to 1963.[11] Numerous biographies have appeared, not only
of Tory prime ministers but also of opposition leaders such as Hugh
Gaitskell and Harold Wilson.[12] Economic and social policy has also
received considerable attention, though usually as part of broader
studies of the welfare state or the British economy through to the
present day.[13] Out of this disparate body of literature, two ideas have
attracted broad, if far from unanimous, support. One presents the
period as the heyday of post-war consensus, an era of bipartisanship
which persisted for a generation after the war. 'Butskellism', named
after Gaitskell and Butler as successive Labour and Tory Chancellors, has been described as 'a fundamental idea in understanding the
politics of the 1950s', signifying cross-party acceptance of the mixed
economy and the welfare state.[14] This trend in policy was said to
reflect a second theme – the ability of Conservative governments, in
spite of periodic difficulties, to deliver growing prosperity. As class
tensions became less apparent, party leaders were increasingly
persuaded of the need for moderate policies that appealed to the

political middle ground, especially to the so-called 'affluent worker'. In the words of Kenneth Morgan, Britain in the 1950s seemed 'remarkably tranquil, marooned in what the Americans once called "the politics of the dead centre", all passion spent'.[15]

Some have been reluctant to accept this picture of affluent consensus. Harriet Jones has questioned the notion of cross-party harmony during Churchill's premiership, and Neil Rollings has pointed to the need for greater precision in the use of terminology. While 'consensus' has been applied to a broad swathe of domestic policy, 'Butskellism' should more accurately be confined to the use of Keynesian demand management in maintaining full employment. By this definition, Rollings claims, there were significant ideological differences between the parties in the 1945–55 period.[16] However, there have been few attempts hitherto to produce an up-to-date overview of the various connecting themes in domestic politics between Churchill's return to Downing Street in 1951 and Labour's victory at the 1964 election. This book sets out to provide such a study. The initial aim, evident in the first four chapters, is to assess how the party battle was conducted in an era of unusually close election contests, and to demonstrate how intimately party fortunes were connected with the performance of the economy. As the beneficiary of improving world trade, Churchill was able to hand over the premiership to Eden in 1955 confident of a second Tory election success, especially as Attlee's final years as Labour leader were plagued by internal feuding. For much of the 1955 parliament, however, the Conservatives appeared vulnerable to economic malaise and to an opposition revitalised under the leadership of Gaitskell. After Eden's resignation was hastened by the Suez crisis, his successor Macmillan trailed in the popularity stakes for as long as the economy remained sluggish. By 1958–9 he was able to engineer a consumer boom sufficient to assist the Tories in securing an unprecedented third successive election victory. Yet by the early 1960s, as we shall see, economic mismanagement combined with a host of other problems – such as the notorious Profumo scandal – to push the government firmly on the defensive until Macmillan's retirement in 1963. The scene was set for Labour's resurgence and Harold Wilson's triumph of October 1964.

The second objective in what follows is to analyse some of the broader questions touched on above, such as the paradoxical relationship between affluence and 'economic decline', the nature and

extent of 'consensus politics', and the changing class composition of
British society and its influence upon electoral behaviour. These
themes are explored in Chapters 5 to 7.[17] By the time Macmillan left
office, the government's policy difficulties were seen as part of a
deeper malaise with roots stretching back over a long period.
Chapter 5 investigates the numerous contemporary critiques which
saw Britain as a 'stagnant society', and looks at scapegoats for the
nation's plight, notably the 'us and them' mentality in industry and
the various political institutions pilloried as part of an outdated
'Establishment'. This is followed by an assessment of what Conservative ministers called 'the opportunity state' – efforts to refashion
the welfare system as set up by Attlee in order to reduce the role of
the state. Chapter 7 looks more systematically at the question of how
far social change, especially the notion of increasing affluence, was
helping to transform voting behaviour. The final chapter extends this
approach by looking at the neglected premiership of Sir Alec
Douglas-Home, Macmillan's successor after an undignified leadership struggle in October 1963. How far, given the sharp fall in Tory
support, was Labour's victory at the 1964 election the result of a
negative verdict on the drift in policy since 1959, as opposed to a
genuine endorsement of Wilson's vision of a 'New Britain'?

The picture which emerges in these pages is that of a nation
uncertain of its economic future, less consensual and more socially
divided than often assumed. In the first place, production and living
standards may have been rising, but so too was the cost of living;
voters were less impressed by the extent of economic progress than
many expert commentators. 'Consensus politics', secondly, is here
portrayed as the unavoidable consequence of elections where both
major parties could command over 40 per cent of the popular vote.
For much of their thirteen years in power the Conservatives believed
themselves to be vulnerable at the ballot box, so compounding
ministerial nervousness about fundamental changes to the post-war
settlement. The persistence of a superficial consensus was reinforced
by the inability of Tory leaders to agree upon what major departures
in policy were desirable. Some of the most radical, libertarian
thinking was to come from Rab Butler, who in office proved to be
less progressive than his espousal in opposition of new Tory 'charters'
made him appear. Churchill spoke of a 'ladder' which the ambitious
might climb, while Eden emphasised the need for a 'property-owning
democracy' and Macmillan prided himself on 'never had it so good'

pragmatism. The post-Suez strategy, aimed at encouraging consumer satisfaction, worked well when the priority was to restore morale. But with a full parliamentary term ahead after 1959, 'Supermac' had few guiding principles to fall back on when promises of greater prosperity turned from an asset to a rhetorical albatross. By the early 1960s the government was also under heavy assault for inequalities that persisted in welfare provision, especially in the areas of housing and education. This reflected, thirdly, the enduring nature of class divisions across the period. Improving living standards could not disguise the frequency of 'razor-sharp class skirmishes' and the 'stifling sense of corsetry and social tension' within British society.[18] A strong correlation continued to exist, it will be argued, between social class and voting behaviour. The 'affluent worker' may have played a part in determining electoral outcomes; but so too did the neglected development of middle-class disaffection with Conservatism.

Electoral insecurity and lack of an agreed ideological framework underpin what was arguably the central weakness of Conservative administrations after 1951: the failure to modernise. Unlike the 1940s, when national energies were absorbed by war and rehabilitation from its exhaustive consequences, the 1950s provided genuine opportunities for economic and social renewal. Yet few were seized. Rather than facing up to the challenge posed by much stiffer international competition, ministers opted for temporary tax palliatives designed for political gain, notably in the election years 1955 and 1959. Failure to tackle the recurring weakness of sterling resulted in periodic difficulties with Britain's balance of payments, so helping to ensure that uneven development – 'stop-go' – became unavoidable. By remaining lukewarm about much of the welfare system inherited in 1951, the Conservatives allowed the popularity of state-provided services to be eroded, thereby encouraging notions of an expensive dependency culture. What this left was a view that politics centred, above all else, on securing individual advancement via material prosperity. Macmillan especially left the way open for a backlash when raised expectations were dashed. It was not simply that government credibility was undermined by charges of mismanagement. Social critics were agreed, more fundamentally, that Britain had lost its sense of direction and desperately needed a combination of old and new virtues: 'the spirit of 1940, with its blood, toil, sweat and tears – yes, but with unity and comradeship also; how much finer than the spirit of 1960 . . . with its cars and washing machines on the "never-never", . . . its feverish pursuit of a prosperity it cannot really bring itself to believe in'.[19] Those such as Correlli Barnett seeking to explain Britain's 'lost victory' in and after the Second World War, it will be suggested, have been looking in the wrong place. In the 1940s the victory had been won; in the 1950s it was thrown away. In place of 1940s 'hope and public purpose', the 1950s witnessed a retreat from New Jerusalem.

1 Setting Britain Free, 1951–5

Introduction

For much of the British population, the Second World War finally ended in the early 1950s. Ration books could at last be thrown away as austerity gave way to the first stirrings of consumer affluence. Two great symbols of prosperity told the story. The number of motor cars increased from around 2.3 to 3.3 million between 1951 and 1955; and during the same period ownership of television sets quadrupled to over four million. Peace was restored with the ending of the Korean War, and several events during 1953–4 helped to kindle a sense of national well-being:

> Everest had been conquered, an Englishman had been the first to run a four-minute mile, and England had regained, and then held, the Ashes. But far above these, in the summer of 1953, Queen Elizabeth II had been crowned in a flourish of peagantry and amidst bold prophecies of a new Elizabethan age.[1]

What looks with hindsight like a golden age has traditionally been linked with the success of Winston Churchill's only peacetime administration. On the home front the Conservatives found a popular formula that had eluded them since the 1930s: a 'middle-of-the-road' consensual approach that ensured continuity with much of the practice of Attlee's government.[2] The absence of a strong right wing backlash after 1951, claims Anthony Seldon, stands out as 'one of the most important and neglected phenomena in the post-war history of the [Conservative] party'.[3] Yet, as this chapter will argue, moderate Conservatism may have owed less to a convergence of political ideas than to the legacy of two hard fought election contests. Labour support in 1951 remained undeniably solid and any thought of radical departures was cast aside when the government found in 1952 how quickly it might lose popularity. Convinced that the country was still 'left inclined', Churchill in his twilight years became a wary guardian of the post-war settlement.

Churchill Returns to Downing Street

Labour entered the election of October 1951 on the defensive. Attlee's government was widely portrayed as having run out of steam, and was accused by its detractors of presiding over a loss of prestige abroad and a fresh economic crisis at home. Although no seats had been lost by the government at by-elections, opinion polls had pointed for several months to the likelihood of a Churchill victory. The campaign, coming only eighteen months after the 1950 contest, was fought on similar lines. Labour's manifesto again looked to the past rather than the future, promising to preserve post-war advances such as full employment and the welfare state. These, it was claimed, would be undermined by the return of a Tory government. Another indication of the absence of new thinking was the time spent by Labour activists depicting Churchill as a warmonger. This element of the campaign culminated in a notorious *Daily Mirror* headline on election day, 'Whose Finger?' (on the trigger), which led Churchill to seek legal redress. Conservative efforts to exploit Labour divisions of recent months – using slogans such as 'The End is Nye' – were blunted by Bevan's willingness to urge party unity. But with many of the arguments having been rehearsed in 1950, Labour's campaign lacked novelty. Press observers had to resort to detailed descriptions of Mrs Attlee's eccentric driving as the Prime Minister busied himself with crossword puzzles in the back of his car on a nationwide tour.[4]

Such new proposals as were put forward came from the Conservative side. As Party Chairman, Lord Woolton was aware that the main obstacle to Tory success was 'widespread distrust of our motives'. Grim images of the 1930s were so strong that the 'working man thinks we are competent but selfish'. It was therefore not considered sufficient to repeat the formula of 1950: stressing support for welfare reform while seeking to exploit disgruntlement over rationing and shortages. Both themes were reinforced in 1951. Churchill promised to 'set the people free' by removing 'socialist controls', which it was said hampered individual enterprise and perpetuated a miserably low standard of living associated with wartime austerity. But in an effort to show trade union voters especially that 'we are not a class party', two populist initiatives were brought forward: the promise of an excess profits tax, and a pledge to outstrip Labour's housing programme by building 300,000 homes every year. Neither claim, however, was able to dominate the campaign. Unlike 1950, housing was relegated to the sidelines as Tory leaders were forced to spend much of their time countering the warmonger charge. More than half of the party's allocated radio broadcast time was spent insisting that Churchill was out to preserve British national prestige and not to embark on military adventures.[5]

Labour's unrelenting propaganda in the run up to polling day – 'a third Labour government' or 'a third world war' – helps to explain why the result was much closer than anticipated. On a high turnout, there was a small swing of 1.1 per cent across the country, sufficient to give Churchill a narrow parliamentary majority (see Table 1).

Table 1   *General Election of 25 October 1951*

Party	Votes	MPs	Share of vote	Change since 1950
Conservative	13,717,538	321	48.0%	+ 4.5%
Labour	13,948,605	295	48.8%	+ 2.4%
Liberal	730,640	6	2.5%	−6.6%
Others	198,969	3	0.7%	−0.3%
Conservative majority over other parties:	17			

Ironically, it was Labour who seemed to take more comfort from the outcome. Hugh Dalton described the result as 'wonderful', believing the Tories would soon run into economic and electoral difficulties.[6] Closer examination of the figures confirmed that although 21 seats had been lost to the Tories, Labour had polled over 200,000 more votes – the highest total hitherto in electoral history – based upon huge majorities in urban strongholds. Nor was there much evidence of Labour desertions to the Tories, with only an estimated 3 per cent of voters switching allegiance since 1950. Indeed the final outcome owed much to reduced Liberal intervention. With fewer than a hundred candidates in the field, erstwhile Liberal voters divided approximately six to four in favour of the Conservatives; 17 of the 21 Tory gains had lost their Liberal candidates since 1950. Like Baldwin between the wars, Churchill relied on a loose anti-socialist coalition that promised moderation and a cautious approach to government.[7]

The Conservatives were under no illusions that it had been a close run thing. Indeed much of the party's inquest into the election acknowledged the extent to which Labour still influenced the political agenda. It was not yet possible, as Harold Macmillan noted, to dictate the terms on which elections would be contested:

> The truth is that the Socialists have fought the election (very astutely) not on Socialism but on Fear. Fear of unemployment; fear of reduced wages; fear of reduced social benefits; fear of war. These four fears have been brilliantly, if unscrupulously, exploited. If, before the next election, none of these fears have proved reasonable, we may be able to force the Opposition to fight on Socialism. Then we can win.[8]

In the short term, as other senior colleagues recognised, the Tories faced the task of disproving such fears without the benefits of a large parliamentary majority. The Minister of Transport was told by Churchill that no more than five Tory MPs should ever travel in the same aeroplane, so as not to have 'too many baskets in one egg'; and Oliver Lyttelton later wrote it was commonplace to assume that a majority of 40 was the minimum necessary 'on which a Government with any serious programme of legislation could work'.[9] Many newspaper editorials were quick to point out that the result hardly constituted a ringing endorsement of Conservative policies. The *News Chronicle*, saddened by the virtual elimination of Liberalism, spoke of a 'stalemate almost as bad as the last one . . . the country has got rid of a party it does not want in favour of one it does not trust'.[10]

Underpinning the sense of Tory disappointment was a recognition that class-based voting remained deeply entrenched in 1951. Of the Conservative gains, 11 out of 21 were made in the suburban seats of Greater London and the Home Counties, suggesting that Labour was losing ground among those middle class voters who had been part of the 1945 'high tide'. Anecdotal as well as statistical evidence confirmed that Conservative support among manual workers who made up the mass of the electorate remained stubbornly low. Harold Macmillan wrote in his diary that 'wherever I have been, I am impressed by the class solidarity of the Labour vote. They grouse, and tell the Gallup Poll man that they will never vote Socialist again – but when the election comes, they vote the party ticket'.[11] Another post-mortem from a Scottish constituency conceded that the fear of unemployment among workers still ran very deep, and that if 'unemployment comes back we may be out for a generation'.[12] Internal party reports came to similar conclusions about Labour's ability to attract nearly 14 million voters. The Conservative machine, it was claimed, had reached the home but not the place of work; Labour's bond with trade union voters looked stronger than ever. The crusade for a property-owning democracy – providing the security of a job and a decent home – must be taken up immediately in order to strengthen the party 'among the artisan class'. If plans were not drawn up and acted upon before the next election 'we shall lose it'.[13]

Hence the new government's room for manoeuvre was limited from the outset. The need to woo working class voters meant there could be no alternative other than to continue policies designed to maintain the post-war settlement. Nowhere were the implications of the election result more evident than in the shaping of Churchill's Cabinet: as one opposition figure noted, the 'real free enterprisers and deflationists' were kept out. Aside from the Prime Minister's accepted heir-apparent, Anthony Eden, who returned to his wartime role of Foreign Secretary, the key appointment was that of Rab Butler as Chancellor of the Exchequer. Before the election the favoured candidate for the Treasury was Oliver Lyttelton, chairman of the backbench Finance Committee. When Churchill decided instead on Butler, he consoled Lyttelton with the knowledge that it had been touch and go, but that the Chief Whip felt Rab was more adept at 'the House of Commons stuff'.[14] Lyttelton's shortcomings as a parliamentary performer had been long known, as was his reputation as a slick financial operator. What may have tipped the scales, in the view of a knowledgeable Tory backbencher, was that 'Rab's position was much strengthened by the narrow result. In these circumstances it would have been more than ever dangerous to have had the other fellow at the Treasury'.[15] At least two more key domestic posts were similarly influenced by the outcome of the election. In an effort to demonstrate his progressive credentials, Churchill persuaded a reluctant Harold Macmillan to go to the Ministry of Housing, charged with the task of building new homes

that might 'kill me politically'.[16] And in preference to David
Maxwell-Fyfe, whose elecion addresses had 'thoroughly frightened
the unions', the Prime Minister appointed the emollient figure of
Walter Monckton as Minister of Labour. 'Winston's riding orders to
me', Monckton wrote, 'were that the Labour Party had foretold
grave Industrial troubles if the Conservatives were elected, and he
looked to me to do my best to preserve Industrial peace'.[17]

   The second main feature of Churchill's government was its so-
called 'national' character. Monckton was one of several non-Con-
servatives invited to join; others included Gwilym Lloyd George,
who became Minister of Food and later Home Secretary. Overtures
were also made to Liberal leader Clement Davies, though efforts to
absorb what remained of the Liberal Party came to nothing. This
aspect of Cabinet-formation owed less to the election result than to
Churchill's preference for promoting wartime associates such as
Oxford don Viscount Cherwell (Professor Lindemann, known as
'the Prof'), recalled to become the Prime Minister's personal adviser
on economic issues.[18] Indeed in many respects Churchill approached
the whole exercise in the same way as he had in 1940. Aside from
approaching old friends and aristocratic associates (many of whom
like Bracken and Beaverbrook were reluctant to return to the fray),
he favoured a system of powerful ministerial overlords and took little
interest once the senior posts had been settled. Macmillan confirmed
that 'he hardly knew the names' when it came to junior positions,
which were left to the Chief Whip.[19] Underlying these personal
preferences was Churchill's long-standing coolness towards the Conservative establishment. In the words of *The Economist*, the hallmark
of the new team was that it 'was not a Conservative but a Churchill
Cabinet'. The parliamentary party may have been reassured by the
presence of Eden, Butler and Lord Salisbury as Churchill's most
influential colleagues, but they were less happy about the inclusion of
'cronies' and the neglect of younger talent.[20] The average age of
Cabinet ministers was sixty and scant recognition was given to the
youthful 'One Nation' intake of MPs in 1950. The promotion of one
of this group, Iain Macleod, to the post of Minister of Health a few
months later only arose after Churchill happened to be present in the
Commons when Macleod launched a vigorous attack on Nye Bevan's
handling of the health service. Even then the Prime Minister was
overheard asking the Chief Whip, 'Who is this?'[21]

The prospects for Churchill's government thus looked uncertain in October 1951. Constrained by both the electorate and a large defence budget that came with rearmament, ministers were in no position to force the pace. Yet similarities in short term priorities could not entirely conceal longer term differences of 'outlook and purpose'.[22] Question marks hung over the type of lead that would be given by a prime minister in his late seventies. His private secretary confirmed that though his health was good upon his return to Downing Street, he spoke of the possibility of giving way to Eden within a year. In the meantime, Churchill concentrated as in the war on foreign affairs and only concerned himself on the home front with housing, food and labour relations.[23] Few believed that Churchill had much faith in his Chancellor, who at the outset was hemmed in not only by Lindemann but by the appointment of another senior non-party figure, Sir Arthur Salter, as Minister of State for Economic Affairs. Among officials there was alarm that the Prime Minister wanted to reduce the Chancellorship to the status of 'a tax-collector'; a fear only partially reduced by the refusal of the wartime Chancellor, Sir John Anderson, to take on the role of economic overlord.[24] Above all, the new government faced a troubled inheritance, the nature of which had been obscured by the optimistic language of the hustings. One minister said that the skeletons were not hidden in the cupboards, they were swinging like candelabra throughout Whitehall. Harold Macmillan wrote in his diary:

> There is a financial crisis, a foreign crisis, a defence crisis. Everything is in a state of muddle and confusion. It is 1940, without bombing and casualties – but without also the sense of national unity? Can this be somehow created?[25]

Tory Traumas, 1951–2

Financial crisis overshadowed Churchill's first six months in office. The immediate problem lay with a growing balance of payments deficit, described by the Chancellor as 'worse than 1949, and in many ways worse than 1947'. In the face of rising imports and unfavourable trade terms, sterling came under intense pressure;

ministers were soon aware that if the reserves continued to drain
away, the point at which devaluation might become unavoidable
would be reached by April 1952. Butler responded by outlining a
tough deflationary package. He told colleagues that only large
savings – from cuts in imports, a tightening of monetary policy
and a review of all government spending – would persuade the
markets of Conservative resolve: first to salvage sterling and then to
tackle rising inflation and 'crippling rates of taxation', responsible for
expenditure four times larger than before the war.[26] The Chancellor's acceptance of orthodox Treasury remedies cast fresh light on his
'progressive' reputation, as Brendan Bracken noted:

> Our Mr Butler has a stronger digestion than the toughest of
> ostriches. He has evacuated his charters with no sign of a blockage
> & is now preparing to slaughter the do-gooders & easy spenders in
> Government service.[27]

Some of the 'do-gooders' were not happy. One minister, highlighting
the fear of being blamed for renewed misery, asked an official how he
could face voters with the news that the bank rate, unchanged for
over a decade, must now go up, and with it council house rents.[28]
With the prospect of austerity intensifying rather than disappearing,
Bracken wrote that this 'first instalment of deflation has created more
wailers around London Wall than Jerusalem ever knew'.[29]

For a brief moment in February 1952, there was a prospect of
much worse to come. Alarmed by the sight of gold and dollar
reserves draining away before his eyes, Butler launched on unsuspecting colleagues a radical plan to reform Britain's external finances. The ROBOT plan, named after its originators at the Bank of
England and Treasury,[30] proposed to transfer sterling from a fixed to
a floating exchange rate and to make some sterling holdings convertible with the dollar, thereby signalling a determination to replace
state controls with automatic regulation of the market. The Chancellor made clear – in confidential talks with senior colleagues and
officials – that this might have undesirable effects, but he regarded
urgent reform as the lesser of two evils. If no further action was taken,
events might move completely beyond control, with the possible
ruination of sterling and 'major disruption' to the home economy.
Other options such as devaluation were ruled out: coming so soon
after 1949, the financial markets would regard this as a sign that

sterling was in irreversible decline. By acting immediately, Butler argued, the government would at least be able to retain some of 'our major objectives' and would set up forces that brought the economy back into balance.[31] At the outset, it looked as though ROBOT might go ahead, as the Chancellor hoped, with minimal fuss. Churchill wrote to Eden, away in Washington, that those colleagues so far consulted (with the exception of Cherwell) thought Rab's proposals for dealing with the new 'financial super-crisis' were on the 'right lines'.[32] A meeting of ministers on 22 February gave little indication of opposition to come. One of Cherwell's aides noted that Butler's approach was to appeal to the 'masochistic instinct of Ministers', urging them to put country before party even if it might 'mean the end of the Conservative Party for twenty years'.[33]

But in the week that followed, opponents of ROBOT launched a counter-offensive. The most vociferous critic was undoubtedly Cherwell, who used his friendship with Churchill to argue that the dangers facing Britain had been exaggerated. Sterling, claimed the Prof, could only be salvaged by improvements in 'real things' such as productivity and exports, not by a 'reckless leap in the dark involving appalling political as well as economic risks at home and abroad'. He argued that convertibility should be sought from a position of strength not weakness and that the reality behind the cosy phrase 'taking the strain off the reserves' was the likelihood of increased inflation and a return to 1930s-style mass unemployment.[34] Similar advice from another close associate, Salter, helped to change the mind of the Prime Minister; he confessed to not knowing much about technical financial questions, 'but I can't help feeling that when Cherwell and Salter agree there must be something in what they say'.[35] When the Cabinet discussed ROBOT on 29 February, the Chancellor found himself with only three firm supporters; the majority of opponents and waverers were swayed by Lord Salisbury's argument that the nation was not yet ready for such a dramatic change in economic policy.[36] The Chancellor was left, in the words of Robert Hall, Director of the Economic Section at the Treasury, 'exceedingly distressed as he had regarded the thing as his own child to save the country'.[37] By the time Butler came forward with a similar plan several months later, resistance had hardened further, and the Chancellor was forced to accept a compromise that spoke of Britain favouring a 'collective approach' to convertibility in the long term.

At least three misconceptions have developed about the ROBOT episode. The first concerns responsibility for outmanoeuvring the Chancellor. Cherwell's role, though important, has perhaps been exaggerated, not least by his biographer, who argues that efforts to bounce the Cabinet into early action would almost certainly have succeeded 'but for the Prof'.[38] Butler insisted in his memoirs, however, that neither Cherwell's 'detective agency in economics' nor Salter's 'stream of sea-green memoranda' would have carried the day but for the 'cautious conservatism' of senior ministers. In the words of Oliver Lyttelton, the Chancellor's staunchest ally, 'the water looks cold to some of them'.[39] Later recollections by Treasury officials agree that apart from Cherwell, the key ministerial opponent was Anthony Eden; angered that such a major change be contemplated with him out of the country, he tipped the balance on his return and gave Butler's critics time to mobilise their defences.[40]

Eden's crucial influence links to a second misconception, namely the idea that ROBOT was defeated ultimately because its advocacy of economic liberalism came up sharply against the social philosophy of 'Disraelian cohesion' that characterised the early 1950s.[41] Yet rather than defending the post-war settlement in principle, ministerial doubters based their opposition on the likely electoral consequences. Churchill was told by Cherwell that the scheme 'would certainly put the Conservative Party out for a generation. Even a Government with a large majority could not survive such a sudden, complete reversal of policy'. In the present parliament, 20 abstentions by Tory MPs would be enough to discredit the idea and force an election that was certain to be lost.[42] If this was a clinching point for Churchill, then it was even more crucial for Eden, who faced the alarming prospect of inheriting a party in opposition rather than in government. Electoral realities, not any commitment to consensus politics, provides the key to the defeat of ROBOT.

The third misreading of these events suggests that the Chancellor was acting out of character. His official biographer claims that he did not pursue the argument with fire or conviction, implying that Butler's heart was not really in such a radical step away from post-war economic orthodoxy.[43] Again, the evidence would suggest otherwise. Not only did Butler continue to float variations on the ROBOT plan for some months to come, he also continued to believe in later years that 'setting the pound free' would have improved Britain's economy in the long run, sparing future governments the traumas of stop–go policies and further devaluation.[44] From the moment he went to the Treasury, Butler showed himself sympathetic to much of the alternative economic strategy worked out by the Conservatives in opposition. While there would be no frontal assault on the welfare state, he could agree that government spending and taxation were much too high. Similarly, inflation would only be controlled if efforts were made to tighten monetary policy. In practice the early months of the new administration highlighted the difficulties of escaping from Labour's legacy. Yet the Chancellor had every intention of trying. He had few qualms, after the shelving of ROBOT, in introducing a tough spring budget. This announced a further rise in bank rate, more import cuts and the slashing of food subsidies by £160 million. For some commentators, this was a courageous effort, unrivalled by Labour budgets since the war. Others felt consumption needed to cut back even more, and Robert Hall noted how Butler, like all Chancellors, forgot how much policy was a compromise between 'principles, the practical difficulties of what the country will stand, and the cowardice of Ministers', who had ruled out tighter rationing or 'much else that might hurt'.[45]

Threats of more controls and rationing were the last thing expected by an electorate promised better times ahead. By-elections during much of 1952 showed a small but consistent swing towards Labour, and the Conservatives fared badly in local elections. Press commentators agreed that the government's honeymoon was bound to end, given the need to tackle the economic crisis, but ministers could be blamed for failing to convince voters that they had inherited a poisoned chalice.[46] Reports to Central Office from the constituencies noted the degree of apathy and frustration among Tory supporters unable to comprehend the need for such harsh medicine. The government had in fact rejected the idea of issuing a 'state of the nation' address, despite being urged to do so by the 1922 Committee, which was anxious to demonstrate 'how many skeletons H.M.G. had found'.[47] Ministers were left in no doubt, moreover, that industrial workers remained suspicious of Tory intentions. A group of 'working men Tories' in Leeds wrote to the Prime Minister to tell him that 'Labour lies' about Churchill reducing living standards were being swallowed on the shop floor.[48] Voter opinion – as in the case of ROBOT – reinforced ministerial caution about alienating working class voters. In the aftermath of the local elections, Churchill decided to suspend planned increases in rail fares, a move which contradicted the principles of the budget and left one Treasury official lamenting that 'Ministers seem to me to be much worse than their predecessors'.[49]

Panic over rail fares was one of several signs of Tory nervousness during mid-1952. Lord Salisbury urged the Prime Minister to go slow on election pledges to denationalise road haulage and steel; both proposals, he said, were 'violently controversial and of an essentially party character', at a time when national unity was essential. Churchill then hardly endeared himself to colleagues by raising one of his familiar appeals in times of trouble: the possible need for coalition. With unemployment edging upwards, he also raised the prospect of public works programmes. In order to guard against further unpopularity, he urged Eden to accept cuts in the huge defence budget rather than looking for further economies in housing: it would be a great pity, he said, 'to ruin the only achievement at home which is comprehended by the public'.[50] Macmillan, though he could rely on over 200,000 unfinished houses left behind by Labour to bolster his first-year returns, was reputed to be desperate to leave his post but was told 'he must stick to his hod'.[51] The Prime Minister was downcast by the local election results, and confided to his doctor that things were 'much worse than the war'. Mutterings about his leadership developed rapidly in the summer, and political observers wrote that unless rectified, charges of indecisiveness could be even more damaging than unfulfilled promises of setting the people free.[52]

Doubts over the economy went to the heart of the government's malaise. Although emergency measures to rescue sterling were beginning to pay off, Treasury officials remained anxious that no medium term strategy was yet in sight. Robert Hall noted that economic policy 'can hardly be said to exist'. The Chancellor himself asked the Chairman of the backbench Finance Committee, Ralph Assheton, what was required to restore diminishing City confidence in ministers, receiving the reply:

> The vital thing . . . is to have a definite policy and to carry it out. Broadly we can either continue the socialist policy and increase controls, or we can go for freedom. I hope you would not consent to remain in office unless the freedom policy is adopted. This will involve pretty fundamental changes including a big cut in expenditure, moving towards convertibility as soon as possible,

followed by a substantial cut in income tax and the ending of food rationing.[53]

Over the summer of 1952 Butler warned colleagues that longer term priorities had barely been addressed. He told Churchill that he still regretted the ROBOT decision because policy currently lies 'between two stools': without the benefits of either full planning or the discipline of the marketplace.[54] While his own preference was – like Assheton – for making cutbacks that would enable the nation to live within its means, others remained to be convinced. One MP, David Gammans, wrote that if by-elections began to be lost all talk of a full-length parliament would become nonsense. It was no use, he said, 'harping on freedom and opportunity' when the nation was still 'security minded': fear of unemployment, as in the Lancashire textile trade, was so strong that maintaining high employment levels must remain the central objective.[55]

By the end of the year, however, government fortunes were beginning to improve. Butler was able to claim credit for a much healthier balance of payments position, although nearly half of the improvement was the direct result of falling import prices and improved terms of world trade.[56] *The Economist* noted that at last an opportunity was arising to make a fresh start; it would now depend on ministers restoring enterprise in place of state control in order to show themselves as a 'Conservative party and not a "me too" party'.[57] Voters also signalled that a corner had been turned. Instead of a by-election defeat, which would have thrown into doubt the government's capacity to last a full term, the Conservatives increased their majority in the marginal seat of High Wycombe. Nor was the situation in the Commons as precarious as originally feared. Although Labour set out to repay in kind the type of harassment used by Tory MPs during 1950–1, the opposition's campaign of attrition was abandoned as it became clear that Churchill enjoyed a safer cushion of parliamentary votes than Attlee had after 1950. Conservative backbenchers who made waves tended to do so in small groups, varying in composition from issue to issue; the government's majority was rarely threatened and the task of the whips was easier than anticipated. Above all, government popularity increased as evidence mounted of disarray on the Labour benches. Far from sustaining vigorous opposition, Attlee's party was showing every sign of having pushed the self-destruct button.

The Turn of the Tide

'What is really significant', wrote Labour MP Richard Crossman on the first day of the 1951 parliament, 'is the cheerfulness and morale of the Party, compared with its state of semi-disintegration just before the election.'[58] But within months pre-election divisions in the Labour ranks were resurfacing with a vengeance. In March 1952 57 MPs defied the party whips by refusing to back an official amendment to the defence estimates, thereby marking the first major act of public defiance by the Bevanites. At Westminster, Bevan's supporters constituted not so much 'a party within a party', as critics alleged, but rather 'the Smoking Room within the Smoking Room'.[59] What made the Bevanite challenge so significant, however, was that for the first time in a generation, the left had a leader capable of attracting support throughout the Labour movement, particularly among constituency activists. The increasingly high profile of the Bevanites set alarm bells ringing on the opposite wing of the party. Those prepared to speak out, such as Herbert Morrison and Hugh Gaitskell, began to enlist the support of concerned back-benchers and trade union leaders such as Arthur Deakin, leader of the Transport and General Workers' Union (TGWU). Deakin pressed for tough disciplinary action after the revolt over defence estimates and, following a protracted inquest, it was decided that MPs could only receive the party whip if they stood by majority decisions of the Parliamentary Labour Party (PLP). The dispute over defence also convinced Attlee to stay on as leader for the time being. He calculated that if he stood down, there would be little to stop the succession of Morrison, whose hardline approach to the Bevanites was certain to make matters worse.[60] In the event, divisions multiplied alarmingly in spite of Attlee's attempt at conciliation. Nowhere was this more evident than at Labour's annual conference in the autumn of 1952.

'The Morecambe Conference', recalled Attlee loyalist Douglas Jay, 'was memorable as one of the most unpleasant experiences I ever suffered in the Labour Party. The town was ugly, the hotels forbidding, the weather bad, and the Conference, at its worst, hideous.'[61] Normal courtesies were cast aside as right-wing speakers found themselves jeered from the gallery; Deakin was so provoked at one point that he shouted at delegates 'Shut yer gob.'[62] What was more, the advance of Bevanite sentiment was reflected in support for a motion demanding further nationalisation of 'key and major industries'. The most bitter feelings were reserved for the elections to the constituency section of the National Executive Committee (NEC). When the results were announced, two of the party's old guard, Morrison and Hugh Dalton, had been knocked off the Executive by two leading Bevanites, Crossman and Harold Wilson. News of Morrison's defeat was greeted with howls of delight on the conference floor, and Wilson was heard to remark that 'Nye's little dog has turned round and bitten Dalton where it hurts.' Many present considered the conference the worst in Labour's history, and there was no sign of any improvement. Concerned that Bevanism might threaten the party's electoral prospects, Hugh Gaitskell hit back with a provocative speech calling for an end to 'mob rule by a group of frustrated journalists'. In its turn, *Tribune* (the house journal of the Bevanites) launched savage attacks on trade union leaders, prompting a rebuke from the NEC for playing into Tory hands by driving a wedge between Labour and the unions. Dalton wrote in his diary that 'nothing is getter better. More hatred, and more love of hatred, in our Party than I ever remember.'[63]

This feuding reflected in part a battle for the leadership. With Attlee likely to retire in the not too distant future, both left and right were manoeuvring for the succession. Beyond this, Bevan spoke of an ideological clash over 'party purpose', between fundamentalists wanting more nationalisation and 'revisionists' who favoured the creation of a less traditional agenda. But most disputes in the early 1950s were on foreign-policy issues such as German rearmament and nuclear weapons. Neither side had as yet formulated a coherent programme to apply to domestic politics, and shared more common ground than was apparent, particularly over the achievements of the post-war government. There was, indeed, a sizeable 'centre' element within the PLP, many of whom believed that internal feuding was a futile distraction. What this really left were differences of political style and emphasis, compounded by a hardening of individual loyalties. The whole dispute became, in the words of Douglas Jay, 'what Thucydides, in his account of the civil war in Corfu, calls "statis": faction for faction's sake in which the protagonists know which side they are on, but usually cannot remember why it all started.'[64] In the aftermath of the Morecambe conference, Attlee took a firm stand. At the first meeting of MPs in the new parliamentary session, he secured agreement for a resolution banning all unofficial groups within the party. Thereafter, instead of a 40-strong group, Bevanism at Westminster was confined to a smaller number of Bevan's closest intimates. Bevan also felt, having secured policy advances at Morecambe, that the time was ripe to mend fences. His willingness to stand again for shadow cabinet elections signalled a desire to re-enter the party mainstream, and opened up a period of 'armed truce' throughout 1953. On all sides, there was a recognition that Churchill's government could only be seriously challenged if Labour displayed unity.

By early 1953 the opposition could not avoid the reality of a government beginning to enjoy the fruits of economic advance. In addition to an improved balance of payments position, Britain's reserves were rising and inflation at home was slowing considerably. Having carried out a 'rescue operation' on sterling in his first year, the Chancellor could plan his second budget in more optimistic circumstances. He wrote to Churchill that attention could turn to encouraging investment in productive industry and to tax concessions in order to stimulate demand.[65] In this he was supporting an agenda that found favour among all sections of the party. The Prime Minister himself had told Butler in the early stages of his budget preparation that Labour had bequeathed:

> a swollen bureaucracy and a level of taxation previously undreamt of in time of peace. It would of course have been much eaier for us to slash these back immediately the war ended if we had then been returned to power. It is more difficult now. But the effort, though greater, must be made. We cannot afford to let it become accepted, as an inevitable feature of the post-war world, that the country must have a non-productive bureaucracy . . . and a standard rate of income tax at 9/6d [47.5p] in the £.[66]

Under similar pressure from backbenchers, the Chancellor opted in April 1953 for an expansionary policy. Sixpence [2.5p] was cut from all rates of income tax, purchase tax was reduced and a pledge made to abolish the excess-profits levy. For the first time since the war, a budget had been introduced with no new taxes or increases to existing taxes.

Butler was given a rapturous reception by Tory MPs. The Chief Whip reported that on the Finance Committee there was almost 'complete ungrudging support' for the budget.[67] Economic commentators were also impressed. There was some concern that consumer purchasing power had been given precedence over improving productivity, but the package was nevertheless said to mark 'a change of direction, a turning of the fiscal tide', and a step away from Labour's economy of restrictions.[68] Butler certainly added to the discomfiture on the opposition benches, where attacks on the budget appeared confused and weak. Combined with the attention given to the Queen's coronation, 1953 developed into an *'annus mirabilis'* for the government. On the back of rising consumption and a vigorous expansion of house-building, national output rose by 4 per cent and remaining controls began to disappear. Denationalisation of road haulage and steel was finally able to proceed, and economic recovery added to the growing reputation of Monckton as a minister capable of defusing potentially damaging industrial disputes, thereby further confounding Labour predictions. Such was the government's improvement in fortunes that over the summer of 1953 the possibility of an early election was widely discussed. *The Economist* summed up the second session of the parliament by saying that the uncertainties besetting ministers twelve months ago 'have been dispelled by a mixture of good management, good luck and weak opposition'.[69]

As the difficulties of 1952 began to recede in memory, opinion polls registered a shift in opinion. In part this was due to Labour's inability to get its act together. Brendan Bracken wrote early in 1953 that the government 'is doing well at the moment. Bevan is doing a better job of work for the Tories than Woolton ever could do.'[70] After the spring budget, ministers could more confidently claim credit in their own right – with spectacular success at the Sunderland South by-election of May 1953, the first time in nearly thirty years that a party in government had captured a seat from the opposition at a by-election. Reports from the constituency indicated that Labour activists were at odds over the choice of a non-local candidate, and on polling day traditional party supporters were reluctant to turn out.[71] The young Conservative candidate, Paul Williams, had the advantage of both Liberal intervention and being known in the area after fighting the seat in 1951. His agent attributed the Tory majority of 1,175 above all to Butler's 'favourable budget' only weeks before, giving credibility to the idea of an improving economy and undermining Labour claims that working-class living standards were deteriorating.[72] Sunderland South made headline news as neither main party had lost a by-election seat in 85 contests since 1945. But the movement of votes was in line with an improved showing for the Conservatives evident over several months. The first eight contests of 1953 showed an average swing of 1.66 per cent towards the government, sufficient if repeated at a general election to deliver a majority of over 70 seats.[73]

Behind the scenes, ministers questioned how long their new-found good fortune might continue. The Chancellor told colleagues that the budget prospects for 1954 were 'menacing', and that unless new expenditure cuts were found he may be unable to maintain moves towards reduced taxation. The Minister of Labour's willingness to compromise was regarded by sections of party opinion as giving the green light to union threats of strike action. Within the Cabinet, some bracketed Monckton with Churchill's reference to General Munro at Gallipoli – 'He came, he saw and he capitulated.'[74] But the major cause of anxiety, sufficient to explain Labour clawing its way back to level pegging in opinion polls by the end of 1953, was uncertainty about the future of the Prime Minister. For over 18 months since returning to Downing Street, Churchill's age had not adversely affected his leadership. When asked how long he proposed to remain in office, he had replied: 'Till the pub closes.' But in June 1953 the Prime Minister suffered a massive stroke. His own doctor doubted if he would last the weekend, and his private secretary, John Colville, began to make contingency plans for a possible succession. With the assistance of newspaper proprietors such as Beaverbrook, the real nature of Churchill's illness was concealed from both parliament and the public. Within a month recovery was on the cards. Colville wrote that Churchill was determined to bring off a final triumph, like Disraeli at the Congress of Berlin in 1878. After visiting him in August, Brendan Bracken noted that 'retirement is not in his vocabulary'.[75]

But there was to be no return to business as usual. Once raised, questions about Churchill's stamina refused to go away, and the episode led to increased tension among ministers who knew the full story. A particular complication had resulted from a serious illness simultaneously affecting Eden, which meant that plans were formulated for a caretaker administration under Lord Salisbury to take over for six months in the event of Churchill's death. In the meantime, Rab Butler was left to combine the roles of Prime Minister, Chancellor and Foreign Secretary in the Commons. Some of Rab's supporters felt he should advance his own claims to the premiership.

Backbenchers wrote in confidence urging him to make 'one or two great speeches' and asking: 'Were Bonar Law or Baldwin "legitimist" successors?' The Chancellor knew that doubts existed about the heir apparent; Eden stood accused of never having 'scored a six off his own bat'. But he also recognised his own shortcomings: his reputation as a Chamberlainite appeaser in the 1930s was not forgotten, and he decided to stick to the role of loyal subordinate.[76] For Eden these events were doubly frustrating. He first had to watch from his sickbed to see if his emerging rival for the leadership might attempt to snatch away the prize he had long coveted; he then witnessed the Prime Minister complete his recovery with a party conference triumph in October that ruled out a general election for some time to come. His hopes raised and dashed, Eden was said to 'long' for Churchill to retire.[77] Other senior Tories were equally convinced that things could never be the same again. Lord Woolton, surveying the effects on public opinion of uncertainty about the succession, privately believed that 'we should be defeated' if the Prime Minister carried out his promise to continue for another two years. Only an early handover to Eden, he claimed, could 'save the Party from disaster'.[78]

Churchill Bows Out, 1954–5

There was much to play for as the parliament moved into its later stages. The Conservatives had yet to resolve their leadership dilemma and it was said that if Labour – having patched up a party truce – could find a real sense of direction it might win a forthcoming election by 'looking like an alternative government; at the moment it merely looks like a congenital Opposition'.[79] Much would depend upon whether Britain's economy remained on an even keel. The Chancellor sought to ensure this by introducing a 'standstill budget' in April 1954, with limited concessions made to stimulating new investment in industry. Some colleagues favoured a bolder strategy. Lord Woolton, who described the budget as 'the dullest thing that anybody ever created', argued for extra tax cuts as a priority, only to be told this would involve undesirable increases in borrowing. On the whole, the party was prepared to accept Butler's line: that rising productivity would gradually allow room for more tax cuts and a reduction in the onerous burden of government expenditure.[80] In the short term, this approach continued to produce dividends. Although the ending of food rationing in mid-1954 may have been due 'much less to Conservative principles than to the favourable turn in the terms of trade', it was inevitably depicted by ministers as an example of setting the people free to spend their own money as they wished.[81]

However, there were two dark clouds on the horizon. In the first place, there was growing concern within the party that the Minister of Labour was 'so anxious to prove that the Conservatives are the true friends of the workers that he will distribute other people's halfpence without a moment's hesitation'.[82] Far from acting against restrictive practices or unofficial strikes, ministers continued to give way in order to avoid major industrial disputes – notably on the railways – thereby adding to a wage spiral during 1953–4 that saw salaries rising three times as fast as output. The second problem was whether the budgetary position could be maintained in the year ahead:

> The miracle has happened – full employment without inflation, and this despite the heavy burden of defence, the rising burden of social services, and some reduction in taxation. But 'the miracle' must not be followed by disillusionment. The forecasts for 1955–56 . . . do not show the margin necessary for further reliefs.[83]

Yet with no imminent sense of danger, ministers paid little heed to exhortations for vigilance in future spending plans. Churchill himself rejected proposals to increase bread prices and school meal charges because he was averse to jeopardising the 'buoyant mood' in the country. By the end of 1954 consumer confidence was drawing in larger numbers of imports, sufficient to make 'some tightening up necessary' and threatening the balance of payments position.[84] The Chancellor responded swiftly. By again raising the bank rate and reintroducing controls over hire-purchase facilities, he hoped to avoid 'any appearance of infirmity in the Government's purpose'.[85] Whether he would be so tough in the 1955 budget, with an election looming, was less certain.

Worries about the economy played a part in ministerial thoughts about when a general election should be called. As Party Chairman, Woolton was tempted by the prospect of an early contest on the grounds that the peak of prosperity may have passed. Butler opposed such a move, having removed any anticipation of an election with his cautious budget. Tory leaders remained anxious that in spite of

Labour divisions – rekindled when Bevan resigned from the Shadow Cabinet in 1954 – the government had been unable to build up a commanding opinion poll lead. In September Woolton reported that experienced agents were noting how 'high prosperity' was little appreciated by voters, who regarded derationing of food as their 'due right' rather than a Tory achievement.[86] Middle-class voters were disappointed that 1954 had not witnessed further tax reductions; tax rates still compared unfavourably with 4s 6d [22.5p] before the war.[87] Unable to produce fresh policies that went beyond a compromise between left and right, Labour was making little headway in crucial by-elections. At the Liverpool West Derby contest in November the Conservative majority was nearly doubled. 'They have tried cost of living', wrote Harold Macmillan; 'they have tried abolition of food subsidies; they have tried rents; they have tried pensions – none of them has proved winners'. But ministers were anxious that all their endeavours since 1951 might be undone because of the unresolved difficulty of Churchill's retirement. Woolton continued to believe the party faced electoral disaster unless there was 'a complete change in the structure of the government and a new P.M.'[88]

From the spring of 1954 onwards concerns about Churchill's erratic handling of Cabinet business began to multiply. One colleague described him as 'gaga', and senior ministers such as Butler contemplated the unpleasant task ahead: convincing Churchill it was time to go without causing undue offence and jeopardising the prospect of a smooth sucession.[89] The frustration of ministers became ever more obvious. In April Woolton hinted at resignation unless Churchill went soon and allowed Eden time to 'play himself in' before an election. During the summer Macmillan was bold enough to tell Churchill to his face that he was not alone in requesting his early departure:

> All of us, who really have loved as well as admired him, are being slowly driven into something like hatred. Yet we know that illness has enormously altered and worsened his character. He was always an egoist, but a magnanimous one. Now he has become almost a monomaniac.[90]

The Prime Minister, however still held the upper hand. He found the thought of giving up office more abhorrent the closer it came; he also knew that ministers would find it difficult to turn him out without ruining the party's election prospects. Fortified by this thought, Churchill reneged on a promise to retire before the 1954 conference and decided to reshuffle the Cabinet instead.[91]

By this time bitterness was creeping into the whole retirement question. 'Winston is trying to double cross Anthony', wrote one minister, raising the question of whether 'some of us should resign and break up the Govt.'[92] This prospect inched closer over the winter of 1954–5, as political observers spoke of a parliament that had exhausted it usefulness and was incapable of taking new initiatives. In December Churchill told colleagues they would have to resign if they wanted to force the issue; he conceded that if a large number did go an election would be unavoidable, but in such an event he would tell the country it was not his doing. In the end it took such a threat to force the issue. By late February 1955 Churchill had agreed to retire on 5 April, but again tried to backtrack in order to participate in a proposed international summit. On 14 March Eden tried to get an assurance that Churchill would not lead the party into another election, but was angrily told it was not a matter for Cabinet discussion. According to Woolton, this was the last straw. 'Eden said that if Churchill changed his mind, as he had done on three previous occasions when he had said he would retire, he proposed to go.' Butler and Salisbury had said they would follow suit and Woolton agreed 'we could not be fooled around any longer'.[93] The failure of the summit to materialise sealed matters. Churchill complained that he was being 'pushed out', though as Macmillan observed:

> Now that he has really decided to go, we are all miserable! Happily, we shall forget the last few months (which have been very trying and nerve-racking, especially for Eden) and we shall only remember the greatness and grandeur of this unique man.[94]

Conclusion

Reaction to Churchill's retirement was muted owing to the coincidence of a newspaper strike in April 1955, though few doubted it had been a triumphant finale to an illustrious career. Churchill could claim to have delivered on his 1951 promises – 'work, food and homes' – and left Eden with every prospect of electoral success, especially after Labour's 'armed truce' gave way to a resumption of more open warfare in 1954. Unable to accept collective responsibility, Bevan resigned from the Shadow Cabinet and found himself on the verge of expulsion from the party after a bitterly resented attack on Attlee's defence policy in March 1955. Above all else, the outgoing prime minister had stayed long enough to see off the years of rationing and austerity. Full employment had been combined with control of inflation, consumer spending power had been boosted through tax cuts and a concerted attack had been made on bureaucratic controls. In the past three years, Rab Butler said in July 1954, 'we have burned our identity cards, torn up our ration books, halved the number of snoopers, decimated the number of forms and said good riddance to nearly two-thirds of the remaining wartime regulations. This is the march to freedom on which we are bound.'[95] Two qualifications though must be added. In the first place, economic recovery owed as much to external forces as to government policy. For more than two years, Britain benefited enormously from the fall in world commodity prices as the Korean War came to an end; this alone provided foreign-exchange income approximating to an extra £400 million purchasing power per year. The role of luck, secondly, should not be overlooked. It was not simply that global expansion made possible both high spending and reduced taxes. If the Tories had won a larger majority, it was noted in 1954, they would almost certainly have been compelled, 'by the dynamic of their own propaganda while in Opposition, to attempt a dash to freedom which would have brought them to electoral disaster within two years'. Even then it turned out to be 'sheer good fortune' that the Chancellor was defeated over 'setting the pound free', thereby leaving the way open to exploit unprecedently favourable economic circumstances.[96]

Nor should the moderation of Churchill's administration be equated with a new consensus, a genuine narrowing of party differences in policy and ideology. As we have seen, the closeness of the election result in 1951 made it extremely unlikely that the Conservatives would challenge the basis of the mixed economy and the welfare state. *The Economist*, which created 'Mr Butskell' in 1954 as a symbol of cross-party agreement, itself recognised that 'deadlock' in policy was the inevitable product of two close election contests and a government with a small majority. 'There is a real risk that the country will get used to it, and that it will become the general assumption that nothing much can ever be accomplished under the British parliamentary system.'[97] In these circumstances, it was notable how far the Conservatives sought to emphasise differences in economic strategy. Aside from a revived interest in monetary policy and a desire for early convertibility, the assault on controls signalled a wish to undercut 'socialist planning'. What Butler called 'the march to freedom' was conducted so vigorously that Tory supporters themselves questioned the pace of change, for example over the scrapping of building controls in 1954.[98] Reliance on budgetary policy, moreover, did not necessarily amount to an endorsement of Keynesian demand management to maintain full employment. More traditional concerns such as balancing budgets and seeking free trade still heavily influenced official thinking, and it was only improved world trade that prevented tensions among ministers from surfacing, while at the same time giving a misleading impression of continuity with Labour policy.[99]

The impression of continuity was reinforced by two further factors. One was the scale of the task facing the Conservatives in 1951. Aside from the electoral tightrope that had to be walked, ministers knew that economic improvement was not sufficiently strong to contemplate any rapid undoing of Labour's legacy, as the Cabinet Secretary hinted to Churchill in 1954:

> The Socialists fashioned the Welfare State on the principle that Whitehall can supply many of the citizen's needs more cheaply and more intelligently than he can himself. They took his money away, on the basis that they would provide free many of the services for which he had previously paid . . . If, therefore, Ministers conclude – as Mr Butler does – that we have got to go on 'for years and years in a long, slow grind' with income tax at 9/6d in the £ and surtax at its present levels, they will, in fact, be deciding that a Conservative Government must perpetuate, or at least be powerless to alter, the pattern of society which the Socialists set out deliberately to create.[100]

A second consideration was the inability of senior ministers to agree upon a coherent framework for radical departures in policy. After being absorbed in the crises of 1952, illnesses to both Churchill and Eden in 1953 left the Chancellor carrying a day-to-day burden

unknown even to his Labour predecessor, Stafford Cripps. The three
leaders 'with the stature to lift the party's eyes further than the length
of a three line whip were wholly prevented from doing so'. As a
result, the Tories never set out an agreed basis for change: the
rhetoric of 'freedom' vied with Eden's 'property-owning democracy'
and Churchill's 'ladder up which all can climb and . . . net to catch
those who fall off'.[101]

What was left then was consensus by default. The 1951 result,
combined with the inability of the Tories to map out a clear
direction, meant that Churchill's government spent much of its time
tampering with Labour's post-war settlement, 'probing its weak spots
and subtly shifting its priorities', but without fundamentally reshaping the agenda of politics and moving only incrementally to retract-
ing the boundaries of state control and to freeing up the market.[102]
Yet in terms of longer term aims, there remained a chasm between
the parties. Tory references to greater liberalisation, lower taxation
and decontrol found no echo in Labour rhetoric about the abandonment of fair shares and the need for economic planning as the only
safeguard of prosperity. Whereas the label of Butskellism was to live
on in years to come, a sharply contrasting picture of the Chancellor
was painted by the *New Statesman* in 1954. Far from being a closet
socialist, as some claimed, Butler might more realistically be seen as
the new 'ideologist of inequality', the minister who had done more
than any other to show that free enterprise was compatible with full
employment, and inequality with the welfare state. It was Butler who
had shown how the post-war settlement could be used to 'maintain
the differences of wealth and status which are essential to stability'.[103]
What was more, as Churchill left the political scene, the opportunity
was opening up to move more rapidly on the 'march to freedom'. For
the first time in a generation, it was no longer necessary for political
argument to focus on the meat ration or other hardships. Attention
could turn to the type of society that should be created in Britain
over the next decade; the only thing missing for Churchill's successor,
Anthony Eden, was a fresh mandate from the people.

2 'The best prime minister we have', 1955–7

The Failure of Anthony Eden: Personality or Policy?

'It is fortunate for Britain that there exists to succeed Sir Winston a leader who is a world statesman in his own right', wrote the *Yorkshire Post* in April 1955. Sir Anthony Eden's greatest asset, it was said, was his ability to 'command respect in the Cabinet room, in the House and in the country'.[1] Few prime ministers had arrived at Downing Street with such glowing tributes ringing in their ears. The conventional wisdom was that Eden had everything going for him: film-star good looks and an impeccable ministerial record made him ideally suited to lead a confident party anticipating electoral victory. He had been closely associated with the spirit if not the detail of a 'property-owning democracy', and he ambitiously championed a genuine 'partnership in industry' instead of outdated class warfare. In short, he 'incarnates as well as any man the new Conservatism' of the 1950s.[2]

Eden's inability to live up to expectations – long before the Suez Crisis abruptly ended his career – has often been attributed to personal failings, such as his lack of experience in domestic politics and his highly strung temperament. But if he proved unexpectedly ill-suited to the demands of leadership, it was also the case that Eden's inheritance was more problematic than assumed. He came to power when deep-rooted economic problems were becoming impossible to conceal, and an early election victory ironically added to the anxieties of party management. As one senior Tory noted: 'whereas in the last Parliament our supporters were inhibited from criticism both by the Olympian position of the then Leader of the Party and by the smallness of our majority in the House, they now feel that both these inhibitions have gone, that the Party is firmly in power for some three or four years, and they can really have a go without rocking the boat'.[3] In such circumstances, as this chapter will show, it was not surprising that Eden flattered to deceive.

The 1955 General Election

It all started promisingly enough. Two interrelated questions faced
Eden when he arrived in Downing Street. Should he reconstruct the
Cabinet and should he call an early general election? Conscious that
Churchill had carried out a major reshuffle in 1954, the new Prime
Minister opted for continuity: Butler stayed on at the Treasury, and
the only change of note was Harold Macmillan's promotion to
become Foreign Secretary. Eden left open the possibility of more
wide-ranging changes in the near future, for after only ten days in
office he announced late May as the election date – a decision
requiring a degree of courage. As Party Chairman, Woolton noted
that the Conservatives traditionally under-performed in summer
elections, when voters were believed to have more interesting things
to do than go to the polling booths. Eden could hardly fail to be
aware that the Tories had not outpolled Labour since 1935, and any
misjudgement would condemn him to one of the shortest premier-
ships in history. But to off-set this, unemployment was low, the
balance of payments favourable and 'electorally, so far as one could
judge, the tide appeared to be with us'.[4] In view of opposition
divisions and the government's excellent by-election record, even the
cautious Woolton was predicting a majority of at least twenty seats.[5]
The Prime Minister was therefore taking only a modest risk, one
which he claimed publicly was necessary to end uncertainty, but
which he privately agreed owed much to the fear that rising prices
might cause a sterling crisis later in the year. 'As you know,' he
confided to Churchill, 'I have been tempted to try to show that we
can be a good Administration for at least six months before appealing
to the country but I am increasingly compelled to take account of
these distasteful economic factors.'[6]

A further reason for an early appeal to the country was that
Butler's scheduled budget could provide a launch-pad for the Tory
campaign. On 19 April the Chancellor, to the delight of his backbenchers, announced two highly popular measures: the standard rate
of income tax was reduced from 9s to 8s 6d in the pound, and the
raising of personal allowances removed over two million from
liability to tax altogether. With the benefit of hindsight, these
changes have been criticised as an abandonment of the Cripps
tradition of refusing to use the budget for overtly electioneering
purposes. At a time of 'overfull' employment (with twice as many

vacancies as men out of work) extra consumer purchasing power from reduced taxation was also certain to have inflationary effects.[7] At the time, Butler cited some powerful arguments in his favour. Treasury officials argued that the tightening of monetary policy earlier in the year – raising the bank rate and imposing a credit squeeze via hire-purchase restrictions – had already steadied an overheating economy. Hence it was consistent to continue with a strategy of reducing taxes, especially as more than half the available budget surplus was kept in reserve. Eden later expressed himself 'astonished' at Butler's moderation: to give away less than half the surplus was 'prudent in any year and restrained in an election year'.[8] Yet the diary of Robert Hall, Chief Economic Adviser at the Treasury, put a different gloss on government thinking:

> The economic picture hardly changed, that is, it seemed if any-thing to need a stiffer Budget, but almost everyone felt that it would be politically impossible to do nothing: it was a question of how to make it look as little like bribery of the electorate as possible . . . even if we run a few balance of payments risks in the process.[9]

The budget provided the ideal basis for Eden's campaign. His main theme was that since 1951 the Conservatives had delivered unprecedented prosperity; he offered the prospect of Britain doubling its standard of living within 25 years.[10] Eden's desire to show that a new chapter was unfolding explains why Churchill, much to his annoyance, was sidelined by Tory organisers. Behind this decision lay the recognition at Central Office that Churchill's pugnacious electioneering style was no longer appropriate. In contrast, Eden sought 'middle of the road' support by short constituency tours that avoided triumphalism. This helps to explain the low-key campaign that unfolded, though equally important was Labour's inability to mount a forceful challenge. Neither appeals to the memory of the 1945 government nor attacks on rising food prices did much to stir voters. The opposition's main problem was how to inject life into what Dalton described as the 'most tedious, apathetic, uninteresting and . . . worst organised' of all the elections in which he had fought.[11] Even Attlee's request that Eden repudiate his 'dirty' claim that Labour would bring back rationing failed to enliven proceedings. Perhaps the main cause of what some called the quietest

campaign since 1929 was the absence of doubt about the outcome.
Eden maintained a steady opinion poll lead after the first week; local
elections in mid-campaign showed an erosion of Labour support; and
Gallup found that irrespective of party allegiance 52 per cent of those
polled expected a Conservative victory, compared with only 22 per
cent predicting Labour success. The *Daily Mirror* slogan 'Keep the
Tories tame' summed up Labour's defensiveness throughout; by
polling day the opposition seemed less concerned with outright
victory than with preventing a government landslide.[12]

In the event Eden secured a solid but not overwhelming victory.
On a much reduced turnout (down by 5.7 per cent to 76.8 per cent
since 1951), the Conservatives increased their majority by over 40
seats.

Table 2 *General Election of 26 May 1955*

Party	Votes	MPs	Share of vote	Change since 1951
Conservative	13,286,569	345	49.7%	+ 1.7%
Labour	12,404,970	277	46.4%	−2.4%
Liberal	722,405	6	2.7%	+0.2%
Others	346,554	3	1.2%	+0.5%

Conservative majority over other parties: 59

The swing across the country was small though relatively uniform.
Tory gains were made from Halifax to Hornchurch, and several seats
in the Midlands showed swings well above the national average of
1.1 per cent. Liberal intervention and the redrawing of constituency
boundaries appeared to have negligible effects. The outstanding
feature of the result was a drop in Labour support: down by one
and a half million votes since 1951. This amounted to one in ten of
those who previously supported the party. If this fall had been
uniform in all constituencies, the Conservative majority would have
risen to over 80 seats. Two forces, however, prevented a landslide.
The first was an unexpectedly strong Labour showing in some
agricultural areas, and the second was the impact of differential

abstentions: the number of party supporters bothering to vote was significantly lower in 'safe' seats than in Labour-held marginals. This led *The Economist* to conclude that 'It is possible to mobilise the Labour loyal to save "our member, Mr X", but it is not so easy to whip up Labour enthusiasm with the battle cry that "we can turn that Tory rascal, Mr Y, out."'[13]

Press observers were agreed about the causes of Eden's triumph. Put simply by the *New Statesman*, 'the nation felt comfortably satisfied and in no mood for a change'. Primarily this was attributed to rising living standards: 'a great many working people are "doing nicely, thank you", and they don't bother to ask why'.[14] An equally strong theme in newspaper reaction was the impact of Labour's internal warfare; this was considered crucial in explaining why for the first time in living memory the opposition was unable to benefit from the 'swing of the pendulum'.[15] The parties endorsed these views. Hugh Gaitskell, for example, spoke of Labour feuding as a key factor, while an internal Tory report noted the ease with which Attlee's attacks had been fended off:

> The 'cost of living' made little headway in face of the higher standard of living. The 'crisis round the corner' carried little conviction in face of existing prosperity and a confident Chancellor . : . 'Fair shares' had a modest run but was defeated by the threat of a return to rationing and restriction. In a relatively quiet campaign the Conservatives held the initiative throughout. The Socialists were always on the defensive – on rationing, nationalisation and controls in particular. After three and a half years of Conservative Government the nation felt on the whole satisfied and in no mood for a change. The Conservatives were talking the language of 1955. The Socialists seemed dull and old-fashioned by comparison.[16]

The 1955 election was a bitter disappointment for Labour. The apathy of party workers was widely commented on during a lacklustre campaign, and the future did not look any rosier. According to the *Daily Mirror*, Labour leaders were 'too old, too tired, and too weak', and the party's organisation was 'pathetically inferior'.[17] Yet it would be misleading to depict the outcome as part of a process of irreversible decline. Labour could still command the loyalty of over twelve million voters, and as H. G. Nicholas – author of an

earlier Nuffield election study – pointed out, the result was in line
with previous post-war contests:

> It is a picture which reproduces with surprising fidelity what we
> have already seen in 1951, 1950 and even in 1945 – the image of an
> electorate astonishingly evenly divided and striking immovable.
> The only distinction that last Thursday's voters can claim to mark
> them out from their predecessors is that they preferred to express
> their endorsement by staying at home rather than by marking
> their ballot papers.[18]

However, it should not be forgotten that the total number of
Conservative voters had fallen since 1951, this in spite of an
electorate enlarged by some 300,000. Senior Tories expressed the
concern that, given all the circumstances, the government had not
done better still. The ghost of 1945 had been laid to rest; it was no
longer credible to argue that Eden would turn the clock back. But
there were few signs of the party winning new converts. If affluence
was the key to success, then it was only slowly driving the working
classes into middle-class patterns of voting. As one internal report
concluded, 'it is clear that there are many people at present disillusioned with Socialism who, nevertheless, have a prejudice against
voting Conservative'.[19] For a leader only weeks in office, however,
such notes of caution paled besides the plaudits he received for
securing an increased majority. As far as Eden was concerned, it
was so far so good.

Eden on the Defensive

The prime minister's honeymoon was brief. Election victory heightened expectations about what might follow, though for a variety of
reasons Eden's prospects were less rosy than they appeared. Rab
Butler later wrote that Churchill's tardiness in retiring left Eden
feeling 'thwarted' and 'stale' by the time he reached No. 10,[20] and
this was not the only difficulty of living in the shadow of an illustrious
predecessor. Whereas Churchill had been unassailable by virtue of
his age and reputation, Eden was not immune to criticism from
within party ranks, especially as a comfortable majority offered the
prospect of several years in power. Nowhere was the contrast

between the two regimes more evident than in the relationship between senior ministers. As Hugh Dalton noted, there was 'no friendship at the top here' between Eden, Butler and Macmillan.[21] In Churchill's absence, the ministerial triumvirate found it difficult to conceal their intense personal rivalries. Butler was reported to have boasted that on domestic issues he would lead the new Prime Minister 'from behind'. On the day he took over, Eden did nothing to rebut Lord Woolton's suggestion that it would be best to 'get rid of Butler'.[22] Relations between the Prime Minister and his Foreign Secretary were no better. Eden and Macmillan 'simply did not like each other', and were soon at loggerheads over the direction of British policy towards Europe and the Middle East.[23] Cabinet colleagues also felt less inclined passively to accept Prime Ministerial outbursts of bad temper (not unknown in Churchill's day), compounded by what one called Eden's 'chronic restlessness'.[24] One MP said that Eden's refusal to 'leave his ministers alone' implied a lack of confidence in Downing Street; this in time was to have a corrosive effect that trickled down via junior ministers to the backbenches.[25]

The electorate at large were more concerned about shortcomings in policy. It was only a matter of months before the economic optimism of the spring was replaced by an atmosphere of crisis. After an election in which the Tory case was based upon the promise of a buoyant economy, it came as a shock to discover that Britain's balance of payments was deteriorating rapidly, reaching a deficit of over £450 million in the first half of 1955. With unemployment still falling, moreover – down to only 200,000 – it was evident that Butler's tightening of monetary policy earlier in the year had failed to cool down an overheating economy. In late July the Chancellor had no choice but to announce an intensification of the credit squeeze, calling upon banks to reduce their advances. By this time the pound was coming under pressure on the foreign exchanges, accentuated by rumours of a move towards convertibility between sterling and the dollar. In September Butler told the International Monetary Fund that sterling would remain within fixed margins and be defended by Britain's reserves. But it was clear that further anti-inflationary measures would be necessary to convince the markets of the government's resolve. As ministers began discussing what form these measures should take, the Prime Minister appeared shaken by his rapid reversal of fortune. 'In the midst of this economic turmoil', he noted in his diary, 'it is fair to recall that I did sound a warning last December and pressed for a February election. . . . Rab was the one who upheld Winston in rejecting any such suggestion.' Butler was now aware of the scale of the problem, but 'when it comes to action the result is poor'. Whatever happened, 'we must not appear like the hard faced men of 1918'.[26]

The friction between Eden and his Chancellor was evident in Cabinet. Both men agreed that if inflation was to be tackled, the government needed to admit that Britain was living beyond its means. This implied both expenditure cuts and increased taxation, though what precise form these should take proved contentious. The Prime Minister strongly opposed Treasury demands for an end to bread subsidies; this he felt would give the government a 'hard-faced' reputation. After agonising over when to act, so adding to a growing reputation for indecisiveness, Eden finally gave the go-ahead for an emergency budget in late October 1955. This proved to be unpopular as well as humiliating for a Chancellor so recently credited with helping to engineer electoral victory. Sharp cutbacks were announced in local authority building programmes, and various forms of indirect taxation were increased. The extension of purchase tax to kitchen and other household goods allowed Butler's package to be labelled the 'pots and pans Budget', which as Eden bitterly reflected was hardly a rallying cry for his property-owning democracy.[27] Altogether the Chancellor clawed back about two-thirds of the tax reliefs provided in the spring. Hugh Gaitskell, seeking to prove his credentials as favourite to become the next Labour leader, made a wounding attack in which he accused Butler of deliberately deceiving the nation about the state of the economy at the time of the election. By the end of the year it was clear things would get worse before they got better: the balance of payments was still in the red and inflationary pressures continued unabated.

Elsewhere on the home front there were further signs of vacillation. With growing numbers of immigrants arriving from British colonies, ministers took a hard look at the possibility of introducing entry controls, but eventually decided not to act.[28] A similar uncertainty characterised policy towards the unions. Shortly after the general election, a threatened railway strike forced Eden to declare a state of emergency. By mid-June, Monckton's conciliatory skills had secured the acceptance of binding arbitration procedures, thus averting a serious dispute and allowing ministers to turn to longer term needs.

The Cabinet was told there was unlikely to be a more favourable opportunity to take 'wise action' that might improve industrial relations.[29] But attitudes in the party were hardening against the Minister of Labour's industrial 'appeasement'. Many activists felt that the need for sacrifices all round was not appreciated by union leaders pressing high wage demands. Monckton conceded that a situation of overfull employment had led employers to outbid each other for skilled labour, creating a feeling of irresponsibility among workers. He remained opposed though to secret ballots before strike action or to legislation outlawing unofficial strikes, which he believed would be 'politically inexpedient and ineffective in practice'.[30] As a result, the Cabinet Committee on industrial policy set up by Eden in the summer made slow progress. In November senior ministers met a TUC delegation at Downing Street to explore the possibility of an agreed wages and prices policy, but in the aftermath of a rise in purchase tax, 'there was no meeting of minds'. Several months later the Cabinet Committee was disbanded after rejecting modest reforms such as a compulsory 'cooling off' period before a strike could be called.[31] Eden's desire not to offend trade union voters was proving as strong as Churchill's.

The Prime Minister's popularity was in any case sinking rapidly by the end of 1955, partly because of his handling of ministerial changes. It was not long before Eden wished he had appointed a more compliant Foreign Secretary; his diary confirmed he was 'as much irritated by [Macmillan's] patronising tone as by his absence of policy'.[32] On top of this came the problem of a Chancellor whose credibility had been eroded. Eden's solution was to propose moving both his senior colleagues. Well before Butler presented his emergency budget to the Commons – when he received Eden's 'full support' – his job had been offered to Macmillan. In return Rab was asked to 'lead the Commons and handle the party'; Eden admitted he was finding it 'difficult to work with so strong a character as Harold Macmillan'.[33] Neither Butler nor Macmillan concurred with enthusiasm. The Chancellor's advisers warned him not to accept anything that smacked of demotion, suggesting that he should stay put until a recovering economy restored his reputation.[34] Macmillan suspected the Prime Minister of jealousy, and angry at the prospect of an early departure from the Foreign Office, his compliance came with strings attached. He was to become 'undisputed head of the Home Front', while Butler – assuming the titles of

COMING HOME TO ROOST ...

"I GOT SIXPENCE, JOLLY, JOLLY SIXPENCE..."

SPRING BUDGET

TO THE ELECTION

AUTUMN BUDGET

Lord Privy Seal and Leader of the House – must on no account be
appointed Deputy Prime Minister.[35] Wrangling continued behind
the scenes for some time before a compromise was reached. Butler
was denied the title of Deputy but was empowered to preside over
Cabinet in Eden's absence, as he had done since 1952. Shortly before
Christmas the reshuffle was finally announced. Aside from the
movement of Macmillan and Butler, Selwyn Lloyd was promoted
to become Foreign Secretary, and Monckton was replaced as
Minister of Labour by the more youthful and combative Iain
Macleod – the only change 'where Eden conceivably had a policy
end in view'.[36]

The changes received a lukewarm press. To move the two most
senior figures in the government within six months of an election, it
was alleged, could only be interpreted as admitting to the failure of
Butler's policy and to the Prime Minister's desire to 'run foreign
policy himself'.[37] Butler was considered to have been outwitted by
Macmillan, and there was speculation that his position as heir
apparent had been undermined. One leading Conservative noted
that the Treasury was the only carrot Macmillan would accept as 'an
ambitious and potentially dangerous leading colleague'. In the words
of Lord Kilmuir, Macmillan's hard bargain ensured that the move
was intended as 'a step towards and not away from the Premiership'.[38] Butler later wrote that it was from this time that senior
figures such as Churchill and Lord Salisbury decided to 'back
Macmillan', even though Churchill had encouraged Rab to accept
the switch.[39] The poor reception accorded to the reshuffle seemed
to sum up the disquiet felt after six months of Eden's administration.
Evidence that disaffection had spread to voters came a week earlier
at the Torquay by-election, where the Conservative share of the poll
fell by 9.4 per cent compared with the general election. This was a
scale of reversal almost unknown in over 40 by-elections during
the previous parliament. Perhaps the best indication of how the
euphoria of May had evaporated came at the party's autumn
conference, where expectations of a victory rally failed to materialise.
Churchill's son-in-law Christopher Soames reported that Eden had
been well enough received, 'but there is a widespread feeling that
the Government hasn't got a firm grip on affairs – there is too much
drift, and not enough evidence of decision on many outstanding
problems'.[40]

Gaitskell Replaces Attlee

The Prime Minister's problems were compounded by having to face a new leader of the opposition. It was obvious in the aftermath of May's election defeat that Attlee, after 20 years at the helm, would soon retire. But when the PLP met for the first in the new parliament, Attlee suggested continuing in post for a short time. To his critics, this was confirmation that he was determined to spite his most long-standing rival; he clung on until 'Morrison's last hope had vanished'.[41] Attlee maintained that his immediate resignation would deepen division within the party by opening the way for renewed hostility between the supporters of Morrison and Bevan. Whatever his motives, the effect of Attlee's decision was to enhance the prospects of the third contender for the leadership – Hugh Gaitskell. Aside from his forceful attack on Butler's emergency budget, Gaitskell's standing in the parliamentary party was improved by 'Operation Avalanche' – the effort of his old ally Hugh Dalton to dislodge ageing members of the Shadow Cabinet, 9 of whom were over 65. By urging others showing 'signs of senility' to follow his lead in retiring, Dalton helped to encourage the view that Morrison's age made him an unsuitable adversary for Eden. With Bevan's record of rebellion undermining his prospects, Dalton was confident that 'H.G. has the Leadership in the Bag'.[42] This prophecy was borne out when Attlee finally resigned in December 1955. In the PLP ballot that followed, Gaitskell comfortably defeated Bevan (157 votes to 70), leaving Morrison humiliated with only 40 votes in third place.

Gaitskell's personal qualities helped to explain the ease of his victory. As one of his close associates reflected:

> It had become clear to those who feared a resumption of Bevan's excesses that a vote for Gaitskell was now the best way of holding the Party together. Though still under fifty, Gaitskell shared with Stafford Cripps one rare quality which was immensely valued by the solid core of Labour MPs. By calculated lucidity and un-adorned rational argument, he in the end produced a more *emotional* conviction than rhetoric could achieve. Bevan's most splendid speeches entertained, impressed, even enthused. . . . But Gaitskell *persuaded*; and left conviction where there had previously been doubt.[43]

The new leader was not without his critics. Even his friends admitted to a 'streak of intolerance' in Gaitskell's nature which meant that those who opposed him were regarded as either 'knaves or fools'.[44] And for Bevanites, it was impossible to forgive overnight Gaitskell's behaviour since 1951 and his close ties with right-wing union leaders. The claim that Gaitskell was insufficiently radical to head the Labour party – which Attlee once said should always be led from left of centre – was one that was to resurface. So too were accusations that he relied heavily on a narrow clique of friends known as the 'Hampstead set', who like himself tended to be middle class and Oxford-educated. As we shall see, the legacy left by the bitter internal disputes of the early 1950s was to haunt the party for several years.

Gaitskell's triumph did, however, offer grounds for optimism. In the first place, he was more willing than his predecessor to take on board the lessons of electoral defeat and to encourage fresh thinking in domestic policy. The NEC had already sanctioned several studies with the aim of redrawing policy in the light of recent social changes. Under Gaitskell's guidance, this process culminated in what became known as Labour's 'revisionist' agenda. In place of the old style corporate socialism characteristic of Attlee's generation, Gaitskell wanted to see policies underpinned by an ideology that emphasised social equality. Revisionism found expression not only in policy committees; in terms of intellectual argument, Gaitskell's case was strengthened by the publication in 1956 of Anthony Crosland's influential work *The Future of Socialism*. Crosland, an Oxford-trained economist and a close friend of Gaitskell, argued that knee-jerk antagonism towards the evils of capitalism was outmoded. Now that post-war economic management appeared capable of delivering wider prosperity than ever before, attention should be focused more on the ethical tradition in socialist thinking. In order to progress towards equality, Crosland argued, Labour had to draw up a new list of priorities: these might include comprehensive secondary schools for all children, the redistribution of wealth via the taxation system, and increases in public expenditure to remedy injustices in areas such as housing and health. Crosland also believed that socialism could only be made relevant to everyday lives if it shed its association with austerity and puritanism of the Cripps variety. 'Total abstinence and a good filing system are not', he claimed, 'the right sign-posts to the socialist Utopia: or at least, if they are, some of us will fall by the wayside.'[45]

A second promising sign for the new leadership was the muted response of the Labour left to revisionism. Many were outraged by Crosland's assertion that nationalisation should henceforth play a minor role in socialist advance, and Bevan himself was scornful. 'Do we now burn the books?', he questioned. 'Don't we need to bother with William Morris, or Karl Marx, or Keir Hardie?'[46] But Bevan had never been able to construct a persuasive alternative pro- gramme, and the retreat of Bevanism within the parliamentary party was such that there was only a negligible intellectual challenge to the revisionist case. The champion of the 'old left', moreover, believed there was no choice but to make his peace with the new leader. Bevan recognised, albeit reluctantly, that Gaitskell's victory in the leadership contest had decisively ended the internal power struggle for the foreseeable future. After years of failing to make progress on party committees dominated by the organisational strength of his opponents, Bevan came to the view that he must play the role of loyal lieutenant, especially after he agreed to become first shadow Colonial Secretary and then shadow Foreign Secretary. The party's prospects were also an important consideration. Gaitskell was not only likely to have a honeymoon period; he was also facing a Prime Minister whose personal level of approval had fallen dramatically from 70 to 40 per cent within a matter of months. Labour was already moving back into an opinion poll lead by the time Gaitskell took over, and as long as Eden remained in office, it seemed reasonable to believe there would be no repeat of the 1955 defeat.

'The best Prime Minister we have'

At the beginning of 1956, the Prime Minister's ability to survive was being questioned. After reflecting on Eden's Cabinet changes over Christmas, newspapers usually loyal to the Conservative cause resumed their sniping. *The Daily Telegraph*, amongst the most fulsome in its praise of Eden six months earlier, caused particular consterna- tion by calling for the 'smack of firm government'.[47] Anti-Tory papers gleefully joined in, some running stories that the Prime Minister might soon resign in favour of Butler or Macmillan. Butler made matters worse when, under persistent questioning from a journalist, he agreed with the view that Eden was the best available leader. This was widely misreported as the claim that Eden 'is the best Prime Minister we have', words which could easily be interpreted as a 'back-handed compliment'.[48] Ignoring the advice of those who felt he should let things blow over, the Prime Minister confronted his critics. First, he took the unusual step of issuing a statement saying that rumours of his imminent resignation were false. Then in a speech at Bradford he turned on 'cantakerous newspapers', adding that 'this country is not on its way down, and this Government is not on its way out'. The barrage of press criticism died down quickly thereafter, especially after Eden met leading editors to reassure them that his new team was working well.[49] But doubts about the Prime Minister's leadership had hardly been dispelled. According to one of his fiercest critics, Randolph Churchill, by this time 'there were many of his colleagues who felt that he was inadequate to the task and that he would have to be replaced as quickly and as kindly as possible by someone with a more robust political stamina'.[50]

Some reporters took a more relaxed view. The government's troubles, it was noted, were no greater than those faced by Churchill in the first year of his 1951 administration. Backbench Conservatives may have been restless but they were far from rebellious, and it was nonsense to think that the Prime Minister could be overthrown within a year of his election triumph without seriously jeopardising the party's hold on power.[51] Those in the know added that there seemed to be a personal dimension to the attacks in the *Daily Telegraph*, originating in a quarrel between Lady Eden and Pamela Berry, wife of the newspaper's editor-in-chief. The Prime Minister certainly believed that a 'personal vendetta lies behind it'.[52] *The Economist* saw both irony and hidden danger in 'this premature insurrection'. The main irony was that despite accusations of dithering, decisions were actually being made more rapidly than in the latter stages of Churchill's regime. Most worrying, claimed *The Economist*, was the possibility that the crisis as described above 'may strengthen Sir Anthony's hand to be a weak Prime Minister': by not wishing to court more unpopularity, he could be tempted to ease up in the essential battle against inflation.[53] Herein lay the central cause of Eden's difficulties – fear that the economy was out of control. In this sense Eden's prospects looked less promising than those engineered by Churchill within eighteen months of coming to power; the good fortune that helped to bring prosperity in the early 1950s had evaporated. The author of the most wounding attacks in the *Telegraph* later insisted there was no real plot against the Prime Minister: it was 'just that people were rather fed up'.[54]

If Eden hoped his new Chancellor would instantly restore the government's fortunes he was mistaken. Macmillan, like most incumbents of his office, was alarmed when he 'saw the books'. The position, he wrote, 'is *much* worse than I had expected. Butler had left things drift', and the exhaustion of Britain's reserves could lead to 'total collapse' within a year.[55] Senior ministers began emphasising in their speeches the 'plagues of prosperity': the difficulty of delivering both full employment and steady prices. This was a way of preparing the public for more bad news. On 24 January the Cabinet accepted in principle the need for further cutbacks in expenditure and another rise in bank rate. But as with Butler, the Prime Minister found himself at loggerheads with Macmillan over points of detail. When Eden maintained his opposition to the abolition of subsidies on the price of bread and milk, the Chancellor issued an ultimatum. 'I don't want to threaten the Cabinet', Macmillan wrote, but he then proceeded to do so by insisting he would resign, knowing that the Prime Minister could ill afford to lose two Chancellors in rapid succession.[56] Faced with the possible collapse of his administration, Eden agreed to a compromise which Macmillan later said conceded 'four-fifths of my demands'. On 17 February a new emergency package was announced, including the reduction of bread subsidies with abolition to follow later in the year. Bank rate rose by half a point to five per cent; hire-purchase deposits were increased; and public expenditure was to be further reduced. On the same day Brendan Bracken wrote to Lord Beaverbrook to say that the Prime Minister had suffered another setback:

> Your prophecy that your former Under-Secretary [Macmillan] would make trouble for Eden has swiftly been proved. He sent in his resignation yesterday on a cunningly contrived issue which would have gravely embarrassed his boss and would have given your former Under-Secretary the credit for being the only virtuous and strong man in the government. A truce has been patched up, but how long it will last is anybody's guess.[57]

The Prime Minister did though reassert his authority in finalising the budget. Macmillan argued that three separate attempts to tackle inflation by mild measures over the past year had failed. In order to maintain international confidence and avoid a crisis later in the year – with the betting on 'compulsory devaluation' – he proposed drastic remedies. These included putting 6*d* back on income tax and making swingeing cuts in defence spending.[58] This time it was Eden who refused to give way, ruling out further tax increases. In this he was supported by Butler, anxious not to see his election-winning formula of the previous year overturned. 'Rab says he will resign if this is done', noted Treasury adviser Robert Hall, adding that 'no one knows whether to believe him or not'.[59] Personal calculation helps to explain why Macmillan, having threatened to resign on the smaller matter of subsidies, never went to the same extreme on issues he described as the 'real test for the government'. Resignation in February would have made him a natural focus for disaffected Tory MPs, especially right-wingers anxious to see tough measures. But he was unlikely to attract the same level of support if he went out on the rallying cry of more income tax and defence cuts. The Chancellor thus had to content himself with a broadly neutral budget. Most attention focused less on a small increase in tobacco tax than on the encouragement to saving offered by the introduction of premium bonds. On the whole Macmillan's entertaining delivery and upbeat talk about balanced expansion earned a favourable reception. By mid-1956 Eden was trying hard to make the case that the corner had been turned. He told MPs that the balance of payments was improving, inflation slowing down, and that with publication of a major White Paper there was a growing recognition that steady prices and full employment could be secured only if the whole community understood the need for 'restraint and foresight'.[60]

Voters, however, remained unimpressed. Although at one of six by-elections held in the early months of 1956 (Leeds North East), the Conservative share of the vote showed an improvement, the remainder continued the pattern seen at Torquay. Tory majorities fell sharply at the expense of the Liberals in some seats, such as Hereford and Gainsborough. Labour came close to capturing Taunton, which it regarded as 'the key to the West Country', garnering support on the new housing estates that had supported Eden in the 1955 election.[61] After a three-month gap the government struggled again at Tonbridge in June, where an 8.4 per cent drop in the Conservative vote saw a majority of 10,196 reduced to 1602. This contest attracted much greater press attention as it seemed to indicate that disquiet had reached the party's heartlands. Some observers claimed that Tory abstentions had been caused by the imposition of an outside candidate, but most believed the result showed how the government needed to improve the economy while convincing 'the body of traditional Tory supporters that they are getting as much considera- tion from the Government as, say, the trade unions have had since 1945'.[62] While home owners faced rising mortgage charges, middle- class bitterness was directed at manual workers apparently securing large pay rises. What Eden faced, it was claimed, was nothing less than a 'middle-class revolt'. During the spring two new movements had been formed on the fringes of mainstream politics: the People's League for the Defence of Freedom and the Middle Class Alliance. Both aimed to restore the middle classes to 'their former place in the community', and posed the danger of enticing into their ranks 'a solid section of Conservative supporters'. Although the number of defections by rank-and-file activists was as yet limited, the threat was sufficient for the Party Chairman, Oliver Poole, to warn publicly of the dangers of splitting the anti-socialist vote.[63]

By the summer of 1956 doubts about Eden were multiplying. One of the Prime Minister's speeches had been so poorly received that an American correspondent noted how backbenchers were 'profoundly gloomy'; there were parallels here with the downfall of Neville Chamberlain, for any further setbacks might lead to 'the sort of rebellion that I watched in late April and early May 1940'.[64] In these circumstances, the absence of a credible successor was vital to Eden's survival. Rab Butler was regarded as a waning force after his departure from the Treasury. He made only two major speeches in six months as Leader of the House; colleagues warned him about 'aloofness' from MPs; and there were rumours that he might go to the House of Lords, thereby ending any leadership ambitions.[65] Eden's reputation had nevertheless sunk further. The impression of a government unable to control events could, it seemed, only be countered either by a strong economic recovery or a major foreign- policy triumph, neither of which seemed likely. In July 1956 the diarist Harold Nicolson noted how he attended a party at which Nye Bevan:

talked to me about the decay of the present government. He attributes it entirely to Eden, who, he says, is much disliked, weak and vacillating, and, in fact, hopeless. He was not talking as an Opposition leader, but as a student of politics. I heard the same thing at the Club today. . . . To choose Eden had been a mistake, since he was not a strong man. He interfered with his colleagues and did not control them, and gave the impression to the House that he did not know his own mind. Now when I hear a man abused like that, I immediately wish to take his side. But I fear that it is all too true.[66]

On the same day President Nasser of Egypt nationalised the Suez Canal. The opportunity for a dramatic recovery in the Prime Minister's fortunes had suddenly, and quite unexpectedly, presented itself.

The Suez Crisis and Resignation

The high drama of Suez dominated British politics in the autumn of 1956. Britain's reputation abroad was to be seriously impaired and instead of securing a triumph, Eden was humiliated and forced to resign – ostensibly on grounds of ill-health – early in 1957. The Prime Minister's initial response, to compare Nasser's unlawful action with those of Hitler in the 1930s, commanded widespread approval. But how to react as the weeks of crisis unfolded became hotly disputed, both at Westminster and beyond. Public opinion appeared divided over whether British military intervention was justified, and there were contradictory signals: opinion polls showed a narrowing of Labour's lead, but by-election results continued the anti-government trend evident earlier in the year.[67] Gaitskell held the opposition together by emphasising the need for a diplomatic solution: 'law not war'. On the Conservative side, a small group of moderates opposed talk of military intervention, but the majority favoured any action that might secure British oil supplies through the canal. They therefore welcomed an Anglo-French assault early in November – justified on the pretext of separating Egyptian and Israeli forces – and were stunned when the operation was suddenly halted in the face of hostile world opinion. After riotous scenes in the Commons, where a sitting had to be suspended for the first time in thirty years, intense pressure was put on disgruntled members of the 'Suez Group' not to vote against the Prime Minister. Despite their opposition to a ceasefire and the withdrawal of British troops, the 'tough men' of the right mostly came into line when threatened with the 'unspeakable [alternative] of a Gaitskell government'.[68] The possibility that Eden's majority would fall so far as to ensure his downfall – as happened to Chamberlain in 1940 – was averted. By late November government unity remained largely intact, impaired only by the resignation of two junior ministers and the Press Secretary at No.10, the latter of whom was speeded on his way with a flying ink pot.

The pressure on the Cabinet had nevertheless been relentless, with the greatest strain being borne by the triumvirate of senior ministers. In the face of opposition from a minority of colleagues, Eden threatened the break-up of the whole administration on 4 November: 'if they wouldn't go on then he would have to resign'.[69] The Prime Minister's poor health increasingly became a factor. Suffering from exhaustion, it was decided he should leave the country for a period of complete rest. On 23 November he left to recuperate at the Jamaica residence of novelist Ian Fleming. Randolph Churchill jibed that when German troops were left to fend for themselves at Stalingrad, 'even Hitler did not winter in Jamaica', and speculation that Eden might have to resign began to gather pace. In the Prime Minister's absence, Rab Butler once more found himself at the helm, respon-sible among other things for ensuring that Eden was consulted at his remote holiday outpost. Butler felt that medical advice made Eden's decision to leave the country unavoidable, but came to regret being left in charge when the government was so clearly out of step with international opinion. As he later observed, he now faced 'the odious duty of withdrawing the troops, re-establishing the pound, salvaging our relations with the US, and bearing the brunt of criticism from private members, constituency worthies and the general public for organizing a withdrawal, which was a collective responsibility'. Butler's notorious ambiguity – formally supporting Eden but indis-creetly expressing reservations behind the scenes – seriously damaged his reputation. He later claimed that he was never opposed to the defeat of Nasser, and was sorry the operation had not been carried out more expeditiously, but wherever he went during the difficult weeks of Eden's absence, Butler 'felt the party knives sticking into my innocent back'.[70]

The third key minister during the crisis, Macmillan, ironically found his political standing enhanced. The Chancellor had been confident that Suez would not place undue pressure on sterling, and his belief that the United States would fall into line explained his strong support for a hard line. But after playing down warnings from his officials, Macmillan was unable to ignore the American pressure which threatened to deplete British reserves to the level at which devaluation had been unavoidable in 1949.[71] Within hours he moved, in the acerbic view of Brendan Bracken, from 'wanting to tear Nasser's scalp off with his own finger nails' to becoming 'leader of the bolters'.[72] The Chancellor was alleged to have threatened resignation unless there was an early ceasefire, and in Eden's absence he championed the view that restoring American backing was more important than holding out for specific terms before withdrawing British troops. This turnaround was interpreted by some as a desire to remedy his misreading of President Eisenhower's intentions, a failing he never concealed in his memoirs. Others, however, suspected a deliberate challenge to the Prime Minister, some even claiming that he pushed Eden into Suez in order to hasten his downfall.[73] While this may be an exaggeration, there were signs that Macmillan saw new possibilities opening up once Eden had left for Jamaica. Unlike Butler, the Chancellor was able to limit his public appearances, so avoiding being linked in the public's mind with the decision for British withdrawal. When he did speak, most notably to the 1922 Committee, his language was replete with references to Munich: reminding MPs that Butler had been a supporter of appeasement in the 1930s. The majority of those present were said to have been impressed, though one critic recalled that the 'sheer devilry of it verged on the disgusting'.[74] On 7 December Bracken wrote that a serious challenge was emerging:

Macmillan is telling journalists that he intends to retire from politics and go to the morgue. His real intentions are to push his boss out of No. 10 and he has a fair following in the Tory party. The so-called diehards think better of him than they do of Eden or Butler.[75]

But the Prime Minister as yet had no intention of retiring. Bracken said Eden had told him 'he fully intends to brazen this out', and seemed to be the 'least rattled' of all ministers. Butler confirmed that when Eden returned from Jamaica on 14 December, looking bronzed and restored to health, 'it wasn't clear that he wasn't going to continue as Prime Minister at all'.[76] This resolve was shaken when Eden received a frosty reception. Aside from scathing newspaper headlines – such as 'Prime Minister visits Britain' – there were embarrassing scenes in the House of Commons when only one Tory MP cheered Eden's arrival. Things were no better when he met the 1922 Committee on 18 December. Many backbenchers were still angry about the early curtailment of the Suez operation, and were not reassured by the Prime Minister's claim that he would act in exactly the same way again. According to one member present, Nigel Nicolson, this remark was greeted 'in almost complete silence'. Instead of striking a chord of defiance, it only confirmed doubts about Eden's judgement: why send the troops in if the operation was not going to be carried through? From this moment, Nicolson said, he must have realised that party support was draining away.[77] Although he confided to a colleague his fear about being a 'Prime Minister at half-cock', it required a renewed deterioration in Eden's health over Christmas to force the issue. When asked if he could last out 'till the summer or Easter at the earliest', the opinion of three leading consultants was unanimous: another breakdown was likely within six weeks if he continued in office. This information was conveyed in confidence to Butler, Macmillan and Lord Salisbury on the morning of 9 January 1957. By 5 o'clock surprised members of the Cabinet were told that the Prime Minister had resigned.

Historians have generally accepted that this abrupt departure can only be explained on medical grounds. Whatever his reception in December, Eden knew that the party still preferred him to Butler. It was hard to see, prior to the doctors' intervention, what could have toppled him in the short term.[78] Others have been reluctant to conclude that medical advice alone forced Eden to go. One biographer claims that Butler initiated moves to persuade the Prime Minister that his position was untenable.[79] Support for this can be found in Bracken's uncorroborated reference to a deputation led by Butler and Salisbury, which allegedly gave Eden an ultimatum on his return from Jamaica: the Cabinet would remain supportive until Easter, but would then seek a change of leader unless the Prime Minister's health was fully restored. 'If', Bracken told Beaverbrook, 'Churchill had had such a greeting from his colleagues he would have told them to go to the furthermost part of hell, but as you know very

well, Eden has none of Churchill's pugnacity.'[80] This could, of
course, explain Eden pressing his doctors on whether he could
continue until 'Easter at the earliest'. But there may also have been
a further factor at work. On 20 December, after a stressful debate in
the Commons, the Prime Minister was goaded into saying that he
had no prior knowledge of Israel's intention to invade Egypt. It
remains difficult to ascertain how worried Eden was that this would
be revealed as a lie by one of the few who knew otherwise, whether in
Israel, London or Washington. He must have been aware that any
such revelation would force him to resign in disgrace; his memory of
appeasement cannot have overlooked the fate of Foreign Secretary
Samuel Hoare in 1935. Writing in confidence to Beaverbrook,
Bracken said that, though his colleagues were willing to put the
knife in his back, the main reason for Eden's departure was 'a secret
stuffed with dynamite'. This was the secret of collusion: 'our friend
brought himself down and needless remorse unnerved him'.[81]

Conclusion

With hindsight, leading Conservatives tried to make out that they
suspected Eden might not pass muster all along. Interviewed much
later in old age, Harold Macmillan claimed that 'Winston thought
Anthony would wreck it – that's a reason why he held on for so
long.'[82] The circumstances of Eden's departure, in the aftermath of
Suez, have made it easy for historians to claim that personal failings
provide the key to understanding his troubled premiership. According to his detractors, Eden was guilty of everything from indecision
and lack of imagination through to obsessive vanity. His mismanagement certainly left the party in a state of turmoil. One back-
bencher noted how weeks of anxiety had produced the danger of an
'absolute split' in Conservative ranks, with up to 100 MPs being
hostile to early withdrawal from Suez and a smaller group of between
10 and 20 opposed to staying on without any apparent advantage.[83]
The bitterness that resulted was not easily forgotten. The small
number of anti-invasion rebels all incurred the wrath of local party
activists, who across the country rallied strongly behind the government; four MPs were deselected and others found their careers
blighted.[84] While an 'absolute split', threatening the early break-
up of the administration, was ultimately averted, it was difficult to

dispute the view of Edward Boyle – one of the two ministers to resign – that the end result brought no credit to the Tory cause:

> Nasser is still there, the canal is blocked, the economic outlook is appallingly black, Stalinism seems to be waxing again, and British influence in the Near East has sunk to a new low point. How any self-respecting Conservative Association can at this juncture circulate pamphlets about Eden entitled 'This is his finest hour' I simply cannot imagine.[85]

But if Eden lacked the qualities that would enable him – in the language of April 1955 – to continue commanding respect in 'the Cabinet room, in the House and in the country', it should not be overlooked that he became the scapegoat for ill-conceived decisions that were taken collectively. Aside from being implicated in the Suez débâcle, senior colleagues were responsible for errors of judgement that saw the first appearance of 'stop-go' in the post-war economy. The downturn of 1955–6 has been attributed even by sympathetic writers to 'short-term, self-defeating expedients', notably a pre-election budget that fuelled inflation and made painful remedial measures unavoidable.[86] Butler was forced to leave the Treasury in humiliation and Macmillan spectacularly misjudged the capacity of Britain's reserves to hold up in an international crisis. On the home front, the Conservative leadership as a whole, and not Eden alone, found itself floundering in the face of changing economic circumstances. Certainly the stagnation of the economy meant that Eden's election victory, which afterwards assumed an air of inevitability, was unlikely to have been so easily achieved at any other time during 1955–6. It was small wonder that, in spite of a larger parliamentary majority, the Conservatives had still not progressed far in domestic policy beyond the legacy of 1951. What was termed in the previous chapter 'consensus by default' remained the order of the day. When Eden left office, just as when Churchill came to power over five years earlier, many assumed that Labour might shortly return to power. The problems that had beset and ultimately undone the 'best Prime Minister we have' were not therefore likely to disappear overnight. As we shall see in the next chapter, his successor was in for a rough ride.

3 'Never had it so good', 1957-9

Introduction

'Inflation', said *The Economist* in 1957, 'is like sin. Everybody is against it, but it goes on.'[1] By the time Harold Macmillan became Prime Minister in January 1957, policy-makers regarded rising prices as the central challenge to Britain's future economic stability. Inflationary pressures had persuaded Eden's government to reverse the expansionary policies of the early 1950s. Macmillan, as a former Chancellor, was fully aware of the dangers that lay ahead, conceding in private that 'the country simply did not realise that we were living beyond our income, and would have to pay for it sooner or later'.[2] Yet this concern is not usually associated with the new incumbent at Downing Street. Rather, many have taken at face value the rhetoric of public utterances about the nation 'never having it so good'. The late 1950s are often remembered as the era of 'Supermac', the great actor–manager who swiftly transformed his party's fortunes after Suez and harnessed the tide of prosperity to sweep to inevitable victory in 1959. The reality, it will be argued here, was less straightforward. As we shall see, Tory unpopularity survived well beyond the departure of Anthony Eden, and continued well into 1958 while the economy remained in the doldrums. Macmillan took a considerable time to establish himself as a popular leader, and two years into his premiership was not sufficiently confident to face the electorate. When victory came in October 1959 it derived ultimately from a lack of trust in the Labour alternative and in a short-term expansion of the economy that could not be long sustained. Ministers, not least those who resigned from the Treasury, recognised that fresh dangers threatened rising living standards unless changes were made; but the desire for party advantage came first. Inflation, like sin, was set to continue.

Macmillan Triumphs Over Butler

Eden was replaced as Prime Minister within 24 hours. Two senior
government peers, Lord Salisbury (Lord President of the Council)
and Lord Kilmuir (the Lord Chancellor), agreed on the procedure to
be adopted for the succession. They would consult members of the
Cabinet and other leading party dignitaries before advising Queen
Elizabeth on the choice between two candidates – Rab Butler and
Harold Macmillan. Kilmuir later outlined the sequence of events that
followed Eden's announcement to a surprised Cabinet on 9 January:

> Bobbety [Salisbury] and I asked our colleagues to see us one by
> one in Bobbety's room in the Privy Council Offices. . . . There
> were two light reliefs. Practically each one began by saying, 'This
> is like coming to the Headmaster's study.' To each Bobbety said,
> 'Well, which is it, Wab or Hawold?' As well as seeing the
> remainder of the ex-Cabinet, we interviewed the Chief Whip
> and Oliver Poole, the Chairman of the Party. John Morrison,
> the Chairman of the 1922 Executive, rang me up from Islay the
> next morning. An overwhelming majority of Cabinet Ministers
> was in favour of Macmillan as Eden's successor, and back-bench
> opinion, as reported to us, strongly endorsed this view.[3]

Most newspapers were wide of the mark in predicting Butler as the
likely successor on 10 January. By late morning of the 10th the
Queen had received advice from Lord Salisbury and from Winston
Churchill, who also 'went for the older man'.[4] By three o'clock
Macmillan, having spent the morning reading Jane Austen's *Pride
and Prejudice* – 'very soothing' – had been summoned to Buckingham
Palace and invited to form a government. During the evening he
took the Chief Whip, Edward Heath, to celebrate with champagne
and oysters at the Turf Club.[5]

The leadership crisis was swift, though it was by no means free of
controversy. In the first place, important questions of procedure were
raised. One minister felt Salisbury and Kilmuir had no authority to
act at such short notice; another maintained that he was never
consulted.[6] Suggestions were also made subsequently that Lord
Salisbury, whose personal preference was for Macmillan, influenced
the outcome by calling in uncommitted Cabinet members at the end;
seeing strong backing for Macmillan on the sheet of paper before

them, the pressure to go with the tide became irresistible.[7] No one involved has corroborated this view, however; nor was it obvious who else might carry out the consultation process. Both Salisbury and Kilmuir could claim to be ideally placed, as respected members of the House of Lords, to offer speedy and impartial advice. They could also claim to be following the precedent of 1923, when senior party statesmen stepped in to assist an outgoing prime minister, Bonar Law, considered too unwell to take charge of soundings to determine a successor. It was noticeable that Labour's immediate response – to question the propriety of the succession – was not followed up when Gaitskell returned from a foreign trip. Clearly a constitutional crisis could have developed (along with a deep split in Tory ranks) had Eden declared a strong preference for Butler. Macmillan states that he 'gathered from Anthony' whom he saw later on 10 January – 'that he had neither been asked for his advice nor had volunteered it'.[8] Some historians have challenged this, citing evidence from Eden's private papers in which he informed the Queen about Butler's success in stepping in during his own absences.[9] But if this was ever intended as an endorsement – which was not at all clear – it was never repeated in public by Eden.

Controversy also surrounds the question of how far Macmillan's triumph was determined in advance. Although Eden's departure was sudden, his ill-health inevitably provoked speculation before Christmas 1956 about a possible change of leadership. In such an event, the Suez group of Tory MPs in particular were determined to block the emergence of Butler. At Cabinet level, as Butler later discovered, there were several younger ministers – including Thorneycroft, Eccles, Lennox-Boyd and Sandys – who were making known their private preference for Macmillan in anticipation of Eden's departure.[10] While Butler was taking comfort from public opinion, which made him the preferred successor, Macmillan was cultivating support where it mattered – inside the party. Edward Heath conceded that there hadn't been much negotiation but there had been 'contacts'.[11] The distinguished journalist Henry Fairlie went further, claiming that 'while Eden was still Prime Minister, recuperating in the West Indies, his Chancellor of the Exchequer was arranging his removal and his own succession'.[12] Notions of any full-blown conspiracy are, however, difficult to square with Eden's determination, until receiving firm medical advice on 7 January, to remain at the helm. What was more, Butler – though bitterly disappointed by his

treatment at the hands of 'our beloved Monarch' – could hardly cry
foul when his rival was so obviously the party's choice. Whatever
system had been used for gauging opinion, it was unlikely to have
produced a different outcome. Butler had to accept that his support
was minimal among ministers and that even natural 'Butlerite' MPs
were switching sides.[13]

The real mystery remains why Macmillan was so overwhelmingly
preferred. Butler's key role in helping to deliver electoral victory in
1955 appeared to have no bearing on Conservative opinion. What
clearly did was the legacy of Suez. It was an open secret that Butler
shared the privately expressed view of Churchill: 'If I had had an
operation on my inside I would not have attempted to invade Suez
by slow convoy from Malta!'[14] In Eden's absence, it was Rab who
had to oversee the humiliating withdrawal of British forces, so
making himself a target for disgruntled members of the Suez group.
Unwilling to admit that the operation had been a mistake, backbenchers took out their anger towards Nasser on Butler, who had
shown himself to be 'sensible' but not very 'heroic'.[15] By contrast,
Macmillan enhanced his standing despite being, in Harold Wilson's
jibe, 'first in, first out'. Initial enthusiasm for intervention, followed
by recognition that American hostility necessitated withdrawal, at
least had the virtue for Tory MPs of demonstrating toughness. In this
respect considerations of character, formed over several years, played
their part in determining the leadership question. Whether justly or
not, many in the party shared Churchill's view that 'Harold is more
decisive'. Whereas Butler was regarded as a masterful intellectual
and administrator, Macmillan – the supreme tactician – was much
less content to sit back and let fortune take its course. His rise to the
top mirrored that of his mentor Churchill in 1940. He, too, had faced
a powerful rival for the succession, Lord Halifax (supported, ironically, by Butler among others). He also combined public loyalty to
the party leader, Neville Chamberlain, with an iron determination to
strike when the moment came. Butler was in no doubt that one major
cause of the outcome was the 'ambience and connections' of his
rival.[16] In the words of Henry Fairlie: 'it was not surprising that it
was with the Chief Whip that Macmillan chose to celebrate on the
night of his appointment, for what he had to celebrate was the
success of a calculated and ruthless political manoeuvre'.[17]

The new Prime Minister showed similar decisiveness in appointing
his Cabinet. Those suspected of voting for Butler were shunted to the

House of Lords. Peter Thorneycroft moved from the Board of Trade to become Chancellor of the Exchequer, and other 'Young Turks' were rewarded for their support in recent weeks. With the likes of Macleod (Labour), Eccles (Trade) and Hailsham (Education) moving into middle-ranking posts, only five of the 1951 Cabinet remained. Most striking was the ease with which Macmillan rebuffed Butler's request to take over as Foreign Secretary, insisting that Selwyn Lloyd remain in place on the grounds that following Suez 'one head on a charger should be enough'.[18] Despite insult being added to injury, Butler held back from splitting the party, agreeing to serve as Home Secretary and Leader of the Commons. With such a hand-picked team, it was not long before the new leader impressed colleagues with his control of Cabinet proceedings.[19] In part this resulted from a deliberately 'unflappable' style that marked him out from his predecessor. At one early meeting of the Cabinet tranquillisers were placed around the table. Ministers were left to devise policy without constant interference, and could even read on the wall one of the new Premier's favourite quotations: 'Quiet calm deliberation disentangles every knot.' Those around him, according to the senior Tory peer, Lord Swinton, believed they had found a leader of many parts:

> Harold Macmillan was perhaps the greatest all-rounder of the Prime Ministers of the century. He was a scholar, and as such could be bracketed with Asquith. As a party manager he could be placed on a par with the Baldwin–Chamberlain association, for he combined the expertise of both. Add to this a peculiar personal flair for timing and harnessing policy to the popular trend of opinion and the claim as an all-rounder is established. Although his sense of history and an innate taste inclined him to an earlier era, he was extraordinarily modern in mastering the current idiom and images of politics. Altogether a formidable combination in one man.[20]

Little of this was apparent to the public in January 1957. Voters did not immediately take to Macmillan's languid style and Edwardian mannerisms, and it was widely believed that after the turmoil of recent weeks, the government might collapse. Macmillan warned the Queen 'half in joke, half in earnest', that he might not last for six weeks, and his memoirs played up the enormity of the problems he confronted. These ranged from Britain's diplomatic isolation in the aftermath of Suez to the elusive domestic task of maintaining the economy 'at the right level, between inflation and deflation'.[21] This did not, as Macmillan's biographers assume, add up to the most troubled inheritance facing any modern prime minister. In the aftermath of Suez, there was a strong desire for unity within Conservative ranks. The parliamentary party followed the Cabinet in falling into line, and Macmillan's calm confidence at the despatch box – in contrast to Eden – was soon reassuring backbenchers. By the spring of 1957 one journalist reported that Tory MPs had 'absolute trust in their leader'.[22] In spite of sniping from sections of the press, there was little prospect of serious internal rebellion or disintegration from within. Nothing illustrated this better than the abrupt resignation of Macmillan's 'Kingmaker', Lord Salisbury, whose departure over policy towards Cyprus generated nothing more than a few adverse headlines. Time was also on the new Premier's side. Labour demands for an early general election not only reinforced Conservative unity; they pointed up how the 1955 parliament was not yet half way through its full term. Macmillan thus had a reasonable period ahead in which to focus on his overriding task – how to restore faith in the government. If this was to be achieved, economic revival above all else was essential.

1957: In the Doldrums

'In the conduct of affairs,' Macmillan once said, 'what is needed is constancy of purpose with flexibility of exercise.'[23] His overriding 'purpose' in economic affairs was growth and prosperity; the problem was how to achieve it. The new Prime Minister was conscious both of the progress that had been made since the war and of the economic dangers that remained. Aware that the rate of inflation had risen by nearly 3 per cent in the first half of 1957, Macmillan made a speech at Bedford on 20 July in which he coined a phrase that subsequently became his own:

> Let's be frank about it; most of our people have never had it so good. Go around the country, go to the industrial towns, go to the farms, and you will see a state of prosperity such as we have never

had in my lifetime – nor indeed ever in the history of this country. What is beginning to worry some of us is 'Is it too good to be true?' or perhaps I should say 'Is it too good to last?' For amidst all this prosperity, there is one problem that has troubled us . . . ever since the war. It's the problem of rising prices. Our constant concern today is – can prices be steadied while at the same time we maintain full employment in an expanding economy? Can we control inflation? This is the problem of our time.[24]

Seen in context, 'never had it so good' was intended as a warning, rather than the complacent boast it became in later mythology. Macmillan's theme, repeated in follow-up speeches, highlighted the dilemma he faced in 1957. As a self-confessed expansionist, he rejected the idea that inflation could only be tackled by a return to unemployment on a scale associated with prewar Stockton, where he began his political career in the 1920s. But how else could voters be persuaded that rising living standards were not endangered? In the short term at least, Macmillan would have to rely on 'flexibility of exercise', even if this involved unpopular policies.

His pragmatic approach was soon apparent. Within weeks the Cabinet had agreed expenditure cutbacks – notably in defence – 'both to convince the public that the Government were in control of the economic situation and also to restore the external confidence in sterling'.[25] But in the spring budget, the Prime Minister was determined to strike a more optimistic note. Record-level British exports were used by the new Chancellor, Peter Thorneycroft, as a pretext for proposing modest tax cuts, both at the standard rate and on surtax. Using language that echoed his leader, Thorneycroft insisted that rising prices could not be tackled by deflationary means. This did not mean he was unaware of hard choices ahead. Thorneycroft had more economic expertise than many holders of his office, and recognised that without radical thinking there could be no easy return to the expansion of the early 1950s. Britain, he soberly told colleagues, had for too long been living beyond its means: incomes had risen nearly three times as fast as output in the previous eight years. His own preferred option was for an incomes policy, designed to counter inflation and make British goods more competitive in world markets.[26] But this was an idea whose time had not yet come. Most ministers were unwilling to interfere with the traditional processes of free collective bargaining, and Thorneycroft had to content himself with a largely toothless three-man Council on Prices, Productivity and Incomes.

Cabinet discussions in 1957 indicated that the 'trade union problem' was working its way up the political agenda. Tory party sentiment, echoed by sections of the press, believed that high wage demands must be curtailed. Pressure on the government intensified with the emergence of a militant new leader of the Transport Workers, Frank Cousins, an outspoken opponent of any form of wage-restraint. Warnings about 'Mr Rising Price' seemed to fall on deaf ears; Macmillan was faced in the early months of his premiership with a series of strikes, notably in the engineering and shipbuilding industries. 'The truth is', he noted, 'that we are now paying the price for the Churchill–Monckton regime – industrial appeasement, with continual inflation.'[27] Much to the disgust of the employers, who were prepared to take on the unions, Iain Macleod as Minister of Labour in effect conceded a large wage settlement. Ministers recognised that 'sooner or later a firm stand would have to be taken on a wages demand'.[28] But this was not the moment. Macmillan believed he could ill afford a widespread confrontation so soon after the Suez débâcle. He was also, as he made clear to ministerial advocates of a tough line, conscious of the need to balance economic against electoral considerations:

A large section of the electorate now consisted of individuals who were members of trade unions; and the Government's victories in the elections of 1951 and 1955 undoubtedly derived in part from the degree of support which they had obtained from this section of the electorate. It would be inexpedient to adopt any policy involving legislation which would alienate this support and divide, rather than consolidate, public opinion.[29]

In the late summer of 1957 concern about inflation and trade unions was overtaken by an unexpected sterling crisis. With almost a quarter of gold and dollar reserves disappearing in the weeks following devaluation in France, a run on the pound was fuelled by rumours that Britain too might be forced to devalue. The Chancellor's response was to show his resolve to the financial markets. In the words of one observer, 'Thorneycroft I' was replaced by 'Thorneycroft II'; the latter seeking tough deflationary measures of a type ruled out in the spring.[30] Cabinet colleagues again objected,

this time on the grounds that proposals to cut public-sector investment could be interpreted as abandoning full employment. Tory-
supporting trade unionists in particular would be alienated by an
admission that the Government had failed in their attempt to
manage the economy on a basis of voluntary agreement; and that
it was unable to maintain for more than a brief period the state of
balanced prosperity achieved during 1953'.[31] With devaluation ruled
out as another national humiliation after Suez, Thorneycroft was left
with few means of controlling the money supply. On 19 September it
was decided to raise the bank lending rate from 5 to 7 per cent. This
was accompanied by limited reductions in public investment and an
intensified credit squeeze. By early October the threat to sterling had
receded. Many economists concluded that Thorneycroft had
slammed the brakes on with unnecessary severity, panicking in the
face of a short-lived, externally imposed crisis. Macmillan spoke in
his memoirs of being pressurised into going against his instincts,
though at the time he, too, seemed prepared to defend sterling at
whatever cost. What he was less prepared for was the way in which
the Chancellor – having discarded any inkling of an expansionary
strategy – embarked on a wholesale anti-inflation crusade.

Thorneycroft's difficulties provided a golden opportunity for the
Labour opposition. Shadow Chancellor Harold Wilson was quick to
attack the September package as a serious setback for production,
investment and employment. 'What a far cry this is from the
complacency of July – or the April budget with those lavish concessions to surtax payers.'[32] Much of Labour's energy in 1957, however,
was spent in working out compromise policies that would satisfy left
and right in the run-up to an election. This process was most striking
in defence policy, culminating in Bevan's renunciation of unilateralism at the annual conference in Brighton. The same trend was
evident in domestic affairs. With sullen acquiescence from Bevan,
the party's policy sub-committee on public ownership produced
Industry and Society, a document which committed a future Labour
government to little more than the renationalisation of steel and road
haulage. In spite of accusations of a sell-out by *Tribune*, the new
strategy was overwhelming backed by delegates at Brighton, and
Gaitskell was credited with a triumph which avoided the need to
make any potentially damaging commitments on public ownership.[33] Whether Gaitskell's patient pursuit of consensus was the right
approach in the minds of voters had still to be tested. Some observers

believed Labour was good at exploiting government unpopularity. Others though felt the chance to champion a dynamic, high-wage society was being lost. Gaitskell, it was said, was too busy playing an old tune: 'he has, all the time, to prove his faith, whether about bombs or about nationalisation'.[34]

For much of 1957, Tory strategists worried about trailing in the opinion polls; Labour's lead was never below five points throughout the year. In April one minister told colleagues that the government 'lacked a clear policy theme with which to dispel the mood of frustration'. His suggestion of clothing the bones of the 'Opportunity State with some attractive flesh to give pleasure to the middle class' never proceeded far.[35] Indeed, the grumbling of the middle classes, evident in Eden's day, continued unabated, with complaints to Central Office that those on fixed incomes were being ignored. In late summer Lord Hailsham was brought in as Party Chairman in an effort to restore morale. Although this helped to galvanise Tory activists – especially when he gave a flamboyant bell-ringing display at the annual conference – voters remained wary. In the wake of the September measures Macmillan was regarded as the most unpopular Prime Minister in living memory.[36] None of this, however, made a general election defeat certain. In eight Tory–Labour by-election fights since Tonbridge in June 1956, the swing from Conservative to Labour averaged nearly 7 per cent – sufficient to deliver a 1945-type victory. But in eight further contests, the Liberals were the main beneficiaries of protest voting, casting doubt on the notion of widespread enthusiasm for Gaitskell. The government, said one Tory insider, 'does not know clearly where it is going or how to get there', but one thing in its favour was the 'continued irrelevance of Labour'.[37] Whatever the state of public opinion, it was obvious that Macmillan had not immediately transformed Tory fortunes. Far from celebrating his first year as Prime Minister, he was faced early in 1958 with his sternest test yet – the resignation of his entire Treasury team.

Thorneycroft's Resignation

The crisis originated in the Chancellor's conviction that economic priorities had altered decisively since September. In order not to 'finance inflation', Thorneycroft urged that current expenditure for

1958–9 should be frozen at 1957–8 levels. As prices had risen in the meantime, this would inevitably involve cutbacks in services.[38] In December 1957 he became alarmed that Prime Ministerial calls for restraint were not having the required effect: the proposed increase by spending departments of £153 million was the largest projected annual rise in peacetime. He warned that this was an intolerable position for a government pledged to sound money and a strong pound:

> With relatively few assets and large debts we continue to live upon the scale of a great power. We have the most expensive defence forces in Europe. We have joined the nuclear 'club'. We claim at the same time a very high standard of life. We seek to lead the world in the social services we provide. All of this is very hard to change. But we must recognise that our failure in one year adequately to face the problem sows the seeds of precisely the same kind of problem in the year which follows.[39]

Aware that the Prime Minister was due to leave on a lengthy Commonwealth tour early in the New Year, Thorneycroft was anxious to settle the estimates and proposed a series of economies. These included abolishing family allowances for second children, increasing National Insurance contributions and raising charges for school milk. From the outset, Macmillan had doubts about what could be achieved. 'The Chancellor', he wrote in his diary on 22 December, 'wants some swingeing cuts in the Welfare State expenditure – more, I fear, than is feasible politically.'[40]

After Christmas the crisis intensified. Macmillan continued to hope that good sense would prevail in the traditional fight between the Treasury and spending ministers. He argued that anti-inflationary reductions must be vigorously sought, but added that 'the precise amount of these reductions was less important than the ability of the Government to demonstrate that they were adhering to their aim of limiting the quantity of money in circulation'.[41] On Friday, 3 January, Thorneycroft ungraciously made clear his dissatisfaction with cuts totalling only £100 million. Several colleagues were provoked into angry resistance by the Chancellor's determination to eliminate the entire increase of £153 million. In a revealing admission, the Cabinet minutes emphasised that the abolition of family allowances for second children (having not hitherto been paid in respect of first children) would seriously undermine 'the only post-war social service which a Conservative Government could claim to have created'.[42] The Minister of Pensions, John Boyd-Carpenter, recorded what happened as Thorneycroft pressed his case beyond the £100 million mark:

> Cabinet met at 11.00 a.m. Atmosphere was tense, and I was told by a colleague that at a meeting on the previous day of a small inner group (P. M. , R. A. B, Quintin Hailsham and one or two others) Chancellor had said he would resign if he could not get 1958/59 estimates pretty well down to 1957/58 totals. . . .
>
> On civil side, P. M. suggested £30m. should be attempted, or indeed pruned 'from the Civil Estimates as a whole'. Chancellor said he wanted £30m. certain from 'Welfare', and to be free to seek other economies on rest of civil side. Iain Macleod said this was like Hitler tactics. . . .
>
> P. M. then said he would adjourn Cabinet, and if on Monday agreement couldn't be reached, following discussions at weekend, he would have to consider question of placing resignation of Government in hands of the Queen. He would regret this very much after all we had been through. . . . It seemed a tragedy in the present state of the world to break up the Government over about half of one per cent of national expenditure.[43]

By the time ministers reconvened for an unusual Sunday meeting of the Cabinet, attitudes had hardened. Thorneycroft insisted that his credibility rested on imposing the same restrictions applied to public investment and the private sector since September last; without this, the position of sterling would be jeopardised. Most ministers took the view that sterling had stabilised over recent months and that a small increase in spending was unavoidable owing to long-standing commitments. In addition, any modest rise in inflation that resulted would be less damaging than the renewal of excessive wage claims, certain to follow welfare cuts. In summing up, Macmillan refused to yield any further. The Chancellor, he said, had the right to request support for an agreed policy of disinflation. 'But disinflation, if enforced to the point at which it created a stagnant economy or provoked a new outbreak of industrial unrest, would defeat its own ends.'[44] The following morning Thorneycroft resigned, accompanied by his two junior ministers at the Treasury, Nigel Birch and Enoch

Powell. Journalists, duped into thinking the Cabinet had met to discuss foreign affairs, desperately sought to keep up with the events of what Macmillan called an extraordinary day:

> Thorneycroft's [resignation] letter was in brutal terms, calculated, if unanswered, to do the maximum injury to sterling. It sought to give the impression that he alone in the Cabinet stood against inflation. Cabinet met at 11. I read out the letter, which was received with a good deal of indignation. . . . I offered post of Chancellor of the Exchequer to Heathcoat Amory, now Minister of Agriculture. He was rather hesitant, but accepted.[45]

Inwardly, the Prime Minister was seething with anxiety that the government might break up. But determined to demonstrate coolness under fire, he left as scheduled for his Commonwealth tour on Tuesday, 7 January. At London Airport the resignations were nonchalantly dismissed as 'little local difficulties' – a pre-prepared phrase which the Party Chairman later said reflected 'more panache than accuracy'.[46]

Macmillan nevertheless survived this latest trauma easily enough. Cabinet opinion, led by Rab Butler – again left in charge during the Prime Minister's absence – remained supportive. Butler's claim that the full cuts would overturn in hours policies on education and social welfare 'to which we have devoted the services of our lives' was interpreted in some quarters as a veiled threat of resignation – posing a him or me choice for the Prime Minister.[47] Hailsham, keen to impress as Party Chairman, swiftly despatched telegrams to regional and local organisers putting the government case; an action that incensed the Treasury ministers. In spite of this, Thorneycroft refused to champion a backbench revolt. His resignation speech centred on the view that Britain was attempting too many commitments, but also underlined his loyalty to the government. In these circumstances, Labour's inevitable onslaught had little effect. Gaitskell claimed that the Conservatives were 'visibly crumbling', though when the issue came before parliament Tory MPs overwhelmingly rallied behind their absent leader; an opposition motion on economic mismanagement was heavily defeated.[48] Macmillan's nerves of steel had again been decisive. By threatening an early election, he pushed his opponents over the edge after they had overestimated their own importance to the government' survival. By insisting that everything possible had been done to secure economies, the Prime Minister persuaded most observers that an inflexible Chancellor – egged on by dogmatic juniors – had resigned over the 'chickenfeed' of £50 million rather than great issues of principle. By mid-February Butler was able to write to Macmillan that the 'atmosphere of bitterness entirely disappeared' after the estimates were finally settled.[49] *The Economist* noted that upon his return the Prime Minister would find that the 'sickly political baby' he left behind had perked up: 'Mr Thorney-croft, after leaving an array of time bombs ticking under the Treasury bench, has nobly refused to set them off.'[50]

The resignation crisis had involved more than 'chickenfeed'. In the mind of Macmillan at least, it represented a challenge to his authority. Across the other side of the world on his overseas tour, he harboured suspicions that Thorneycroft 'may be calculating on another "sterling crisis" this autumn and the breakup of the Government in conditions which would allow him to seize the leadership of the party from me and Rab'.[51] What the dispute did appear to represent, more fundamentally, was a clash of opposing views, between Tory deflationists and the Butler–Macmillan advocates of 'solvency with social progress'. Neither school of thought, it may be argued, was as consistent or blameless for the outcome as its supporters claim.

The Treasury ministers have been retrospectively credited with foresight in proposing monetarist solutions to Britain's economic ills. In the battle against inflation, claimed Nigel Birch, 'we were fighting to win and they were not'. Thorneycroft also remained unrepentant, writing in 1976 that 'those of us who stood then were certainly very isolated and very much alone. What is certain is that the dangers of which we warned, the perilous path which we saw opening out ahead, have been tragically fulfilled.'[52] At the time, the Treasury team failed to persuade either the party or wider opinion of the merits of its case. Even among those who welcomed the attempt to rein in public spending it was noted that the '1957 ceiling' was of no great concern to foreign holders of sterling. The significant savings implied by getting as close as £50 million to 1957–58 expenditure could have been presented to the financial markets 'as a confidence-inspiring factor, while Mr Thorneycroft's resignation is clearly a confidence sapping one'.[53] The crudeness of the Chancellor's ap-proach, moreover, suggested an obsession with short-term cuts rather than any forward-looking vision.

The Cabinet case also smacked of inconsistency. Thorneycroft's retort to charges of deserting the team was that the team had deserted him. Butler for one, having backed the Treasury hardline over 'ROBOT' in 1952, had switched camps. Macmillan, the slasher of food subsidies, had also conceded the force of Thorneycroft's case – not least in his 'never had it so good' speeches – but flinched from pursuing the logic of the September measures. The Prime Minister rejected the accusation that he pulled back for fear of an electoral backlash; his administration, he said, had not shown itself afraid to court unpopularity. Yet privately ministers accepted that underlying the crisis was the simple question: 'were you going to inflate for electoral reasons, or were you going to stick fast to try and stop it?'[54] The answer for most was clear. According to Hailsham, it was 'perverse' to endanger any prospect of electoral revival by allowing the Tories to be presented as the party hostile to social welfare.[55] The outcome was thus ultimately determined by electoral rather than economic considerations. It was difficult to present it as a victory for 'one nation toryism', as cutbacks in services were still to proceed and ministers were aware that government spending as a proportion of national income had been falling steadily since 1951. Macmillan was opposed to deflation as a 'strict puritanical creed' but he was left without a clear alternative strategy. Instead it remained uncertain if inflation was still regarded as the prime enemy, and if so how it was to be tackled. With a more amenable Chancellor in place, the suspicion was that Macmillan had cleared the way for relationary measures that might again raise the spectre of rising prices. Certainly the Prime Minister returned from his Commonwealth tour asserting that 'both a brake and an accelerator are essential for a motor car'. When the crunch came, reflected Enoch Powell, Macmillan was more inclined to use the accelerator than the brake. The conquest of inflation, he said, was sacrificed in the interests of 'buying votes for 1959'.[56]

Enter Supermac

Macmillan had every need of 'buying votes' early in 1958. Thorney-croft's resignation did nothing for public confidence in the government. At the first 'television by-election' in February, Labour captured Rochdale; the Conservative party was pushed into third place, its vote falling dramatically by over 30 per cent compared with 1955. A detailed voter survey found 'a general picture . . . of ill-defined frustration and disgruntlement'. In March two further seats were lost, Kelvingrove to Labour and Torrington to the Liberals. The Prime Minister's performance was compared unfavourably with that of his reliable deputy, the Home Secretary. According to one journal, Macmillan's six-week absence abroad was seen at Westminster as 'the period of the best Prime Minister we haven't had.' Upon his return, Conservative Central Office had to find new ways of 'trying to project in 1958 a Prime Minister obstinately determined to reflect 1908'.[57] During the spring, these 'new ways' unexpectedly presented themselves. In part this was due to Macmillan himself, returning to Britain more confident in the role of world statesman. In May he demonstrated for the first time his mastery of the small screen. In a long interview with two American TV presenters, the Prime Minister impressed viewers with his wide-ranging knowledge of world affairs and sense of humour. More important in the longer term was his exploitation of growing public resentment about trade union militancy. As one minister later recollected: 'Two things together quite suddenly launched the super-Mac period: the Ed Murrow television interview and the bus strike in 1958.'[58]

Industrial unrest had been threatened for some time across the transport sector. Macmillan's strategy was to divide and rule. It would, he told colleagues, 'be prudent to seek to deal separately with the various industrial disputes . . . and to avoid a conflict with organised labour on a wide front'.[59] With this in mind, a compromise pay offer was awarded to railway workers, in spite of 'grumbling' in the party sufficient to revive fears that Thorneycroft was 'ready to pounce'.[60] The way was left open to face the London bus strike that began early in May. This was ideal territory for a 'showdown' with the unions. Bus workers generated less public sympathy than the railwaymen and their potential for wider disruption of the economy was limited. The strike also allowed a hostile press to demonise the Transport Workers' leader, Frank Cousins, as a militant trouble-maker. TUC leaders were equally critical; some told ministers that they wanted Cousins 'taken down a peg'. Confident of victory, Macmillan made it clear he was not prepared to press London Transport to make concessions.[61] Cousins was deliberately left out on a limb. After seven weeks he accepted terms which, as his critics noted, were less generous than might have been secured at the outset.

The Economist hailed a possible turning-point in post-war industrial relations:

> To put its achievement at its lowest, London Transport has helped to slow down the pace of wage inflation. At best, by showing the public that a strike, though unpleasant, is not bound to be a disaster or lead to all-out industrial warfare, it may have done something to alter the fatalism toward leapfrogging wage demands which has been at the root of this country's economic problems since the war.[62]

Any temptation among ministers to follow up this victory with reform of trade union law was, though, resisted. Macleod as Minister of Labour claimed that maintaining cross-class backing was paramount: he argued that the only way of ensuring support from trade union voters was to engineer a return to economic growth and rising living standards.

With the departure of Thorneycroft ('stupid, rigid'), Macmillan believed reflation was at last on the agenda. Sterling stood at its highest point for months, and 'over-full employment' was being eroded by steady rises in the jobless total. But the new Chancellor, though easier to deal with on a personal level ('flexible and courteous'), proved to be no soft touch. Although his background in local government made him progressive on social questions, Amory's experience of the textile trade inclined him towards caution on economic policy. Under the influence of Treasury officials, he argued that to expand too rapidly would provoke renewed inflation, in turn disturbing the new-found confidence in sterling. The result was a standstill budget in 1958. Macmillan was disappointed that 'once again we have to sacrifice the middle and salaried classes to the needs of the wage battle'. But the inclusion of modest tax reductions allowed him to describe the outcome as a reasonable, 'humble little package'.[63] During the second half of the year the case for expansion gained ground. The credit squeeze came to an end as bank-lending limits and hire-purchase controls were removed. Amory believed these expansionary forces alone would be sufficient. The Prime Minister though was not satisfied. 'What is wrong with inflation, Derry?', he would ask, pressing for additional measures of public investment to give a stimulus to employment. When opposed on this, Macmillan attacked the Treasury's 'disgraceful paper. It might have been written by Mr Neville Chamberlain's Government.'[64] Assisted by a sharp fall in import prices, economic activity began to pick up while inflation remained under control. By the end of 1958 bank-lending rates had been reduced to 4 cent and sterling made convertible into dollars; the Thorneycroft crisis seemed a distant memory.

This turn of events made life more difficult for the opposition. Labour leaders found that support for strike action left them open to charges of indifference to inflation. Attacks on 'Tory deflation' became difficult to sustain in the face of Amory's new measures, some consciously designed to steal Labour's clothing.[65] In the meantime, Gaitskell continued to publish policy documents, generally deemed worthy but uninspiring. Confidence in Labour ranks about electoral victory was steadily eroded. Only weeks after the Thorneycroft resignation one backbencher expressed the 'feeling among Members that the Party was not making sufficient impact in the country'.[66] Even at the Rochdale by-election, Labour's share of the vote fell compared with 1955 and the headlines were stolen by the stampede of Tory voters to the Liberals. This inability to inspire trust, one minister wrote, stemmed from a lack of adventure:

> The Labour Party from 1957 to 1959 committed the same fundamental errors of 1950–51. They waited for the Conservative Party to put forward policies, which they then criticized. The notion that they ought to be making the political running never seems to have occurred to Gaitskell and his lieutenants. . . .
>   To adapt Shaw's famous jibe at Rosebery, 'they never lost a chance of missing an opportunity'. I suspect that many of their leaders believed that they only had to sit back and wait for the elections to return to power, but, be that as it may, they certainly made no attempt after Suez to retain the political initiative. By the time they awoke from their dreams of office it was too late.[67]

Certainly 1958 saw a steady improvement in Tory electoral fortunes. Local elections in the spring highlighted the importance of industrial unrest. In line with previous trends, county council contests in April showed a strong movement away from the government. However, at borough elections in May, with strike activity prominent in the news, there was an appreciable swing back towards the Conservatives. On the day after Macmillan compromised in a

PEEp..!

railway dispute, 'the abstaining majors . . . retreated into apathy again'; the North Islington by-election showed a 10 per cent swing to Labour. A series of further by-elections in June – held against a backdrop of the bus strike – suggested that 'Mr Cousins was again a bogeyman'.[68] In August the Tories edged ahead in national opinion polls for the first time since Macmillan came to power, obliging him to dampen speculation about an autumn election. Although the government's prospects looked brighter, the likelihood of an early contest was remote. After Christmas the Tory revival was threatened by rising unemployment, which reached post-war levels only briefly exceeded in 1947. Labour assaults on 'the party of unemployment' brought them renewed dividends, and Conservative strategists noted the party's faltering performance in Northern England and Scotland – areas badly affected by unemployment.[69] If voters had 'never had it so good', this was a claim Macmillan was not ready to put to the test. Before doing so, he had one or two more tricks up his sleeve.

The 1959 General Election

In February 1959 the Prime Minister made a high-profile visit to Moscow, boosting his image as a statesman of world renown. After his return, he moved to trump Gaitskell's claim that the opposition alone possessed the key to economic growth. Ignoring fears of inflation, Macmillan secured increases in capital spending and insisted on a generous budget. Income tax, for some time 8s 6d [42.5p], was reduced by 9d [3.75p] (rather than the smaller amount favoured by Amory); purchase tax was cut; and investment allowances were restored. Altogether, tax remissions cost the Treasury £360 million: far in excess of Butler's pre-election package in 1955. Labour claimed that the budget threatened economic overload, and some experts questioned the scale of the tax cuts when the surplus on the balance of payments over recent months barely covered Britain's rate of lending abroad. It remained to be seen if 'this week's bumper budget is to be the harbinger of economic reexpansion or merely of yet another autumn [sterling] crisis.'[70] But complaints were drowned in a chorus of approval. Amory's assertion that this 'is no spending-spree budget' was swept aside by press and party supporters who trumpeted the return of good times. Hire-purchase debt for consumer goods, it was noted, had risen by £300 million in 18 months; the number of cars had increased from 3.5 to nearly 5 million since 1955; and production was rising at a year-on-year rate of 10 per cent. By the spring of 1959 unemployment was also falling again. Labour chose to debate the subject on the very day improved figures were released, leaving Macleod to quip that when asked to pick their weapons the opposition chose boomerangs.[71]

During April ministers agonised about a May election. Hailsham believed a narrow victory was probable but could not be assured.[72] Local elections that followed suggested this had been an over-cautious assessment. Labour lost heavily in provincial English and Welsh boroughs, falling back to early 1950s levels of support. Macmillan's advisers were confident of a securing a 50-seat majority, and the case for an autumn contest became irresistible. Good fortune, it appeared, had rescued the government:

> Four years ago one could say that two questions seemed likely to decide the outcome of the election in 1959 or 1960. The first was whether the standard of living would rise sufficiently quickly under Conservatism to make Labour's philosophies look out of date to an enriched working class; that has not happened. The second question, then, was whether the remarkable coincidence of short-term advantages that brought victory to the Tories in 1955 could really be expected to come to their aid just before the new election. By what Labour must regard as an appalling fluke, the coincidence seems to have occurred . . . The small recession is over, unemployment is falling, and this time there have been eighteen months of price stability as well. The sun is shining down on Britain's packed beaches in the first hot summer since 1955, and in an atmosphere of easy holiday contentment the literally floating voter feels no burning need for a change.[73]

Preparations for the election had long been under way. In preparatory discussions, Butler had advocated an emphasis on the themes of 'Opportunity' and 'Responsibility'.[74] But the former increasingly took precedence over the latter, and was presented overwhelmingly in materialistic terms. In early 1959 the Conservatives launched a major poster campaign – part of an advertising programme that cost half a million pounds in two years – featuring families enjoying newly available consumer goods. 'Life's better with the Conservatives' ran the accompanying slogan; 'Don't Let Labour Ruin It'. Ministers echoed this line in public speeches. Macleod spoke of giving the new middle classes 'the opportunity they long for instead of the equality they despise'; opportunity was defined in terms of owning a house, a car, a washing machine or taking an overseas holiday.[75] It came as no surprise when Macmillan avoided controversial issues such as trade union reform in the party manifesto. Instead, prosperity was made central, with a renewed pledge to double living standards within a generation. Labour's election platform had also been prepared well in advance. Nationalisation was played down and former Bevanites reassured by promises of improvements in the social services. Economic growth was to follow from innovative planning techniques aimed at raising levels of investment. These promises – painstakingly arrived at in 1957–8 – were much less distinctive in the altered circumstances of 1959. By the summer Gaitskell was privately admitting the prospect of defeat for the first time since Macmillan replaced Eden.[76]

The Prime Minister got the better of pre-election skirmishes over the summer of 1959. In the words of his official biographer, he was 'quite shameless' in exploiting a visit to London by US President Eisenhower; the two leaders featured together in a television broadcast confirming the mending of fences since Suez.[77] But when the campaign itself got fully under way in September, the Conservatives were caught off guard. More so than his predecessor in 1955, Labour's leader was prepared to carry the fight to his opponents. Gaitskell's emphasis on economic expansion and the pledge to raise retirement pensions by ten shillings received a generally favourable press. A four-member Campaign Committee led by Richard Crossman ensured effective co-ordination, and Labour shook the government with its professional TV broadcasts. Gaitskell though made a serious blunder in claiming that improved social provision would not require any increase in income tax. While the effect of a single comment can easily be exaggerated, this incident appeared to mark a turning-point. 'The Lord', said the Tory Chairman, 'has delivered him into our hands.'[78] Ministers relentlessly claimed that Labour was 'auctioneering' for votes with a series of unattainable promises. According to Rab Butler, the opposition's motto was 'a bribe a day keeps the Tories away'. In the run-up to polling day, Tory assaults on Labour's ability to finance its programme paid dividends. Opinion polls moved back in the government's favour, though the high proportion of 'don't knows' made ministers reluctant to make firm predictions of victory.

Wavering voters may have had doubts about a government eight years in power, but when the crunch came these were cast aside. On an increased turnout, the Conservatives won an unprecedented third successive victory in peacetime, increasing their majority to 100 seats. Labour's vote fell by 189,000 (in an electorate increased by 1.1 million) while that for the Tories increased by 463,000. The Liberal share of the poll more than doubled, though this produced no corresponding increase in seats held (see Table 3).

Across the country there was an average swing to the government of 1.1 per cent. Regional variations were more pronounced than in 1955, with the highest swing in the West Midlands (3.15 per cent)

Table 3 *General Election of 8 October 1959*

Party	Votes	MPs	Share of vote	Change since 1955
Conservative	13,749,830	365	49.4%	−0.3%
Labour	12,215,538	258	43.8%	−2.6%
Liberal	1,638,571	6	5.9%	+3.2%
Others	125,000	1	0.9%	−0.3%

Conservative majority over other parties: 100

and Greater London (2.25 per cent), where the Tories made 15 of their 22 gains. Rural Britain generally saw a smaller net swing towards the government, but in two areas – around Clydeside and Greater Manchester – the movement of votes benefited Labour. In terms of social class, the Conservatives had maintained a strong lead among all sections of the middle class. Of those classified as working class – constituting 60 per cent of the total electorate – Labour's lead was mitigated by strong support for the government among non-manual workers; the so-called 'affluent worker' had arrived.[79] The 1959 result was widely attributed at the time to two forces. One was the Prime Minister, who was credited with a series of personal achievements – restoring relations with the USA, reviving party morale and confounding Thorneycroft's warnings of economic ruin. 'Supermac' had come of age – not 'the comic Edwardian dandy but the masterful, dominating, self-confident statesman'.[80] The second main force was said to be the unusual combination at a single moment in time of full employment, stable prices and a strong balance of payments. The *News Chronicle* voiced the common view that 'most electors did indeed believe that they had never had it so good'.[81] Evidence to sustain this was provided by regional trends. Instead of a clear Labour advantage in London, for example, the parties now held an equal number of seats. The high swing of 4.9 per cent in Dagenham reflected a strong Tory performance in areas associated with flourishing industries such as car manufacture. In contrast, the two regions that went against the national trend had suffered higher than average unemployment, notably in the Lancashire cotton trade. In reviewing the election, both parties endorsed newspaper verdicts. Conservative findings stressed two causes of victory: the atmosphere of hope that came with 'peace abroad and rising living standards at home', and the 'general confidence in the Prime Minister's leadership'.[82] Labour's inquest played up the first theme:

> We were defeated by prosperity: this was without doubt the prominent factor. . .

> Prosperity not only hardened the middle class against us but deep inroads were made into our normal working-class support. This was strikingly reflected in our failure to capture the new towns. . .

> There was also grave doubt as to whether we really could pay for our programme. . .

> This and other issues added up to a generally unfavourable image of our party. . . Too many of the electorate saw us as an exclusively class party and a party of restrictions and controls.[83]

Reference to Labour's 'unfavourable image' provides an extra dimension in understanding the election outcome. Macmillan's victory day claim that the class war was obsolete testified to his success in removing some of the suspicion evident at the last election about the 'party of privilege'. In 1955 27 per cent of those questioned by Gallup believed Conservatism stood for the wealthy and rich; by 1959 this had fallen to 17 per cent.[84] What had happened in the interim was a deliberate pitch for upwardly mobile working-class voters, especially young families looking to buy their own property. In this sense it was not so much real improvements in conditions since 1955 – in practice mostly confined to recent months – as Macmillan's ability to identify himself as the most likely provider of future prosperity that made a crucial impact. Conversely, government propaganda managed to portray the opposition, in the minds of the same key voters, as the party of ration books and austerity. After a concerted campaign by big business and Tory Central Office, it was found that the proportion of those who associated Labour with nationalisation had doubled since 1955, in spite of Gaitskell's careful avoidance of specific pledges. Labour compounded this problem with its acknowledged 'failure to project a clearer image of our party'.[85] Within Labour ranks there remained deep ambiguity about afflu-ence, which many regarded as a threat to working-class values and life-styles. This helps to explain why so little attempt was made to imitate the Tory use of mass advertising techniques; Labour spent only £22,500 on its poster campaign in the run-up to the election. The party's manifesto – in 1945 style – tried to contrast the business elite who had 'never had it so good' with the continued suffering of the old, the sick and the unemployed. Internal Conservative findings noted with satisfaction that cries of class war sounded irrelevant, as did 'pictures of a depressed and poverty-stricken Britain which the voter found laughably unlike the world which he saw around him'.[86] Labour thus suffered as much from self-inflicted wounds as it did from economic forces over which it had no control; 1959 was an election as much 'lost' by the opposition as it was 'won' by the government.

Conclusion

In some ways the result was far more crushing for Labour than defeat in 1955. It was no longer possible to blame factional in-fighting, and three successive rebuffs inevitably led to speculation that the party had become obsolete in the face of 'middle classation' and the rise of the 'affluent worker'. The Liberals had demonstrated their ability to pick up a growing proportion of anti-government votes, and if the Tories proved as adept in future at harmonising the economic and electoral cycles, Labour would soon be in terminal decline.[87] Gaits-kell's immediate response was to play down such apocalyptic notions. He pointed out that on balance only three in every 200 voters had switched allegiance, and that with 44 per cent of the total vote Labour still represented 'nearly half the population'.[88] To some listeners this smacked of complacency, though there were sound reasons to doubt the fashionable view that permanent opposition beckoned. The Conservative share of the vote had declined slightly, and Macmillan polled some quarter of a million fewer votes than Labour had in 1951. It would be sensible, concluded *The Economist*, not to read too much into a single result. The opposition had not been 'driven from the field' and commanded the loyalty of twelve million supporters. Rather, the election had reinforced a message evident in 1955: that Labour had not yet learnt to 'cope politically with the social realities of an increasingly affluent society'. This did not mean the task was impossible. If the party's problems stemmed as much from its own failings as from social change, then they were capable of political resolution. 'The parliament of 1959–64 starts with Labour's scarecrows still in place. Where is the man who will rid the Opposition of this troublesome incubus, and come forward to save the Left? On that question, in all probability, the political future of this country hangs.'[89]

The answer could hardly be foreseen in October 1959, though more predictable was the possibility that the government might run into difficulties of its own. Richard Crossman's complaint that Macmillan had sold himself at the election 'as though he were a detergent' was not simply sour grapes on the part of the losers; other voices were raised claiming that crude appeals to materialism were depriving politics of any higher idealism. At the time Tory MPs were scornful; most were grateful that 'the restoration monarch of modern times', as Butler called him, had pulled off a stunning victory. Yet Macmillan's was a high-risk strategy, for if he could not deliver on ever-greater prosperity, 'never had it so good' was almost certain to rebound. With expectations raised, voters were likely to turn on a government that had few overarching themes – none comparable to national reconstruction after the war – to fall back on in times of trouble. Behind the scenes, there were signs before October 1959 that ministers realised a high price was being paid for victory. Painful decisions could be shelved but not avoided indefinitely. Butler spoke in 1958 of a bleak outlook that contained the seeds of troubles 'unsolved during the Labour Party and Winston Churchill regime'; and Amory as Chancellor warned colleagues that commitments planned for 1960–1 onwards 'would far exceed the resources likely to be available and would be liable to provoke a recurrence of the inflationary pressure which was only now being brought under control'.[90] Not long after his election triumph Macmillan started to warn publicly that 'materialism is not enough', claiming that he did have regard to broader national objectives. But the damage was done. By shifting the basis of politics so strongly towards material rewards, he left himself vulnerable to any renewed economic hardships. As we saw at the beginning of this chapter, the Prime Minister recognised that Britain was living beyond its means and would have to pay for it 'sooner or later'; 'sooner' was fast approaching.

4 'Mac: the end', 1959–63

Introduction

'Never before', wrote Rab Butler in the aftermath of the 1959 election, 'has a political party had a greater opportunity than we have at this moment.'[1] With an increased parliamentary majority, and facing a demoralised opposition, the new government looked stronger at the outset than its predecessors had done in 1951 and 1955. Harold Macmillan looked set fair to deliver his main campaign promises: peace abroad and prosperity at home. The main danger, as the Prime Minister recognised, was that of complacency:

> Since Parties depend for their continuing strength upon the new voters coming in, we must not allow the thought to develop over the next year or two that we have done well but that we have completed our task. The cry of 'time for a change' could well be the Socialists most potent weapon at the next Election. It is therefore of great importance that we should present at this and each successive [party] Conference the idea of a continuing programme of useful work.[2]

But what was to make up such a programme? Would the new government, it was asked, 'veer to the right', beginning to map out a more distinctive approach to the post-war settlement than had been possible earlier in the decade, owing to the crises of the mid-1950s and the constraints imposed by a narrower majority? Or would the Prime Minister be content to direct his appeal to the middle ground of politics, continuing efforts to show that 'we are an all-class party', as both Churchill and Eden had before him?[3]

The reality of the next four years was that Macmillan never worked out a successful 'programme'. After a promising start, his grip on the Tory faithful and the nation began to slip during 1962–3. 'Supermac' was to find that galvanising a party traumatised by Suez – and uniting it in time for election success – was an altogether different task from planning ahead for the full life of a parliament. In part the turnaround in political fortunes was due to circumstances beyond government control. Embarrassing ministerial resignations could not be foreseen; nor could the French decision to deny Macmillan what would have been a major diplomatic triumph – British entry to the European Economic Community (EEC), popularly known as the Common Market. The early 1960s also witnessed an upsurge of 'anti-establishment' sentiment, fomented by a new generation of satirists and opinion formers; a theme explored more fully in the next chapter. But Macmillan's own shortcomings equally contributed to the outcome. The chickens came home to roost as it became clear that rising living standards were not as easy to deliver as appeared the case in 1959. Not only did he make serious errors of judgement, over the economy and the sacking of senior colleagues, he also had no strong basis of conviction upon which to fall back when 'never had it so good' rebounded. As we shall see, the pre-war exponent of a firmly grounded 'middle way' in politics increasingly became the 'master empiricist', whose guiding philosophy appeared to be: 'Whatever is both expedient and popular will be done; whatever is inexpedient and disruptive will not be done.'[4] This helps to explain why, when Macmillan resigned after nearly seven years as Prime Minister, 'time for a change' was a potent threat and he left behind a party facing almost certain electoral defeat.

The Heydey of Supermac

For eighteen months after the election, Macmillan remained at the zenith of his power. Basking in the glow of credit for securing a third successive Conservative victory, he was in a strong position to determine personnel and policy. In choosing his new Cabinet, continuity was the main theme: Heathcoat Amory stayed on as Chancellor and Selwyn Lloyd as Foreign Secretary, both staunch Macmillan loyalists. Rab Butler's place as 'number two' was confirmed by adding the Party Chairmanship to his existing duties as Home Secretary and Leader of the House. Those who sought 'creative imagination' rather than the 'mixture as before' were comforted by the promotion of younger ministers, such as Reginald Maudling to the Board of Trade and Edward Heath to the Ministry of Labour.[5] Butler was not to find life easy. He had to stand in when the Prime Minister made his frequent sorties abroad, while also touring the country and listening to the views of party workers, most of whom were 'in favour of birching and flogging'.[6] But as Selwyn Lloyd noted in his diary, the Cabinet worked harmoniously at the outset:

> To what extent is it a seething mass of the ambitious and the jealous? I should say not at all. . .

> Rab is very happy after his [second] marriage. His ego is very satisfied with being Chairman of the Party as well as Leader of the House and Home Secretary . . . His position as Crown Prince is, I think, impregnable, but there are some who say not.

> Derry Amory seems content to go on, although there have been threats of only one more Budget.[7]

Amory did indeed intimate that he wished to return to his business interests, especially after bruising encounters with Macmillan prior to the delivery of his third budget in April 1960. In line with Treasury officials, Amory had been warning for some time that an overheating economy would lead to renewed inflation unless slowed down; he also claimed that the government was not meeting its objective of reducing expenditure as a proportion of GNP. The Chancellor's desire for increased taxation was resisted by the Prime Minister, who argued that:

> following the Budget of last year and the Election last autumn, a deflationary Budget would either be very foolish or very dishonest. Unless it is supposed that we would be thought very modern and up-to-date; like those young ladies who oscillate daily between the stimulant and the tranquiliser, the new progressive Conservatism will turn out to be a policy of alternation between Benzadrine and Relaxa-tabs. I don't like it at all.[8]

Macmillan clearly feared being hoist with his own petard; he wanted to avoid the unpopularity that might follow, as Butler put it, from 'going back on all our talk of prosperity'.[9] In spite of Amory's retort that in existing conditions a standstill budget would be inflationary, the Prime Minister prevailed. Minor reliefs such as the greater release of post-war credits to hardship cases were offset by raising tobacco tax, leaving a negligible net increase of £12 million pounds.

Tory MPs struck a note of 'faint praise', with the Chief Whip admitting it had not been a 'howling success'. Some were annoyed by the increase in tobacco duty though most were persuaded that a neutral budget was a price worth paying to avoid harsher medicine at a later stage. Those observers who spoke of a 'mouse of a budget' had to admit that the government was acting from a position of strength. The economy was still advancing at 'high speed', with full employment and stable prices, and the Chancellor could shift from the accelerator to the brake if dangerous impediments appeared around the corner.[10] The Prime Minister was satisfied that if the budget did not carry off his preferred theme – 'You've got it good; keep it good' – it was at least respected by the public for its emphasis on 'consolidated success'.[11] But in the weeks that followed, Macmillan found great difficulty in persuading Amory of the need for continued expansion. Anxious that high levels of imports would add fuel to inflationary pressures, and determined not to 'drift into crisis', the Chancellor insisted on raising interest rates to reduce domestic demand.[12] The Prime Minister grudgingly consented, though he placed no obstacles in the way of Amory's retirement from high office during July 1960. In his place at the Treasury came Selwyn Lloyd, in turn replaced as Foreign Secretary by Lord Home, leading to accusations that both major departments of state had become 'personal dependencies'. Macmillan easily shrugged off charges that his leading ministers were 'insufficiently distinguished' to pursue independent policies.[13] As parliament prepared for the summer recess, he reflected on a satisfactory first session, modestly informing the Queen: 'Such popularity as we may have been able to obtain among the people is not of our own creation. We owe it to the strange goings-on in the Opposition Parties.'[14]

The Labour party was certainly making the government's task easier by responding to electoral defeat in 1959 with renewed infighting. The ball was set rolling by Gaitskell's ally Douglas Jay, who published a controversial article suggesting that if Labour was to escape from its exclusively working-class image, it might have to consider a change of name.[15] To the left it seemed outrageous that the Gaitskellites – having dictated policy for years – should claim that defeat confirmed the need to move further to the right. Bevan gave vent to his frustration by claiming that Labour had paid the price for fighting not on a socialist programme but on 'pre-1914 Liberalism brought up to date'. This set the scene for a period of

protracted blood-letting. Gaitskell himself opened up a fresh area of
controversy at the annual conference in November 1959. His own
explanation for defeat emphasised long-term social change, but also
argued that votes had been lost because of the party's image –
especially its association in the public mind with wholesale nationalisation. He thus proposed the amendment of Clause IV of the 1918
constitution: that which stipulated the wish to see the 'common
ownership of the means of production, distribution and exchange'.
Even sympathisers in the audience were alarmed. Tony Benn wrote
in his diary that Gaitskell's speech:

> was a ghastly failure because it was constructed in quite the wrong
> way and without regard to the needs of the Party. In effect he
> asked, 'How much of what we once believed will the electorate
> now stomach?' The answer he produced was not surprisingly,
> 'Very little'. But that is not the question you should ask.
>   If he had said, 'Here is the modern world full of causes for us to
> take up. Here is what we must do' . . . . the Party would have risen
> to him to a man. But he is quite incapable of inspiring people.[16]

For many Labour activists, including trade unionists hitherto loyal
to the leadership, Clause IV was the cornerstone of their political
outlook. Gaitskell was not proposing to rule out all future measures of
public ownership; but simply to cast doubt on such a vital symbol of
socialist faith was regarded by many as seeking to 'persuade Christian fundamentalists that they need not believe in God'.[17] After
numerous heated exchanges, the party leader was forced to accept a
compromise, the essence of which was that 'a New Testament should
be *added* as a supplement to the Old'.[18] By focusing on a symbolic
issue – which moderate MPs thought would not be understood by the
public – Gaitskell had deepened divisions without furthering the
process of policy revision. His own advisers had warned him that he
would 'start a battle in the Party that will cause far more trouble
than the thing is worth'.[19] As a result, he has been much criticised for
poor tactical sense. At the outset, however, he cannot have known
that his former union allies would desert him, and Gaitskell himself
was convinced it was not the wrong battle to fight. If, as he believed,
Labour's real problem was its 'class war' image, then it was only by
demonstrating a willingness to change that the party would attract
sufficient new voters to return to power.[20] The controversy had

though made matters worse in the short term. By June 1960 the NEC
felt compelled to condemn personal attacks that were contributing to
the party's 'ever deepening crisis'.[21] And for Gaitskell himself, the
humiliating outcome raised question marks about his ability to
survive as leader.

Unease about the leadership crystallised during the second half of
1960 around another high-profile issue – that of defence. Unlike
Attlee, Gaitskell could no longer rely on solid union backing for a
multilateral defence policy. By aligning supportive elements at the
1960 conference in Scarborough, the Transport Workers' leader
Frank Cousins – the 'bully of the block vote' as one critic called
him – ensured the passage of two unilateralist resolutions. Gaitskell,
convinced that left-wing enemies were out to destroy him, let it be
known he would not accept the view of conference, in theory the
party's supreme policy-making authority. He argued that for Britain
to renounce nuclear weapons unilaterally was intellectually disreputable and electorally disastrous, and he pledged himself to 'fight and
fight and fight again' against the decision. Shortly afterwards, it was
more a case of fighting for his own job. Support had grown for the
view that Gaitskell spent too much time imposing his views on
recalcitrant followers and not enough seeking to match Macmillan
on the national stage. After the death of Nye Bevan in 1960, the
party left agreed to back Harold Wilson in a leadership challenge.
Wilson stood not on the basis of support for unilateralism, but rather
as a 'unity' candidate, opposed to what he said was Gaitskell's
divisive style. In the event, Gaitskell secured a comfortable but not
overwhelming victory in the PLP ballot; at the same time, Wilson
put down a useful marker for the future.[22] What the party gained
was more difficult to see. Tony Benn spoke of a shambles in which
MPs openly went round denouncing each other: 'We cannot survive
as a united Party if this goes on for more than a week or two.'[23]

Public opinion in the early months of the 1959 parliament
reflected both Labour's difficulties and Macmillan's confidence. In
March 1960, the Conservatives scored a by-election victory at Brig-
house in Yorkshire; this emulated Sunderland South in 1953 as only
the second occasion in thirty-six years when the opposition lost a seat
to the government of the day. Local elections in the spring went the
same way. Labour suffered its greatest losses in borough seats since
1948. The party's inquest found that while the results were similar to
the general election, the outcome had been made worse by the 'sharp

outbreak of controversy within the Party' – threatening a repeat of
the Morecambe fiasco in 1952 that so damaged election prospects in
1955. Morgan Phillips, Labour's General Secretary, told the NEC
that the party's morale was at an 'all-time low'. The feeling that
Labour can never win again was gaining ground, he said, and in
both parliament and the localities there were 'clear signs of demor-
alisation'.[24] Any slight weakening of support for the government
brought comfort not to the official opposition but to the Liberal
party, especially in middle-class suburbs and seaside resorts where
Labour had never been strong. This raised the possibility of occa-
sional Liberal by-election victories, as in the previous parliament.
More ominously, if floating voters were to go over *en masse* to the
Liberals, 'it will be Labour's grimmest long-term augury yet'.[25]
However, the main theme of these early months was the continuing
buoyancy of the government, dominated with nonchalent ease by the
Prime Minister. Shortly after his first reshuffle in July 1960, an
opinion poll showed 72 per cent of voters 'satisfied' with his leadership. 'Mr Macmillan remains unchallengeable', it was agreed as the
Conservatives – unlike Labour – gathered for a harmonious autumn
conference at Scarborough.[26] Yet from the spring of 1961 onwards,
perceptions of all-conquering 'Supermac' slowly began to change;
the bubble was about to burst.

'Supermacbeth' on the Defensive

Macmillan's new Chancellor, Selwyn Lloyd, faced many of same
intractable problems as his predecessor. In spite of a reputation for
lacking originality, Lloyd was prepared to experiment with 'planning' as a remedy for the structural problems that left the British
economy trailing behind its international competitors – an issue
explored more fully in the next chapter. But in the short term
inflation remained a threat. After a revaluation of the German mark
threatened another balance of payments crisis, Lloyd was forced to
settle for a cautious budget in April 1961. Although taxes were raised
by £80 million, he brought 'great joy to Conservatives at Westminster' by raising the starting point for the payment of surtax, from
£2000 to £4000.[27] In the early summer, pressure on sterling
intensified. Strike action by dock workers helped to widen the trade
gap, and in order to prevent reserves draining away the Cabinet

agreed to a new package of deflationary measures. In the 'little budget' of July 1961, credit terms were tightened, bank-lending rates increased, and cuts in expenditure projected. Most controversial was a proposed 'pay pause' for public-sectors workers. Noting that average incomes had risen 8 per cent over the past year, compared with increased productivity running at 3 per cent, Lloyd concluded that 'there must be a pause until productivity has caught up'. The Chancellor was given a rough ride in the Commons, with Labour MPs taunting him with cries of 'resign' and 'surtax concession'. Macmillan's press secretary, Harold Evans, conceded that the July measures had 'the most universally critical Press that I can remember for any government proposals'. Those who welcomed the recognition that Britain was living beyond its means doubted the wisdom of imposing 'the biggest immediate cut in demand . . . imposed by a British government on any single afternoon in peacetime history'.[28] Macmillan spoke of the press as 'vapid, ill-informed and spiteful', and Rab Butler struck a more defensive tone than hitherto in noting a perceptible decline in the morale of party workers, occasioned by talk of a stop–go economy and 'uncertainty as to where we are going in major issues'.[29]

The Prime Minister's response was to launch the first of several attempts to give new direction to his administration. In policy terms, he opened up a debate about possible British membership of the Common Market; a 'Grand Design' that might provide a new international direction while also boosting the domestic economy. In terms of personnel, Iain Macleod was moved in October from the Colonial Office, where he had antagonised many 'retired colonels', to take over the roles of Party Chairman and Leader of the House. According to Macmillan, the promotion of a younger, forceful orator 'could help me to recreate a sense of purpose – a movement – almost a crusade' in favour of 'progressive Toryism'.[30] Rab Butler was initially reluctant about a reshuffle which left him, as he said,'shorn of two plumes and retaining the Home Office which is the one hot potato'. He was, however, reassured by being placed in charge of a ministerial group overseeing negotiations with European leaders about entry to the Common Market. Although refused the title Deputy Prime Minister on the grounds that it had no constitutional status, Butler was told by Macmillan that the changes would not affect the choice of his successor, on which he would only say that the Queen would consult close colleagues such as Lord Home when the time came, probably after the next election.[31] There was press speculation after the changes were announced that Macleod was being groomed as a future leader. Having refused to accept the Chairmanship alone, Macleod confirmed he had the highest ambitions by establishing a high-powered committee to begin planning for a general election. The autumn reshuffle failed to disguise emerging signs of unease on the Tory benches. After engineering workers achieved a large wage rise – leaving Macmillan accused of wringing his hands like an 'impotent Pontius Pilate' – the Prime Minister acknowledged the emergence of 'a hard core – ten to twenty MPs on our side – who are so bitter against me and my "progressive" colleagues that they will use every difficulty . . . to work up a large-scale revolt'.[32]

In the early months of 1962, backbenchers began to question openly whether 'Supermac' was losing his sureness of touch. One member of the 1922 Committee caused a stir by using coded language to urge the Prime Minister to think of retiring; another was more forthright in private, calling him 'limp, weary, old and cosy'.[33] The pay pause was proving deeply unpopular with public-sector workers, such as nurses and teachers. Production had slackened since the July measures, retail sales were flat, and morale had not been noticeably improved by Selwyn Lloyd's second budget, which again went for fiscal neutrality. The Chancellor raised a few cheers from his own side by promising to abolish 'Schedule A' tax on owner-occupiers of residential property. But most attention came to focus on new duties proposed for confectionary and ice-cream; even Lloyd's sister could not resist the jibe – 'Well, well! Taxing the poor children's pocket money!'.[34] Economists added on a more serious note that the budget offered no remedies for Britain's more deep-seated problems. The Prime Minister was conscious of this charge, and having hitherto defended Lloyd against critics, his diary began to refer to a colleague who lacked 'fire in the belly'.[35] Macmillan personally took the lead in a second effort to relaunch his government. What he called 'the New Approach' was an attempt to move forward from the pay pause to creating a formal, longer-term incomes policy. Without this, he felt there was no prospect of reconciling the main aims of economic policy: full employment, stable prices, a strong pound and expansionary growth. At the moment, he told colleagues, these goals were 'like four balls in one of those puzzles we had as children – you can get three into the holes and when you get the fourth in, out pops one of the others'.[36] Several ministers took some persuading. Those antagonistic to a move towards planning challenged the ideological basis of the 'New Approach', echoing the view of Chief Whip Martin Redmayne that 'This is not Conservatism.'[37]

Two further factors increased the pressure on Macmillan. The first was a gradual recovery in Labour fortunes. During 1961 Gaitskell made an impressive fightback. A year after the Scarborough decision on unilateralism, support from moderate union leaders enabled him carry a multilateral defence policy. As Macmillan recognised, this greatly enhanced Gaitskell's standing by demonstrating his 'patriotism' and ability to triumph in the face of adversity. A new domestic programme also began to emerge, combining social egalitarianism with planning for faster growth, and an advertising campaign was launched to improve Labour's image among the aspiring classes. By the autumn of 1961 the opposition was edging ahead in national opinion polls. At local elections during the spring of 1962 Labour performed particularly well in areas containing a concentration of marginal parliamentary seats.[38]

Allied to this was a second worrying development: the erosion of government support at by-elections, especially in the face of Liberal resurgence. This trend had been gathering pace since the introduction of the pay pause, and it culminated in a famous Liberal victory in March 1962 at Orpington, a suburban commuter seat adjacent to the Prime Minister's constituency of Bromley. The scale of the Liberal victory – with Eric Lubbock easily overturning a Tory majority of 15,000 – was described by *The Times* as the 'most severe blow' the Conservatives had suffered since 1951. At Tonbridge in 1956, which sparked off similar talk of a 'white-collar revolt', the Tory share of the vote had fallen by 8 per cent; at Orpington it was more than 20 per cent. The party's private inquest attributed the result to 'general discontent of Conservative supporters' on several fronts – a lack of leadership, mishandling of the pay pause, 'weakness' in dealing with the unions, and the local repercussions of a Tory council 'which had skimped local services appallingly in this rapidly growing area'.[39]

Orpington captured the headlines, but senior Tories realised it was consistent with other results. Macleod as Chairman reported to Macmillan that at eight by-elections in March and April 1962, the average decline in the Conservative share of the vote was in excess of

20 per cent. Survey evidence commissioned after Orpington suggested that of all the forces working against the government, economic difficulties were 'more important than all other subjects put together'. Whereas the image of Tory 'competence and care' had been undermined, voting for a Liberal candidate was regarded as a useful, almost 'non-political' form of protest.[40] There was one crumb of comfort. For as long as the Liberals were the main beneficiaries of anti-government sentiment, it was possible that the pattern of 1957–8 might be repeated; Liberal support could fall away and there would be insufficient enthusiasm to elect Labour at a general election. Even when Labour made its first by-election gain of the parliament, at Middlesbrough West in June, its increase in the share of the vote was small compared to the Liberal advance. For Macmillan, though, the differences with 1957–8 were more striking than the similarities. After five years at the helm, he wrote in his diary, 'enemies of the leadership' within the party, 'already numerous, have been strengthened'. In addition, voters 'really are tired of us': only reflation and the excitement of a new initiative such as Europe could overcome the sense of frustration and boredom.[41] Many agreed that the time had come for drastic remedies. One MP wrote in response to local election losses that 'there is a general feeling that changes must be made quickly or if not Party loyalty will be strained to the utmost'.[42]

In the event changes were made quickly, though in such a way that Macmillan's reputation was to be irreparably damaged. One of the initiatives urged upon the Prime Minister by Macleod was a further reshuffle to freshen the government's image: two thirds of the Cabinet had been in place since at least 1957, and there was clearly scope to emulate President Kennedy in the United States by creating a younger ministerial team. An increasingly likely contender for dismissal was Selwyn Lloyd. In June 1962 Macmillan's diary reflected his anger at the 'delay and lack of initiative' shown by the Chancellor in developing a 'guiding light' incomes policy to follow the pay pause.[43] On 21 June Rab Butler offered the unusually forthright advice that Lloyd should be removed, and by early July Macmillan concluded that the only solution to this 'immense human and political problem' was a change at the Treasury probably at the end of the month. An appointment was made with the unsuspecting Chancellor for Thursday, 12 July, to 'give him forewarning in a nice way'.[44] But on the morning of the appointment rumours of impending changes appeared in the *Daily Mail*, following indiscreet comments by Butler. The Prime Minister, believing his hand had been forced, decided he must act swiftly. In an excruciating meeting, Macmillan told Lloyd that the 'situation was desperate' and that changes could not be delayed; a stunned Chancellor left devastated, refusing the offer of a peerage.[45] Overnight the Prime Minister – not wishing Lloyd to suffer alone and fearing a weekend of press speculation – decided to bring forward other planned changes. By the end of Friday, 13 July, seven ministers, one third of the Cabinet, had been dismissed. Several of those removed, including close associates such as Lord Kilmuir, the Lord Chancellor, and housing minister Charles Hill, were never to forgive the speed and brutality of the sackings. Customary courtesies were ignored and the usual pretence of parting on good terms was forgotten. Harold Watkinson, removed from Defence, expressed the common view that they had been 'exposed to the greatest possible degree of unpleasant publicity and stress'.[46]

By the time consequential changes were made, 39 of over 100 government posts were affected in what became known as the legendary 'Night of the long knives'. Why, then, had the Prime Minister gone so far and so fast? As in the case of Thorneycroft's resignation in 1958, he was obsessed with threats to his own position, most imagined more than real. His private comments showed deep distrust of colleagues: Butler was 'round the bend'; Macleod was 'vain and conceited'; Maudling had 'no loyalty'.[47] Weeks after the sackings Macmillan told Lloyd during a secret meeting that a conspiracy had forced his hand, with Butler 'plotting to divide the party on the Common Market, and bring him down'.[48] It was true that Butler had not yet declared himself in favour of entry to Europe, but Macmillan had not hitherto been overly concerned that Rab was seeking to oust him. Indeed, shortly before he had dismissively told Butler 'I don't see why I should make room for you, old cock'.[49] Other ministers were told a different story. Harold Watkinson recalled that Macmillan spoke to him in highly emotional terms, painting 'a picture of a political situation that was beyond my wildest dreams', including forebodings of ministerial revolt centred on Selwyn Lloyd.[50] Lloyd was no more a conspirator than Butler, though his refusal to go to the House of Lords did make him a potential rallying point for disaffected backbenchers *after* his sacking. One reason for bringing forward the remainder of the reshuffle was Macmillan's desire to 'stop intrigue in the House and the party';

endless speculation might allow what he called 'the restrictionist' MPs – right-wingers who favoured more spending cuts – to line up behind Lloyd, especially if the Minister of Labour John Hare carried out a threat to resign in sympathy.[51] This still left senior colleagues bemused as to whether such abrupt and sweeping changes had really been necessary. The Chief Whip later told Butler that he was 'unable to explain all this except that the PM had thought that the Government was in a political decline. For once the unflappable actually flapped.'[52]

Macmillan soon recognised that 'flapping' had been a mistake. Press images depicted a massacre that smacked of panic; the *Daily Telegraph* spoke of the 'Stalinist scale of the purge' and reported the party to be 'pole-axed by shock'.[53] Satirists had a field day, presenting the Prime Minister as 'Supermacbeth', with Lloyd in the role of Banquo. In the Commons Macmillan came under fire and was not helped by one supporter who, as a Labour MPs observed, asked 'whether he should not be congratulated because "he had kept his head, when all about were losing theirs". This provoked the longest spontaneous laugh I ever heard in the House.'[54] Opposition leaders gleefully exploited the implication that one third of the Cabinet cannot have been up to the job. Why, Gaitskell asked, had the Prime Minister stopped at seven sackings? More worrying for Macmillan was the knowledge that 40–50 MPs were being urged by Nigel Birch – who had resigned with Thorneycroft in 1958 – to abstain in the censure vote called by Labour. Birch persuaded Lloyd to insist upon the publication of his resignation letter, which was then used to imply that Macmillan, for a second time, was rejecting a Chancellor who took seriously the fight against inflation. 'Once is more than enough', he magisterially wrote in *The Times*.[55] But any hope Birch had that abstentions might force Macmillan to resign without bringing down the government quickly disappeared. Gaitskell's strong language in the House – 'a desperate man in a desperate situation' – served to rally Tory MPs, who were also threatened with the prospect of an early election. Labour's vote of confidence was easily defeated with no government abstentions.

What, though, was the longer term impact? Some historians have argued that Macmillan benfited in some ways from the night of the long knives. His central aim, of returning to an expansionist agenda at the Treasury, was made possible by the dismissal of Lloyd. In addition, he succeeded in bringing on several fresh ministerial faces;

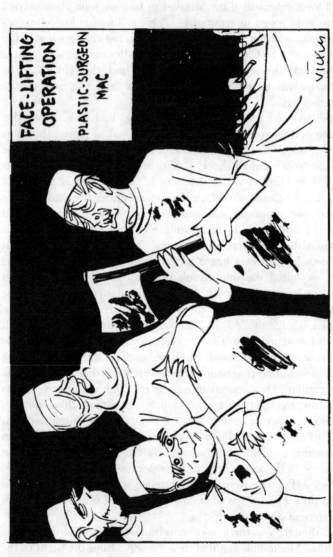

"WONDERFUL JOB, SIR! THE PUBLIC WAS GETTING A BIT BORED WITH THE SAME OLD FACES ..."

not only Reginald Maudling as the new Chancellor of the Exchequer, but also Edward Boyle at Education and Keith Joseph at Housing. This helped to create an impression of energy and initiative, while also suggesting that – with Macleod's reputation suffering as Chairman – Maudling might emerge as another possible successor.[56] The long-time favourite for the leadership, Rab Butler, came out of the crisis with his position strengthened by the additional title of First Secretary of State, deputising for the premier whenever requested. If many have exaggerated the importance of July 1962 – for example the colleague who reflected that 'Macmillan committed political suicide more certainly than if he had himself resigned'[57] – there can no doubt that it was a turning-point. The Prime Minister's 'unflappable' reputation was destroyed overnight. Attention was diverted away from the 'New Approach', with its announcement of a National Incomes Commission, and focused instead on Macmillan's cruel streak. Selwyn Lloyd's impression – of his 'utter ruthlessness, and his determination to retain power by the sacrifice of even his closest friends'[58] – was one shared by the public. Macmillan's personal standing in opinion polls slumped – those dissatisfied with his leadership jumped from 39 to 52 per cent, thereby breaking all previous records. In the absence of an agreed successor, he remained relatively secure, but from July 1962 rumours of plots against the leader on the backbench intensified, as did discussion of the 'retirement question'. The reshuffle backfired in highlighting Macmillan's age; at 68 he was almost nine years older than any other minister and seventeen years above the average of the new team. In November 1962 Butler noted that the Prime Minister was 'feeling more and more the loneliness of his position'.[59]

Despite the severity of the purge, it still failed to arrest the remorseless decline of Tory popularity since the summer of 1961. In spite of a successful party conference, where attention centred on progress in Common Market negotiations, the Conservatives fared badly in the 'little general election' of November 1962 – a series of five by-elections held in the same week. Glasgow Woodside and South Dorset were lost and three supposedly 'safe' seats were only narrowly held. 'The Press exploded into sensational headlines', noted Harold Evans, 'explaining that the days of Macmillan are now numbered as the Party seeks new and more vigorous leadership.'[60] MPs took the results calmly, nervous after the alarums of July about 'doing or saying anything'. Yet there was now cause for genuine alarm. In the first place, the by-elections confirmed that Liberal popularity had peaked and that floating voters were moving straight to Labour, now some 10 per cent ahead in national opinion polls. Labour's more credible image made the electoral outlook 'disturbing', if not yet 'irremediable'.[61] The state of the economy, moreover, was 'perplexing' – as Maudling put it – with things not going 'as we expected'. Unlike 1958–9, structural problems such as rising regional unemployment meant that ministers could not rely on the economy recovering 'anything like as fast or as automatically as before'. Five years on from when the government found itself in similar trouble, the Tories also had to do much better to achieve the same results: 'like a horse that had gone much higher in the handicap'.[62] If there was to be a recovery from these mid-term blues, the Tories needed early policy success and good fortune. Neither was apparent in the early months of 1963, when things went from bad to worse.

All Change at the Top

Two events in January 1963 had a profound influence on the direction of politics in the latter stages of the 1959 parliament. The first was President de Gaulle's 'icy blast from Paris'[63] – the vetoing of Britain's application to join the Common Market – which left Macmillan's government lacking any central strategic direction. The second was the unexpected death of Hugh Gaitskell after a short illness, leaving his adherents in the Labour party shattered. Douglas Jay later said he possessed not only the 'common sense and moral authority of Attlee, but a wider intelligence and a deeper understanding of the economic and social issues of the age' than any contemporary; had he lived, he would have pursued his aims with a 'sureness of purpose' that had not been seen since the 1940s.[64] At the time, Gaitskell's supporters also mourned the uncertainty his death produced. Political commentators pointed out that with the opposition rudderless, Macmillan might be tempted to go for an early election. In the event, the leadership contest which followed was if anything to bolster Labour popularity. In the absence of an agreed Gaitskellite candidate, Harold Wilson won sufficient support from the centre-left of the PLP to defeat two representatives of the right, George Brown and James Callaghan.[65] As his challenge to Gaitskell in 1960 demonstrated, Wilson believed – like Attlee upon whom he modelled himself – that Labour was best led by maintaining unity between the different wings of the party; in other words, that he should not follow Gaitskell's confrontational style. As he settled into his new post, Wilson made a point of including several Gaitskellites in his Shadow Cabinet, in particular persuading a reluctant George Brown to continue as deputy leader. Inevitably the party left, denied influence under Gaitskell, most appreciated the arrival of a dynamic new leader. Richard Crossman spoke of 'psychological revolution in the Parliamentary Party and in the Party in the country', so much so that he was 'irresistibly driven to clichés of the New Frontier and comparisons of Harold with Kennedy'.[66]

Wilson wasted no time in exploiting his provincial, lower-middle class background: 'a reflection of what many people in the early 1960s were seeking: an image . . . of self-help, energy, efficiency and hostility to upper-class pretension and privilege'.[67] He did this by staking out a policy position that played down both the revisionist emphasis on equality and the left-wing case for extending public ownership. Instead, he brought to the fore the theme that socialism was about science. His central thesis was that in order to avoid the stop–go economics of the Conservatives, Labour would champion a new managerial revolution. As the party of professional managers, scientists, technicians and skilled workers, Wilson believed, Labour would stand for modernisation, in contrast to the out-dated image attached to the government. This approach was developed at the the party's annual conference in October 1963. The willingness of Gaitskellites, in the words of Douglas Jay – to refrain from making trouble in the way Bevanites had over recent years – meant that compared with the last time the party met in Scarborough, this was a 'positive love-feast'.[68] Wilson used the occasion to spell out his notion of Britain being transformed by the 'white heat' of the technological revolution. Enthusiastic press reporters agreed that Wilson had triumphed and was proving a formidable opponent. Many endorsed Crossman's view that the new leader had – within a matter of months – provided 'the revision of Socialism and its application to modern times which Gaitskell and Crosland had tried and completely failed to do. Harold had achieved it.'[69] Cooler appraisals noted many potential flaws in the 'white heat' strategy, not least what would happen if technical change did not deliver a high-growth economy. But for the time being Wilson – with his familiar pipe and relaxed, witty TV style – carried all before him.

The Prime Minister, in the meantime, had no choice but to seek new ways of regaining the initiative. Quite how this might be done – after so much had been staked on the abortive attempt to join the Common Market – remained difficult to envisage. As Michael Fraser said, Europe was designed to dish the opposition parties, 'give us something *new* after 12–13 years; act as a catalyst of modernisation; and give us a place in international sun'. Shortly before Gaitskell's death, Macmillan described modernisation as a 'particularly urgent' task in the run up to an election. But with the government waiting for reports that might give substance to modernising rhetoric – such as that from the Robbins Committee on higher education – it was left to the Chancellor to produce some rabbits from the hat. 'When in doubt, reflate' was said by officials to be Macmillan's motto, and in February 1963 he told Maudling that the forthcoming budget 'will be the key to the success or failure of the Government . . . the moment to launch the post-Brussels policy on the home front'.[70] With 'our policies . . . in ruins', Macmillan was not in a strong enough position, as he had been in the past, to override Treasury fears that over-expansion might create a fresh crisis. The Chancellor said 'it was necessary to remember 1959', and his caution was echoed by advice from the Research Department. It was noted that opposition propaganda about 'electioneering budgets' had done little harm in 1955 and 1959, but circumstances had changed. Much of the urgent clamour for tax cuts had disappeared, and there was now greater public concern about unemployment, which at over 800,000 was at its highest level since 1947. Hence the sober conclusion of the Research Department that 'we do not believe that the Party would gain credit if the Budget gave rise to any suspicion that we were manipulating the economy for party advantage'.[71] Maudling's budget did introduce modest remissions on income tax, especially in the lower ranges, but Harold Evans conceded that the press response was one of 'mild disappointment'. The best that could be said for it, in the words of the *Sunday Times*, was that 'a good budget ripens, like a good cheese'.[72]

In these circumstances – with an election unlikely until at least the spring of 1964 – speculation continued to surround Macmillan's leadership. For a brief moment in January 1963, the Prime Minister thought he might benefit from renewed Labour turmoil after the death of Gaitskell. Unlike the opposition, he claimed, the Tories had several strong leadership contenders, including Butler, Lords Home and Hailsham, Maudling and Heath. Once again his optimism was misplaced. Wilson's energy and relative youthfulness was soon being contrasted with the fading appeal of a prime minister approaching seventy. With Labour 15 points ahead in the Gallup poll, its largest lead since the 1940s, backbench muttering about the leadership grew more outspoken. According to Macmillan's son, Maurice, most sections of the party were unsettled: 'ex-Ministers, Baronets, Knights and Burgesses. Even the 1922 Committee and John Morrison were disturbed.' Although there were no organised factions, the Prime Minister himself believed that 'nearly half the Conservatives think that I should retire'. The combination, he told Butler, of 'the Kennedy image plus Harold Wilson at 46 was a potent force in favour of a young man'.[73] But with the 'young men' on his side 'not yet ready for taking over', Macmillan – like Churchill in 1954 – was in no hurry to go. He cleared the air after the budget by telling the 1922 Committee that he would lead them into the next election: the economy might be improving slowly, he told MPs, but it promised to restore party fortunes sufficiently to deliver a fourth election victory. If, however, the Prime Minister thought the leadership issue was finally settled, he was wrong; for in the early summer of 1963 his authority – and that of the entire government – was shaken to the core by the Profumo scandal.

Macmillan's handling of the allegations made against his War Minister, John Profumo, convinced many Tory MPs that without a change of leader, electoral defeat was certain. Rumours of an affair in 1961 between Profumo and a call-girl, Christine Keeler, had been circulating for some time. In March 1963, following questions asked in parliament, Profumo made a personal statement claiming there was no security risk and 'no impropriety' in his relationship with Keeler, who was linked at the same time with a Soviet Embassy official, Captain Ivanov. The Prime Minister accepted this as an end of the matter, believing one of his ministers would not lie to the House and perjure himself in the courts in pursuing libel actions against magazines threatening to run the story. But the rumours refused to go away. In early June, while Macmillan was away on holiday, Profumo confessed that he had lied and promptly resigned. This dramatic turn of events caused a political storm, with the scandal dominating the national newspapers for several weeks. In part, this was due to the rich mixture of ingredients in the story: sex, race, class and national security; as well as a cast list of characters ranging from the aristocratic 'Cliveden set' of Profumo's friend Lord Astor to the low life of Soho.[74] If this was not enough for Fleet Street, it came in the aftermath of another security scandal that had soured Macmillan's relationship with the press. In the so-called Vassall case, a homosexual British spy had been linked with a junior minister who was eventually forced to resign, though the allegations of a relationship proved to be unfounded. Two journalists were jailed in March 1963 for refusing to disclose sources of information; the Prime Minister was among those who felt the press had received its just desserts. Harold Evans wrote that many newspapers 'have accumulated bitter feelings against the Prime Minister and . . . this will be reflected in their writing' unless fences were mended. Revenge was swift, for in the Profumo case – having been warned off for many weeks by libel threats – Fleet Street had the perfect opportunity to get 'its own back for Vassall'.[75]

Attacks on the Prime Minister were thus made with a sense of vindication and vindictiveness. Aside from expected criticism from hostile papers such as the *Daily Mirror*, Macmillan faced a torrent of abuse from the likes of the *Sunday Times*, which spoke of faltering leaders 'unalert to security dangers and indifferent to traditional moral standards'. Most damning of all was the claim in *The Times* that eleven years of Tory rule had brought the nation 'spiritually and psychologically to a low ebb'.[76] Downing Street regarded this as part of a 'Macmillan must go' campaign, aimed at encouraging a ministerial resignation – probably by an outraged Enoch Powell, returned to office after his 1958 resignation – which might in turn force a change of leadership.[77] This threat was averted after the Prime Minister carefully secured full Cabinet backing for his handling of the crisis, but on 17 June he still faced an awkward task in explaining to the Commons why he had not known the full facts earlier. For once Macmillan looked ill at ease at the despatch box. After Harold Wilson's skilfully understated performance – asking about the security dangers and why Macmillan had not personally intervened to interview Profumo – the Prime Minister plaintively admitted he did not 'move among young people'. He had acted honourably but had been 'grossly deceived'. This defence left him open to the charge of incompetence rather than dishonesty: a theme taken up by critics on the government benches, notably Nigel Birch, who finally secured revenge for the Treasury resignations of 1958 by quoting Robert Browning with great effect – 'Never glad, confident

morning again'.[78] Unlike the 'night of the long knives', when
government whips similarly threatened an early election, several
MPs felt moved to join Birch in his protest. Twenty-seven MPs
abstained on Labour's motion of censure, cutting Macmillan's
majority to 69. This was a moral defeat in view of those involved:
'Not only the usual malcontents', Macmillan noted, but 'worthy
people' swept along by the emotion of the issue.[79]

In the next few weeks the government came close to collapsing.
The morning after the censure debate Macmillan faced apocalyptic
headlines. The *Daily Mail*'s 'Mac: The End' vied with the *Telegraph*
headline '*Premier likely to resign soon*'.[80] The satirists followed this up
by depicting Macmillan as completely out-of-touch, employing cruel
jibes such as 'I wasn't told', 'Life's better under a Conservative' and
'We've never had it so often'.[81] With only one in five of those polled
thinking he should stay on, Macmillan inevitably faced a rising tide
of hostility within the parliamentary party. Rab Butler later said 'it
was extraordinary how a gust of wind swept the Commons and the
Conservative Party in favour of a younger leader', with Maudling
the initial favourite.[82] There was uproar at the 1922 Committee
when one MP demanded that Macmillan go in the next fortnight,
adding that 'there were too many pimps and prostitutes in high
places'.[83] Wild speculation abounded about the sexual behaviour
and preferences of ministers, not all of which, it seems, was unfounded. Such was the intensity of rumour-mongering that a number
of ministers chose to confess their indiscretions to the Prime Minister.
Macleod as Party Chairman intervened to insist that this 'madness'
stop, though Macmillan feared he might yet be condemned by
further revelations about 'one important and one unimportant
minister'.[84] Another colleague, who owned up to involvement with
the Duchess of Argyll in a notorious divorce case years earlier, had
actually prepared and was about to publish a letter of resignation; he
was only persuaded not to go ahead by claims that the government
was certain to fall if another scandal broke.[85]

Yet the Prime Minister managed to defy those who were already
writing his political obituary. How then did he survive such a
sustained onslaught? In part this was due to his recovery of poise
in the Commons. On 21 June he gained a breathing space by
appointing an enquiry under Lord Denning to ascertain whether
there had been any danger to national security. Only two of fifteen
letters published in *The Times* on the theme of 'Mr Macmillan's

leadership' were hostile. The Prime Minister was regarded by many
as an innocent scapegoat; there was evidently public sympathy for
the view he himself expressed – that he never thought the government could be 'brought down by two tarts'.[86] Press attention moved
away from Macmillan to focus on the trial and death of Keeler's
associate Dr Stephen Ward. And backbench mutterings were contained by warnings that the Prime Minster's enforced resignation
might precipitate an election that would leave the party out of a
power for a generation. On 28 June Macmillan reiterated his
determination to stay on to the next election if his health allowed:
'I must have the support of the party, and I think I have it.'
Agitation among MPs gradually settled down, and Macmillan's
reputation was enhanced by recognition of the part he played in a
newly announced nuclear-test ban treaty. At the end of July the
Chief Whip told Rab Butler – who was being encouraged to make
clear his own leadership ambitions – that a month ago 'the chicken
was coming out the egg . . . but the shell is now hardening up';
Macmillan had undertaken to go on to Christmas and might carry
on after that.[87] By the first week of August, with one opinion poll
showing a sudden narrowing of Labour's lead, Harold Evans reported that the Prime Minister was 'jauntily and firmly back in the
saddle'; the 'little crooks' on the backbenches had been put firmly in
their place.[88]

Macmillan may have survived, but few would dispute that his
administration was gravely damaged by the Profumo episode. It was
true that the Prime Minister refused to yield to the vitriolic assaults of
Fleet Street or to what Butler called the 'herd instinct' among MPs
that demanded a younger leader. He could also claim that at last
there were signs of Tory support in the country edging upwards; the
mid-term surge for the Liberal party was receding, if not the steady
advance made by Labour. To set against this, Profumo had dis-
tracted ministers from developing policy; there was no new strategy
in sight following the Europe débâcle and an election was drawing
ever nearer. The scale of the crisis was such that Rab Butler – a
shrewd judge of electoral opinion over the past decade – pessimisti-
cally concluded that the party had been brought 'to a very bad way':
'it will be with the utmost difficulty that we shall recapture the lost
ground'.[89] Macmillan himself had suffered grievously. His colleague
Lord Home later said it was the only time he could remember

Macmillan being 'worsted – he so fundamentally hated the whole thing'. This was an oblique reference to his wife Dorothy Macmillan's long affair with Tory MP Bob Boothby , which some felt explained the Prime Minister's refusal to confront Profumo personally.[90] Unlike previous crises, for example the night of the long knives, dissatisfaction with Macmillan had been difficult to contain. As *The Economist* put it, 'the Tories are in the market (a bit shamefacedly) for a new leader'. Many backbenchers who remained silent in public continued to believe in private that Macmillan should go in the near future. One reported that while constituency activists remained loyal, MPs were gravely alarmed about the danger of floating voters turning against a discredited figurehead.[91]

If Macmillan was left a dejected figure, he was also less resilient. He was soon showing signs of discomfort and drowsiness that characterised the early stages of a serious illness. The eventual publication of the Denning Report in late September 1963 produced no fresh embarrassments. The report did criticise ministers for not ascertaining the truth at an earlier stage, but any accusations about security dangers were rejected and press reactions muted; Profumo was considered to be yesterday's story in Fleet Street.[92] But the whole episode had made sufficient impact for Macmillan to agonise over the question of whether he should continue. Rather like Churchill in 1954–5, the answer varied on a day-to-day basis. Harold Evans recorded on 29 September that Macmillan had decided to retire the following January after seven years in Downing Street. During the following week, after 'second, third and fourth thoughts', he settled on 'Operation Limpet'. His main justification for staying on was that as the party could not agree upon a successor – his own preference was for Lord Hailsham rather than Butler or Maudling – he must respond to the 'growing wave of emotion in my favour'.[93] After finally reaching a decision, the hand of fate intervened. On Tuesday, 8 October, with constituency workers congregating in Blackpool for the party's annual conference, the Cabinet backed Macmillan's pledge to continue after lengthy deliberations. But a sudden deterioration in the Prime Minister's condition forced the issue. Macmillan was told he must undergo immediate surgery to tackle an inflamed prostate. Instead of making his way to Blackpool, he had to content himself with sending a message announcing to Conservative activists his intention to resign. The Macmillan era was over.

Conclusion: Macmillan's Legacy

Harold Evans wrote in October 1963: 'the announcement that Macmillan was to go brought some degree of measured assessment of his place and his achievement. How vastly different it looks from the cheap, carping and often vicious criticism of recent months.'[94] Many have agreed that the final few months of his leadership should not obscure the Prime Minister's great skills – his control of the Cabinet and mastery of parliament – and his record of solid achievement at home and abroad. Sympathetic historians have argued that, in spite of the economic downturn of the early 1960s, the affluent society had come to stay, at least in the southern half of England. Britain's average growth rate continued to exceed that of the inter-war period and there had been no return to mass unemployment. Home ownership was rising steadily and that great symbol of the new consumer society, the television set, could be found in nine out of ten homes.[95] If, as was widely accepted, Macmillan had been unable to prevent Britain falling behind its major international rivals, he had at least faced up to the necessity for new departures in policy. More so than many of his younger colleagues, the Prime Minister had sought ways of tackling long-term structural weaknesses of the economy, as his switch to planning and modernisation showed. He may not have left Britain stronger in economic terms than he found it, though he was not alone among modern political leaders in this respect, and he had at least salvaged 'a little dignity from the wreckage. One man alone can do little more'.[96]

However, any balance sheet must take account of Macmillan's legacy for the party and the government. Here – with Labour confident of finally returning to power – it becomes difficult to dispute that the hopes of October 1959 had been gravely disappointed; so much so that one leading Tory reflected in 1963 that voters were certain present policies 'don't work' and were 'convinced the time of the Conservative Government has come to an end and that this is as it should be'.[97] The Prime Minister must ultimately shoulder responsibility for this state of despair. It was not simply that the opposition managed to present economic difficulties as self-inflicted and modernising initiatives as too little, too late. More fundamentally, Macmillan seemed incapable of setting out a positive agenda for the future. He once wrote in his diary that, like Churchill's pudding, 'we have no theme', and in early 1962 those

assessing a leader five years in power argued that his one overriding
failure was 'his refusal to hold out any ideal to his country'. Backbenchers, too, had a creeping sense that 'we were serving under a
Prime Minister who'd lost vision'.[98] The shallowness of Macmillan's
appeal to materialism and unbroken prosperity was openly exposed.
'It was truly said', he privately told colleagues in the bloody aftermath of the night of the long knives, 'that although we had built an
affluent society for the young, we had failed to give them the moral
basis they needed.'[99] Pragmatism based on 'never had it so good'
might triumph when the nation seemed at ease, but when the going
got tough the Prime Minister – lacking any strong ideological basis
for his own politics – could do little more than drift along hoping
something might turn up. 'Supermac', the hero of 1959, had turned
into the ageing and anachronistic 'MacBlunder'; a fitting symbol of
what many were calling in the early 1960s Britain's 'stagnant
society'.

5   The Stagnant Society: Modernising Britain

Introduction

Shortly before the resignation of Harold Macmillan in 1963, *The Economist* reflected on the state of the nation:

> In the gloom of this summer some uncomfortable memories have been stirring. Twenty-five years ago friends abroad were blaming Britain for going to sleep in the face of the the enemy. Now they not only accuse Britons of wanting to contract out of the cold war. They also say that Britain is badly governed, badly managed, badly educated and badly behaved – and the striking thing is that more Britons are saying the same, more stridently still. Every summer visitor to London has been hit between the eyes by this passionate soul searching. All the political parties are going into their annual conferences with plans . . . to put Britain right by bringing it up to date; each promises that, like a detergent, it will wash whiter. The British have become, suddenly, the most introspective people on earth.[1]

Such introspection was not entirely new. Similar bouts of self-criticism had flared up before, for example in the Edwardian period when Britain faced the challenge of emerging industrial powers such as Germany. What was unusual about the anxiety of the early 1960s was that it came at the tail-end of a period when – judged by its own previous standards – the British economy had been performing well. Living standards had risen steadily during the 1950s, unemployment had been low since the war and inflation averaged only 2–3 per cent annually – a record that would have been hailed as a great success between the wars.

Where the problem began was that new standards were being applied. As we have seen, Macmillan's popularity faded rapidly after 1959, and he found himself faced with something more than mid-term blues when a new 'stop' phase in the economic cycle began.

What made criticism more damaging than in previous downturns, for example during 1956–7, was a greater recognition of British shortcomings in an international context. As a host of authoritative reports made clear, Britain's economy may have been functioning more effectively than in the past, but it was failing to keep pace with its major rivals. While the average growth rate of the British economy in the 1950s had been 2.6 per cent, the equivalent figure for France was 4.5 per cent, for Germany 7 per cent and for Japan 8 per cent. Whereas production in Germany was doubling every ten years and in France every seventeen years, in Britain the same increase required 32 years.[2] In 1950 Britain's share in the value of world exports stood at 25.5 per cent; this fell to 16.5 per cent in 1960 and to 13.9 per cent in 1965. In addition, the proportion of GNP devoted to investment in Britain, while rising after 1959, remained exceptionally low by international standards.[3] The decision to apply for membership of the Common Market encouraged further unflattering comparisons, as did the recognition that Britain's status on the world stage was slipping away with the end of Empire. Unlike the late 1940s, when opinion formers took pride in victory and economic recovery, 'decline' became a national preoccupation, stimulating a wide-ranging debate and creating intense pressure in favour of reform.

The government's policy difficulties in the early 1960s were seen by many as part of a deeper malaise. In 1961 the Duke of Edinburgh was said to have remarked that it was 'about time that we pulled our fingers out'.[4] In the search for scapegoats that followed, Britain was frequently depicted – in the title of a popular Penguin special by Michael Shanks – as *The Stagnant Society*. Other journalists and social commentators joined in to create a new genre: 'state of England' literature, usually employing apocalyptic titles such as *The Split Society* and *Suicide of a Nation?* In assessing Britain's collective loss of confidence, this chapter will highlight two particular themes. In the first place, we can see that Britain's problems were usually attributed to the type of problems identified by Correlli Barnett in the 1940s – class divisions and outdated methods, both in industry and in politics. But more so than after the war, when structural reform was never high on the political agenda, and when the resurgence of rival economies could not be predicted, the pressure built up for urgent change. Hence we find, secondly, that a fashionable remedy emerged in the form of 'meritocracy': the idea of replacing the privileged elites who governed Britain with talent drawn from all sections of society; replacing the 'amateur' with the 'professional' in order to face the challenges of the future rather than the past. What will be argued here is that both themes seriously undermined Macmillan, compounding the feeling identified in the last chapter that the government had lost its sense of direction. For a variety of reasons – including bad luck as well as bad judgement – the Conservatives were unable to meet the challenge of 'modernisation' in the early 1960s. The new mood of national uncertainty provided great opportunities for the Labour opposition; the real beneficiary in the short term was to be the arch-meritocrat, Harold Wilson.

Us and Them

The starting point for many commentators and critics was the damaging impact of poor industrial relations on Britain's economic performance. The nature and scope of the problem was spelt out by Michael Shanks, a journalist on the *Financial Times*, who in many ways sparked off the 'state of England' debate among the intelligentsia with his publication *The Stagnant Society* in 1961. As Shanks was well aware, tensions between 'us and them' were deep-rooted in Britain's past and had not, as some assumed, been eradicated by the arrival of post-war affluence. The experience of war and a friendly Labour administration under Attlee had greatly strengthened the position of the trade unions in the 1940s. This was consolidated after the Tories returned to power when full employment and labour shortages enabled union leaders to bargain with confidence. But there was a pronounced upward trend in strike activity from 1953 onwards, as well as a return to industry-wide stoppages unseen since the 1930s. The one-day strike of over a million engineering workers in December 1953 was followed in the next few years by national stoppages among train drivers, dockers, busmen and printers. These groups were at the heart of most industrial unrest, which throughout the 1950s remained modest by international standards and had little impact on the economy as a whole. It was, however, sufficient to prompt renewed discussion – largely in abeyance for a decade after the war – about Britain's 'industrial disease', especially as evidence mounted of a growing trend towards unofficial strikes, instigated not by union officials but by more militant shop stewards championing the grievances of those on the shop floor.[5]

Two important consequences followed. One was the progressive erosion of public goodwill towards the unions, marking a change from attitudes reflected in opinion polls and newspaper columns during the 1940s. The clearest turning-point came with three strikes in rapid succession in 1955, among dock workers, printers and the railwaymen. In each case, conflict arose not over conditions imposed by the employers but over internal union matters: demarcation quarrels between rival unions, concern over wage differentials between skilled and unskilled workers, and attempts to prevent individuals joining a union of their own choice. In the run-up to the 1955 election, while Gallup found public opinion to be in favour of a tougher government approach towards 'unnecessary strikes', it was Labour who suffered most by virtue of its close ties with industrial trade unionism.[6] Public confidence was further eroded in the second half of the 1950s when 'responsible' trade union leaders were increasingly eclipsed by perceived hard-liners such as Frank Cousins, newly appointed head of the Transport and General Workers' Union and a particular target for hostile newspaper editors. The second and interlocking consequence was the growing acceptance of the 'wage-inflation thesis'. As early as 1951 *The Economist* complained that an 'alarming inflation of wage costs has taken grip of the British economy'. If, it was claimed, wage costs continued to run ahead of productivity, then the nation would struggle to remain solvent and secure. Ten years later the message was starker still. After periodic economic crises and with another imminent, *The Economist* voiced the common fear that high wage settlements granted to trade unions were pricing British goods out of international markets. Permanent economic decline beckoned.[7]

Michael Shanks was prompted to describe how this dangerous position had arisen after a visit to Communist-controlled Eastern Europe, which he believed – for all its glaring faults – did have a 'sense of purpose', unlike 1960s Britain. Aside from global forces, he claimed that the main obstacle to revitalising Britain was the outmoded mentality found on both sides of industry. His experience of talking to hundreds of industrialists and employers left the impression that they had little ability to appreciate the everyday concerns of the Bermondsey dockworker, the Lancashire weaver or the Rhondda miner:

How many times in recent years has one heard the following argument from middle class lips: 'But surely these chaps must realise that the country *just can't afford* to pay such-and-such a wage increase, or cut the working week by so much!' . . . But how many members of the middle class apply the same argument to themselves? How many seriously consider cutting their own salary in order to help the national economy?. . .

Thus we have what is in effect a dual standard. For the middle class one's salary is something one negotiates individually with one's employer or one's client according to the law of supply and demand, without regard to the state of the national economy or other extraneous considerations. . .

When it looks at the working class, however, it sees not a number of individual men and women but a huge amorphous army all clamouring for more money . . . In other words, the worker's reward is judged by its effect not on himself but on the national economy. The average middle class member would never dream of thinking of his own income in these terms, but he is perpetually amazed at the obtuseness and selfishness of the worker in not doing so.[8]

The tight community structures of the manual class, Shanks recognised, were under threat from the new world of consumer goods, hire purchase and continental holidays. But if the working-class was dying out, then 'like Charles II it is taking an unconscionable time about it'.[9] In the older working class districts especially (and he suspected, in newer industries such as motor manufacture as well), a sense of separateness remained strong and solidarity a prized virtue. Whereas the middle class tended to operate as individuals, for manual workers the emphasis was on the collective:

This basic attitude of loyalty to one's mates and hostility and suspicion towards all outsiders accounts for most of the things the middle class finds puzzling about working class behaviour. For the middle class likes to believe that we are in truth 'one nation', and that the class war is an outmoded irrelevance that nobody except a few Socialist agitators really believes in any more. . .

In present circumstances, unfortunately, the class war does still exist, in cold if not in hot form. Even if there are no actual hostilities, the armies are kept fully mobilised. The workers . . .

believe that all they have achieved in the way of better wages and working conditions has been through their solidarity – through the activities of their unions and shop stewards, resting always on the workers' determination to strike if necessary in defence of their rights or in support of their claims.[10]

But if the trade unions had played an honourable role as the custodians of working-class values, Shanks also went on to sympathise with the view that by 1960 the unions were the greatest institutional barrier to Britain becoming a genuinely dynamic society. This was not, he stressed, for some of the reasons commonly cited by arch-critics, who blamed wage demands alone for inflation (this, Shanks argued, was too simplistic), or who saw the unions as a Communist-inspired conspiracy aimed at holding the nation to ranson (for which concrete evidence was thin on the ground). Rather, the most credible charges were that the unions had fallen behind the times, failing to recruit rapidly in growing white-collar trades, and had failed to keep their own house in order. The major problems of recent years had been well documented: unofficial strikes, demarcation disputes, the breaking of negotiated agreements, and restrictive practices which saw output being deliberately held back in order to stave off threats of technical innovation – a particular concern in craft unions such as printing and shipbuilding. In many cases, these failings were aggravated by the administrative structure of the unions, which led to minimal contact between union officials and branch members. Shop stewards, unpaid and regarded as more in touch with grass-roots opinion, had increasingly become identified with militancy, and were willing to disrupt work on issues as trivial as the length of tea breaks. Hence the unions, as represented by shop stewards if not full-time officials, were 'too often proving themselves the natural allies of the forces of stagnation and conservatism in industry'.[11]

As a diagnosis of Britain's 'industrial disease', the view of Shanks was widely shared, and brought for example to cinema screens in 1959 in the satirical film by the Boulting brothers, *I'm All Right Jack*. Set in the early 1950s, workers at an engineering factory were depicted as lazy and liable to strike whenever prompted by the domineering Chief Shop Steward Fred Kite (played by Peter Sellers). On union membership, one of Kite's fellow stewards remarks 'It's not compulsory, but you have to join.' Management was similarly lampooned. The bosses of 'Missiles Ltd' were presented as feckless, themselves provoking a stoppage to make a larger profit by diverting an order in a corrupt arms deal. But if this portrait was becoming a familiar one, it did not provide a convenient scapegoat for all of Britain's ills in the 1960s. Who precisely was the villain of the piece? Certainly the trade unions were not seen by the wider public as 'overmighty subjects' who must at all costs be brought to heel. In 1962, at least two out of every three Gallup respondents claimed that, generally speaking, unions were a 'good thing', roughly the same proportion as ten years earlier.[12] As we have seen, Shanks himself pointed the finger at both sides of industry, and other writers were more forthright in decrying the attitudes of employers. Industrial correspondent John Cole wrote that the 'stupid antagonism' of the middle classes had much to answer for, citing the example of the Ford company at Dagenham, which was so bitterly anti-union that it took many years for organised labour to receive employer recognition:

> By that time, not only had a mood of antagonism and rancour settled firmly on the bleak Essex marches where the factory lies, but the rudimentary union organisation bore the seeds of the present chaos. Why do Ford have twenty-two unions operating in their works while Vauxhall have two? Principally, because trade unionism at Dagenham began as an underground movement.[13]

Other writers widened the cast list of possible suspects. In Andrew Shonfield's pioneering study *British Economic Policy since the War*, published in 1958, government ministers were called to account for too frequently adopting deflationary measures to protect sterling whenever the balance of payments was in deficit. This, Shonfield argued, was at the base of British underinvestment compared with its rivals: industry as a result lacked the confidence to plan for the long term, making stability and growth difficult to achieve.[14] The critical tone of Shonfield's work was taken further by another economic commentator, Nicholas Davenport, whose work *The Split Society* attacked Britain's moneyed elite for placing the interests of 'finance capital' above those of the working class. The pursuit of 'hard money' policies in the 1950s, he claimed, together with the dismantling of economic controls, opened up the way for a boom in equity shares as the rich set about profiting from dividends and increased profit margins. The average male manual worker may have experienced a 50 per cent improvement in his real standard of living since 1951, but over the same period owners of capital had enjoyed a rise of 183 per cent in the value of equity shares (225 per cent with net dividends added). It was small wonder, Davenport concluded, that workers maintained an 'us and them' mentality in insisting that wages stay ahead of prices; and that Cousins should demand that 'in a free for all, labour is part of the all'.[15] The issue of who was responsible for Britain's faltering economic performance was therefore too contentious and multi-faceted to provide any easy answer to the 'what was wrong' question. Instead, a more clear-cut target came into view: the 'stagnant society', it was said, stemmed primarily from failing leadership.

The Establishment

In all areas of public life, 'state of the nation' critics claimed, Britain was being ill-served by an old-fashioned and privileged elite, increasingly referred to as the 'Establishment'. By the mid-1960s this was a well-worn term, and few would have quarrelled with the definition given by one of Macmillan's ministers, Reginald Bevins:

> What on earth is the Establishment? I suppose I could define it as a power group, operating on the scenes, but mostly of course behind the scenes. The vital thing to grasp is that its influence is all-pervasive. Unlike a Masonic Order or a political party or the Salvation Army, it has neither rules nor ritual nor identity. It is invisible, but it is ubiquitous.[16]

When the phrase first came into usage, in the middle of the 1950s, it was not always used pejoratively. In 1955 the journalist Henry Fairlie provoked controversy by talking of an 'Establishment' that included not only the Prime Minister and the Archbishop of Canterbury, but also 'lesser mortals' such as the Chairman of the Arts Council, the Director-General of the BBC, and the editor of *The Times Literary Supplement*.[17] In the debate that followed, some questioned the use of the term, saying it was not startling to discover that Britain – like any other nation – had a governing class. Others praised the Establishment as a source of stability. Henry Fairlie

noted that membership was difficult to define and constantly changing; hence it was possible to argue that the elite within British
society staved off the danger of becoming fossilised by continual
renewal.

But by the early 1960s references to the Establishment had become
more uniformly critical. The tone was set by a collection of essays
published in 1959 by a young historian and novelist, Hugh Thomas,
who defined the Establishment as 'the present-day institutional
museum of Britain's past greatness'. Contributors to his volume were
generally agreed that 'the fusty Establishment, with its Victorian
views and standards of judgement, must be destroyed'.[18] Perhaps the
most forceful advice on how this might be done came from the Balliol
economist Thomas Balogh, in 'The Apotheosis of the Dilettante', a
sharp critique of the recruitment and ethos of the senior civil service.
Balogh attacked what he called the 'myth of a perfectly working
government machine', and lambasted the non-specialists who rose to
the top through a recruitment process that favoured those with 'good
connections and no knowledge of modern problems'. He was especially critical of the Treasury, which dominated Whitehall and itself
highlighted the 'cult of the amateur'. For Balogh, therefore, the
restructuring of the civil service was an essential first step towards the
creation of a more dynamic, forward-looking economy.[19] The civil
service was one of the areas investigated in what became one of the
most influential studies of the Establishment, Anthony Sampson's
Anatomy of Britain, published in 1962, and widely read among the
nation's opinion formers.

Sampson, an *Observer* journalist, corresponded with or interviewed
200 prominent individuals in order to see who runs Britain, 'how
they got there, and how they are changing'. What he found was that
traditional elites were alive and well, not only in Whitehall but also
at Westminster and inside the major financial institutions. He began
by pointing out the surprising resilience of the upper class, which
constituted only a tiny minority of the population. The aristocracy,
he noted, were 'much richer than they seem' and their influence over
British politics had far from disappeared as some assumed. Who
would have guessed that over a century after the 1832 Reform Act, in
1962, 'the Prime Minister, the Foreign Secretary, the Governor of
the Bank of England, [and] the Chairman of the Defence Committee
. . . would all either belong, or be closely related to, the old
aristocratic families?' Sampson constructed an elaborate family tree

to show how, while many of the landed elite had retreated to their country estates, others had maintained an informal 'network of inter-marriages with political and financial powers'. While every nation had its power elite, it was this network of extended family ties that accounted for the special flavour of the British Establishment. While insiders might regard their position as beneficial to the nation, Sampson noted that an alternative view had gained ground in recent years – one which saw the Establishment as a:

> closed, self-contained circle which favours hereditary amateurs against self-made professionals, produces 'old-boy' agreements between banks and businesses, and acts as a drag on ambition and dynamic.[20]

Central to the analysis – and to that of other 'state of England' critics – was the importance of the public schools and Oxbridge as a training ground for the governing elite. In spite of wartime threats to make education a genuine agent of social change, the independent schools had thrived in post-war Britain, with an estimated increase of 20 per cent in pupil numbers. Eton above all had emerged 'with more stability and prestige than ever', its products still going on to the Foreign Office, the civil service and the merchant banks in the same high proportion as before. Etonians were marked out by the social exclusiveness of their ancestry rather than academic prowess; the Headmaster proudly noted that 60 per cent of the intake had Old Etonian fathers. Although high fees restricted attendance at public schools to only 5 per cent of the nation's children, their influence upon the power structure of Britain remained unmistakeable. A survey in the 1940s had shown that of 830 bishops, judges, magistrates, higher civil servants, governors of Dominions and directors of banks, three quarters came from public schools, nearly half from the top-tier 'Clarendon Schools' such as Eton, Harrow, Rugby, Winchester and St Pauls. Since the war, Sampson concluded, the public schools had gradually become aware that there was no longer an Empire for their products to govern.

> But no one visiting a public school can fail to be struck by the continuity of these isolated communities: they roll on with their Latin jokes, their founders' prayers, their fags and private languages, still perpetuating vestigal aspects of a Victorian world.[21]

The universities told a similar story. Oxford and Cambridge remained the preserve of the wealthy and exceptionally talented, helping to explain why Britain fared so badly in international comparisons for the provision of higher education. In 1957 a United Nations survey showed that Ireland, Turkey and Norway alone among 28 nations analysed had a lower number of university students per million of population than Britain. Only 4 per cent of British schoolchildren went on to higher education, compared with 30 per cent in the United States. The domination of Oxbridge remained much as it had for hundreds of years. Its 18,000 students were 'one of the most elite elites in the world', figures suggesting that in the twentieth century Oxbridge had provided 87 per cent of permanent secretaries and 72 per cent of cabinet ministers. At the same time, the background of those reaching the dreaming spires was not changing as rapidly as some assumed. In 1957 on average half of those entering Oxbridge were from the public schools, with many grammar schools opting to send their pupils to less regarded provincial universities. The quasi-aristocratic atmosphere of Oxbridge, Sampson noted, had been largely unaffected by post-war pressures, as was the unchanging calendar of boat races, college balls and 'summer frolics'. At Christ Church, he found:

> the dominant group is still made up of beaglers, sports-car drivers, champagne-party-givers and future Conservative MPs. From the annual newsletter, which records the KCMGs, the ambassadorships and cabinet changes of alumni, one might suspect that the whole of government provided a kind of aftercare treatment for Christ Church men.[22]

However, Sampson – like Michael Shanks – was not oblivious to elements of change within British society. While the public school–Oxbridge network still monopolised large areas of public life (in diplomacy, the services and the City of London, as well as politics), 'new centres of power' were more likely to be the province of grammar school and Redbrick-university educated products. This was true, for example, of those professions which between them controlled business and commerce: accountancy, insurance, science and engineering.[23] Hence Anthony Sampson concluded that it was more accurate to speak not of a single Establishment but a 'ring of Establishments', between which there were only slender connections.

But he had little doubt where power and prestige really presided, for the British way was to honour the old institutions, with their 'pageantry and rigmarole', rather than the new ones. His experience in preparing the book convinced him – in summing up – that Britain's problem in 1962 was essentially one of leadership:

> Briefly it is that the old privileged values of aristocracy, public schools and Oxbridge which still dominate government today have failed to provide the stimulus, the purposive policies and the keen eye on the future which Britain is looking for, and must have . . . The old fabric of the British governing class, while keeping its social and political hold, has failed to accommodate or analyse the vast forces of science, education or social change which (whether they like it or not) are changing the face of the country . . . Britain's malaise, I suspect, is not primarily a malaise of the ordinary people, but a malaise among the few thousand managers of our society who failed to absorb and communicate new challenges and new ideas.[24]

In the circumstances of government unpopularity in the early 1960s, the Establishment thus became a convenient scapegoat. In the realm of academic debate, the concept was still open to criticism. To outsiders such as American writers Almond and Verba, the stability of its democracy was the central feature of British political culture in 1963. Nearly half of respondents in a 1950s survey mentioned the system of government as something they were proud of when asked, a proportion higher than in other countries studied except for the USA.[25] But this research pre-dated the abrupt mood change that followed the 1959 election, and ran counter to the increasingly sceptical attitude towards leadership developing within Britain itself. This mood was taken up by a new generation of satirists quick to condemn the 'old guard'. In October 1961 a London nightclub called the Establishment was opened, providing a platform for young comedians to lampoon political leaders and others in positions of authority. A wider audience still was reached by the hitherto unthinkably daring television show *That Was the Week That Was*, which began its first series in the autumn of 1962. In the words of its presenter, David Frost, the programme's biting portrayal of ministers represented a revolt of youth, directed against the ageing Establishment.[26] Even those who still preferred other terminology – such as the 'managerial class' – were agreed that drastic changes were necessary. In the words of one critic, those groups who governed Britain did so 'with little or no reference to each other, and with no sense of a common purpose'.[27]

Modernisation

It would be misleading to imply that all 'state of the nation' critics in the early 1960s either diagnosed Britain's problem in the same way or advocated identical remedies. For Michael Shanks, the main task was to make trade unionism 'stronger and more coherent'. If TUC authority was strengthened, enabling it to deal more effectively with abuses and leading to streamlined unions reflecting modern industry, then it would be possible to 'finally lay to rest the ghost of the thirties'.[28] For others, the primary need was to maximise leadership potential by thoroughly overhauling recruitment procedures to top positions, thereby widening the scope for talent wherever it was found.[29] What did tend to unite social critics was the view that, in order to rediscover its sense of direction, Britain needed to be 'modernised'; institutions, policies and values would all need to be brought up to date, otherwise the goal of reinvigorating the economy and recovering lost prestige would remain elusive. Implicit in 'state of England' writing was the assumption that the government had gone neither far nor fast enough in addressing the new agenda. There was no doubt that ministers were alert to the wide-ranging debate opening up after 1961. Macmillan told colleagues that modernisation would determine the fate of his administration, and his decision to go for Common Market membership was intended to provide the Tories with a forward-looking strategy both at home and abroad. But modernising rhetoric brought few dividends while Macmillan remained at Downing Street, as we can see by looking at the government's approach to the two key areas of industrial relations and political leadership.

In the early 1950s conciliation had been the watchword of Conservative policy towards the trade unions. Sir Walter Monckton was chosen by Churchill as Minister of Labour specifically for his lack of partisanship, and from the outset he tried to 'do justice in the many disputes' that arose between employers and labour, aiming always to reduce the field of conflict to the 'narrowest limit' so that agreement might be reached.[30] This conciliatory approach ensured – as Churchill intended – that the TUC's recently acquired status as an 'estate of the realm' was not jeopardised, though it did lead to rumblings of discontent within the party. Grass-roots party opinion still hankered after punitive measures to reduce the 'power' of the unions – a desire that intensified as Monckton's willingness to compromise led to complaints that inflationary wage settlements were being sanctioned in order to avoid industrial unrest. Much of the later criticism of Tory 'industrial appeasement' ignores, however, both the political and economic realities of the early 1950s. The closeness of the 1951 election alone made it imperative that large numbers of working-class trade unionists should not be alienated. Rapid economic growth, moreover, meant that wage increases were pegged below the general level of price increases, while at the same time maintaining full employment. In these circumstances, few considered the period as one of lost opportunity for reform. If Churchill could be criticised for discouraging open discussion of issues such as the quality of management or restrictive practices on the shop floor, there was at the time little external pressure for the reform of voluntarism as a guiding principle in industrial relations.[31]

The 1955 parliament saw much soul-searching but no decisive change in government policy. If the decade after 1945 had seen an extension of the 'wartime mentality' in industrial relations, Eden was the first Prime Minister to be faced with a new 'post-war ethos', reflected in increased strike activity and more hardline employer attitudes.[32] Ministers resisted pressure from within the party to legislate on issues such as strike ballots, and opted instead to publish a more authoritative statement on the dangers of wage inflation. The government's White Paper of March 1956 warned that if prosperous economic conditions 'are exploited by trade unions and businessmen, price stability and full employment become incompatible'.[33] While holding both sides of industry to account for mounting difficulties, the government's statement proposed no new mechanisms for imposing wage restraint, and Eden himself conceded that the White Paper had received 'a somewhat indifferent reception by the press and the public'.[34] Many employers were disappointed to find that no change of direction followed the arrival of either a new Minister of Labour, Iain Macleod, or a new Prime Minister, Harold Macmillan. Employers in the engineering and shipbuilding trades were dismayed to see Macleod back down from an initial willingness to support their

"YOUR INTENTIONS MAY BE STRICTLY HONOURABLE, SIR WALTER, BUT WHAT ABOUT THOSE FRIENDS OF YOURS?"

opposition to high wage claims. Macmillan was similarly equivocal in 1957 when threatened with industrial unrest which he felt the government could not tackle head on so soon after the Suez fiasco. Pressure for a more interventionist policy steadily mounted. In 1958, as we have seen, the Tories reaped electoral rewards after standing firm during the London bus strike, and Macmillan appointed – in an educative if not regulatory role – an independent Council on Prices, Productivity and Incomes. By the end of the decade, the so-called 'laissez-faire collectivism' of the early 1950s was being supplanted by more active corporatism in industrial policy.[35]

The shift in emphasis became more pronounced after 1960. Reform of trade union law was still resisted, both for electoral reasons and because ministers believed the impact would be marginal. The government's task was to encourage via informal negotiations the breaking down of 'attitudes of mind which think in terms of "they" and "us"'.[36] But several forces led Macmillan to consider introducing for the first time a statutory wages policy. Ministers and officials, including those at the Ministry of Labour – now under John Hare – were impressed both by the apparent success in France of 'indicative planning' and by independent surveys confirming the wage–price spiral as the main cause of inflation. Over the past decade incomes had risen by £10,000 million while productivity had increased by only £3000 million. These figures persuaded even Treasury sceptics of the need for drastic action, taken initially in the form of the 'pay pause' announced by Chancellor Selwyn Lloyd in July 1961. In spite of breaches by public-sector workers, such as the railwaymen, Lloyd followed up the pay pause with the idea of a 'guiding light' of 2.5 per cent increases during 1962. As Macmillan told Cabinet colleagues, what was being sought was an *acceptable* incomes policy, one which offered trade unionists rewards not just restraint.[37] Hence the TUC was invited to join the newly formed National Economic Development Council (NEDC), which proposed an annual target of 4 per cent growth in the economy. For the Prime Minister, industrial planning was only one aspect of a wider package of modernising measures; this would take in reform of the nationalised industries and included wide-ranging inquiries by experts such as Beeching into the railway network and Robbins into higher education.

In practice, Conservative 'planning' offended as many as it pleased. Ministers might comfort themselves that the pay pause brought home the realities of the wage–price problem more than any exhortation over the past decade. But the pause was deeply unpopular with trade unionists, who had been denied any prior consultation, and with the wider public. Discussions with thousands of voters revealed that while there was support for pay increases being related to higher productivity, the policy was resented as discriminatory against particular groups of workers and unfair coming so soon after surtax concessions to the rich.[38] Much goodwill had therefore been lost by the time Macmillan resorted to a 'guiding light' and a National Incomes Commission to offer 'independent' advice on major wage claims. The TUC refused to co-operate with what were regarded as attempts to penalise ordinary workers while the better off were asked to make no corresponding sacrifices. Many trade unionists saw the initiatives of 1961–2, and the Contracts of Employment Act that followed in 1963, as an eleventh hour conversion by a faltering administration – a view reinforced by the divisions within Tory ranks over industrial planning. Some Cabinet ministers, Macmillan conceded, were 'laissez-faire minded', and belonged to the ' "more teeth" school of thought', agreeing with the party's Industrial Relations Committee that compuslory strike ballots were more urgently required than a 'new [NEDC] monster'.[39] The view of most Tory MPs and activists appeared to be an acceptance of planning as unavoidable, but regrettable.[40] On this issue, there was plenty of scope for Labour to make the running by claiming that its closer ties with the unions made it more likely to deliver economic growth combined with fairness to all sections of the community.

Further damage was caused to Macmillan's reputation by his inability to extend modernisation to the area of political institutions and leadership. As we have seen, the composition and structure of the civil service was a frequent target for social critics, yet institutional reform had been a low priority for the Conservatives since 1951. After Churchill's abandonment of his attempt to restore wartime practice with a system of ministerial 'overlords', interest in reshaping Whitehall to the needs of a new age dwindled. In 1954 Tory Chairman Lord Woolton noted regretfully that the Cabinet had never placed the machinery of government on its agenda.[41] Lack of innovation resulted in part from the inertia of the 'higher divinities' of postwar Whitehall, Edward Bridges and Norman Brook, neither of whom saw the need to reform the service over which they presided. 'Outside critics', in the words of Peter Hennessy, were brushed aside as if they were ignorant and parasitical fleas on a flourishing, healthy body.'[42] Once this complacency was threatened by growing criticism in the late 1950s, Macmillan did consent to internal changes. Most notably, moves were made to transform the mechanics of long-term public expenditure planning and control, culminating in the Plowden Report which sanctioned surveys to forecast future commitments and the availability of resources. But this did not prevent the opposition seizing the initiative by proposing more fundamental reform. Wilson in particular cleverly made the case for institutional change as an essential prerequisite for creating a more dynamic economy. He outflanked the Tories by promising new departments such as a Ministry of Technology, plus a Department of Economic Affairs to break once and for all the 'dead hand' exercised by the Treasury over the Whitehall machine.[43]

Failure to undertake reform of British institutions was symptomatic of a major flaw in Macmillan's modernising strategy. By the early 1960s the Conservative party itself was regarded as a central part of the Establishment which it had become so fashionable to pillory. It was difficult to take seriously promises of radical change from a party so firmly committed to old traditions. Anthony Sampson was not alone in pointing out just how far the Tories were still dominated by an 'old boy network'. Of the 65 ministers appointed to various posts by Churchill in 1951, only 8 were not public-school educated; 10 years later the figure had risen – to 17 of 69 appointments – though the change was barely noticeable in the Cabinet. Two thirds of Eden's Cabinet had been to a Clarendon school. Macmillan was accused of denying real influence to rising Tory meritocrats by favouring wealthy relatives, and even after the reshuffle of July 1962, nearly half the Cabinet consisted of Old Etonians. In the 1955–64 period only two Conservative backbenchers could be described as coming from a working-class background; by contrast, a large proportion had been to Eton and Oxbridge.[44] When Conservative popularity remained high, the social composition of the party was not necessarily a disadvantage. Studies of the 1959 election had pointed to the importance of the deferential working-class Tory, those who believed 'it's in the blood for them, running the country'.[45] But if the governing class failed to live up to expectations, perspectives could change. The Profumo affair proved so damaging because it appeared to expose double standards on the part of those who publicly championed old-fashioned morality –

refusing, for example, to liberalise laws on divorce or homosexuality
– while adopting a different code for themselves in private. Gallup
found more than half of those questioned 'horrified' by the episode,
suggesting Conservative credibility as 'natural rulers' had been badly
dented.[46]

Sex and security scandals, combined with de Gaulle's veto, left
Macmillan's search for a new dynamism in tatters. *The Economist*
doubted if Profumo was at the root of national unease:

> Vastly the largest event for Britain in 1963 was the barring out
> from Europe . . . Up to then any British reappraisals had a focus
> and a setting . . . Since then British policy and British politics have
> sometimes seemed rather like a decapitated lizard which for a time
> goes twitching blindly on.[47]

What modernisation had taken place was easy to depict as half-
hearted and ineffective. Michael Shanks pointed out that it was all
very well to initiate the Beeching Inquiry into the rail network, yet it
was not presented as part of any integrated transport policy; a
'similar vacuum', he maintained, existed in relation to fuel policy,
the distribution of industry and land use.[48] Social critics were agreed
that much more fundamental changes were required. Both poor
industrial relations and backward-looking leadership might be
tackled, it was felt, by greater meritocracy: allowing talent to flourish
from whatever quarter it came, so as to encourage a society with
'fewer social frictions, less antagonism and hostility between classes
and groups, a greater degree of dynamism and common purpose'.[49]
These words belonged to Shanks, though they could equally have
been spoken by Harold Wilson, who made the modernisation agenda
his own. Britain was falling behind its competitors, the youthful new
Labour leader maintained, *because* the talent of the majority was
being held back by a failed elite. 'We are all modernisers now', Rab
Butler remarked; but some were more convincing than others.
Macmillan, having only recently traded on his embodiment of
Britain's past – with his languid Edwardian style – was incapable
of taking on the role convincingly. As John Ramsden notes, 'the
problem only increased as he himself aged, at just the moment when
sweeping changes in the popular culture of the Western world were
bringing forward the spirit of youth'.[50]

Conclusion

The notion of Britain as a 'stagnant society' in the early 1960s did not
go uncontested. In his outspoken fashion, Henry Fairlie decried the
ceaseless number of books and 'special numbers' on the 'state of
England', attacking what he called their phoney obsession with
decline and crisis. Fairlie insisted that Britain was 'as free and orderly
and kindly a country as any in the world'; he suspected that those
who called for dynamism were encouraging authoritarianism and
paid scant regard to possible victims of change such as the old and
the weak. He ventured that Britain had little to learn from France
and Germany about the ordering of a free sociey, and he claimed
that class differences were more imagined than real and 'scarcely
mattered a whit'.[51] While a sense of crisis can of course be easily
exaggerated, what was striking about the work produced independ-
ently by writers, journalists and social critics was its agreement
upon broad fundamentals. A common starting point – which Fairlie
was unable to contradict – was that Britain lacked the sense of
purpose that had been evident in the war years and its immediate
aftermath. Anthony Sampson's extensive interviewing led him to
portray 'a country that doesn't believe in anything, and is confused
about its direction', while others spoke of the 'feeling of belonging to
the only nation without aim or inspiration'.[52] In the words of *The
Economist*: 'It is, above all, the sense of direction that has to be looked
for before it can be said that all this soul-searching is realistic and not
just sentimental.'[53]

'State of the nation' critics also disagreed strongly with Henry
Fairlie about the importance of class tension. The evidence presented
in this chapter suggests that class divisions – far from withering away
as Macmillan claimed in 1959 – persisted into the 1960s at all levels
of British society. Indeed for social critics the debilitating effects of
class were at the heart of everything that was wrong with the
'stagnant society'. Arthur Koestler, the editor of one of the most
extensive 'special numbers' on the 'state of England', forcefully
rejected the assurances of 'wishful thinkers' that class divisions were
on the wane. Post-war affluence, he said, may have dulled glaring
economic inequalities, but had left in tact 'psychological apartheid'.
Having lived on both sides of the Channel, Koestler was able to
introduce a comparative note:

Most European countries went through a series of social revolutions in 1789, 1848, 1918, and 1945, which abolished or eroded the social and educational class-barriers to a considerable extent. This country was spared these bloody upheavals, but at a price which now makes itself increasingly felt. Instead of flames coming out of the roof, it saw the rafters crumbling with slow dry rot. It preserved its anachronistic class structure . . . as unique in the Western world as are its weights, measures, and currency . . . In this oldest of all democracies class relations have become more bitter, trade union politics more undemocratic than in de Gaulle's France or Adenauer's Germany. The motivation behind it is neither communism, socialism, nor enlightened self-interest, but a mood of disenchantment and cussedness.[54]

Here then, implicit in the work of a broad swathe of influential writers, was a damning critique of Conservative rule since 1951. Contemporaries were not slow to point out that Harold Macmillan, as Prime Minister since 1957, shrank from the task of presenting sober realites to the nation. To adopt whole-heartedly the modernisation agenda would be to admit that much was wrong, to concede, as Koestler put it, that the British people were 'riveted on the past', with their 'gaze turned backward and inward'. Yet, as we have seen in previous chapters, Macmillan was the master of 'avoiding conflict, postponing pain'. More than one historical account has concluded that, unlike de Gaulle, he was too willing to compromise for the sake of short-term popularity; hence priority was given to consumer spending rather than greater investment on infrastructure projects such as factories, railways and ports. What Macmillan finally lacked was 'a compelling sense of national purpose and the determination to convince the public of the need to look to the long term'.[55] *The Economist* article cited at the beginning of this chapter claimed it was all to the good that politicians and pundits were vying with each other in 1963 to produce prescriptions for a host of problems: for remodelling the machinery of government, for updating the structure and content of British education, for widening the catchment area for civil servants and managers, for providing industry with modern facilities and recruits. 'These', it concluded, 'are the right, necessary agenda for a contemporary Britain'.[56] The question it did not pose was: why had this agenda not been addressed in the past decade?

6   The Opportunity State: Welfare Policy under the Tories

Introduction

Almost without exception, 'state of England' critics in the early 1960s regarded educational reform as an urgent national priority. Arthur Koestler summed up what many felt:

> It is our out-dated educational system, out-dated in almost every respect – 11-plus, streaming, curriculum, segregation by class and sex – which perpetuates the iniquities of the past. It tears the nation apart and provides, generation after generation, a new crop of unwilling combatants for the cold class war. Equal opportunities for equally gifted children regardless of the status of the parents seems to me the basic axiom on which a free society must be built.[1]

Some historians and political scientists, writing with the benefit of a longer perspective, have defended the welfare record of successive Tory governments – in education as in other areas of social policy. Certainly Labour accusations in 1951 that the welfare state would be threatened by the Conservatives proved to be wide of the mark. Official statistics showed that, far from dramatic cutbacks, expenditure on services such as social security, health and education rose from £1537 million in 1950 to £3171 million in 1959; followed by further steep rises in the early 1960s. Ministerial resignations from the Treasury in 1958 have been interpreted as the defeat of hardliners unable to resist a remorseless rise in public spending. Hence there was much evidence of 'post-war consensus', an all-party commitment to minimum standards of social welfare that was to persist until the 1970s.[2]

Those such as Ben Pimlott who have attacked the 'myth of consensus' paint a different picture. On one level, rising expenditure owed much to the inevitable consequence of demographic change, such as increasing numbers of schoolchildren and pensioners. At another level, any consensus between the parties was skin deep, a temporary compromise between hostile groups rather than a genuine agreement about fundamentals.[3] Other recent writers have sought to reconcile these contrasting viewpoints. Rodney Lowe notes that party divisions were strong after 1951 both over particular policies and underlying philosophy, with Labour seeking a more equal society through state intervention and higher taxes if necessary, whereas Tories sought only that degree of intervention and taxation compatible with market efficiency and personal initiative. But for various reasons, such as the need to appeal to the electoral middle ground, these divisions did not prevent broad continuity or the expansion of existing welfare programmes.[4] Here, in reviewing social policy across the 1951–64 period, it will be argued that the Conservatives did bring into power the outline of an alternative agenda. What followed was an attempt to turn Labour's 'welfare state', based on universalism and collective provision, into an 'opportunity state', stressing selectivity, individualism, and private over public provision. Efforts to refashion Labour's legacy were enough, as we shall see, to occasion some fierce party exchanges, notably over housing and education. At the same time, the inheritance of 1951 proved stubbornly resistant to change; fear of an electoral backlash, over health and pensions in particular, meant that some existing provision went unreformed. The 'opportunity state' never became sufficiently developed – in either intellectual or practical terms – to provide a convincing, popular alternative. By 1964 the Tories were left vulnerable to the charge made by Arthur Koestler and many others: that opportunity for the few came at the expense of the majority.

Phases in Welfare Policy, 1951–64

Successive parliaments after 1951 saw subtle adjustments in social policy. In opposition during the late 1940s, the Tories had not accepted passively Labour's version of the welfare state. While conceding a greater role for state provision than in the past, Tory reformers working under Rab Butler's guidance at the Conservative Research Department questioned the cost, structuring and principles of newly provided services in health, social security, housing and education. The party chose to oppose the introduction of the

National Health Service (NHS) on the grounds that the variety and independence offered by 'voluntary hospitals' was being ignored. What emerged was a more distinctly 'liberal' agenda, one which challenged the universalism of the Beveridge insurance system and the tax-based financing of the NHS.[5] Party differences over how welfare services should be provided were accentuated by contrasting views on taxation and public spending. The recovery in Tory electoral fortunes after the war relied heavily upon middle-class disquiet, not only over rationing and austerity, but over tax rates and what was alleged to be extravagant spending on social services. Many party workers and supporters agreed with the view of the *British Medical Journal*, which claimed in 1950 that the nation was 'facing bankruptcy because of the Utopian finances of the Welfare State'. As a result, pressure built up for an incoming government to bring spending under much tighter control.[6] In the 1950–1 elections, Labour charges that Churchill would destroy popular services were vigorously denied, for fear of alienating working-class voters. Simultaneously, Tory leaders tried to reassure middle-class backers that it was possible to have welfare reform with a Conservative face.

This delicate balancing act was reflected in social policy as it unfolded in the 1951–5 parliament. The closeness of the 1951 result ensured that, in the short term, cautious pragmatism triumphed over the desire to push forward an alternative agenda. Ministers who had denounced waste in opposition became reluctant to sanction large cutbacks once in office, despite early Treasury raids on education and health.[7] Several forces combined to dictate a 'steady-as-she-goes' policy. Local authority power, civil service inertia, a prime minister determined to play safe and demographic change all played a part, the latter exemplified by increased numbers of schoolchildren requiring the employment of 25,000 additional teachers. Above all, plummeting popularity in the early months of the Churchill administration persuaded ministers that any wholesale assault on welfare spending would play into the hands of Labour propagandists. Those who complained that the party had softened its line on the social services through 'funk' rather than courage or conviction had to take comfort from continued downward pressure on public sector investment.[8] Changes to the structure of investment finance in 1953 freed up private funds to build cinemas, shops and office blocks, but at the same time drained resources away from new infrastructure projects in education and health. At the 1955 election, thanks to a rapidly improving economy in 1953–4, ministers could claim to have squared the circle. Tax cuts had assuaged middle-class opinion, while Labour predictions about attacks on the welfare state had been confounded. Instead, there had been a 'consensus born of constraint', with expenditure on the social services increasing roughly in line with inflation but declining marginally as a share of national income.[9] 'In sum', notes James Cronin, 'the Conservatives largely acquiesced in the maintenance of the social programmes put in place during the late 1940s, but spent hardly a shilling more than was required by the exigencies of politics and the growing demand for services.'[10]

With the security of a larger majority, ministerial rhetoric and policy began to shift after 1955. Eden made much of his 'property-owning democracy', and Macmillan as Prime Minister after 1957 spoke of an 'opportunity state' that stressed greater individual choice than associated with a collectivist 'welfare state'. When new economic strains emerged over the winter of 1955–6, the government chose a set of priorities, both social and economic, that constrasted sharply with what Labour had done in office and proposed in opposition. Far from meeting demands for welfare concessions to safeguard the poor, the Cabinet removed what remained of subsidies on council housing, bread, milk and school meals. This provoked a furious Labour attack on what was said to be a diminished commitment to full employment. In 1949 the Labour Chancellor, Stafford Cripps, while seeking disinflation, had raised food subsidies in order to hold down prices and so preserve wage restraint. By removing subsidies, increased prices were certain to stimulate higher wage demands and so create a climate in which employment would become more scarce – a fear borne out by slowly increasing levels of unemployment in the second half of the 1950s.[11] Public-sector investment continued to suffer, and ministers also conducted a far-reaching review of the social services, noting that costs looked likely to rise faster than any corresponding expansion in gross domestic product over the next few years. In the event, ministers defended the status quo, though as we can see from the working of the Social Services Committee in 1955–6, they did so for reasons which highlighted the differences between opposing front benches.

Treasury officials began by urging ministers to consider 'the long-term approach'; five-year advance planning would help in controlling expenditure.[12] But under the chairmanship of Rab Butler, the Social Services Committee found difficultly in identifying even short-term economies. The Minister of Housing, Duncan Sandys, refused to attend; cuts in health were out of the question once the government-commissioned Guillebaud Report recommended further expenditure in 1956; and Eden as Prime Minister was known to back educational expansion. Treasury officials also overplayed their hand by basing their case for cuts on figures suggesting that since 1951 social spending had risen by 35 per cent, compared with a 25 per cent increase in GNP. Unless this gap was closed, it was suggested, further economic crises were unavoidable. Ministers were not slow to point out that 'expenditure on the social services, although tending to increase each year in absolute terms was in fact taking a decreasing proportion of national income'.[13] Treasury attacks were resisted, in other words, primarily on the grounds that welfare expenditure was already being tightly controlled. The Chancellor was told that most members of the Committee felt defence should be the main target for cutbacks. By the end of 1956 – to the dismay of leading civil servants – Macmillan had decided to accept Butler's advice that 'the whole thing should be quietly buried'.[14] Thus when Peter Thorneycroft urged deeper savings in the face of a fresh sterling crisis in 1957, several options had been closed off by the Social Services Committee. Talk of withdrawing family allowances from second children was rejected as too damaging electorally. Thorneycroft's resignation as Chancellor in early 1958 left the government's dilemma unresolved: should the welfare state be attacked, maintained or reformed?

No clear answer was provided before Labour returned to power in 1964. There was evidence both of new thinking and rising expenditure. Within the Conservative Research Department, it was agreed that tax cutting no longer had priority over welfare expenditure, and that a middle way should be sought between the extremes of universalism and selectivity.[15] In 1961–2 welfare expenditure, whether as a proportion of public expenditure or as a proportion of gross domestic product, was no higher than it had been a decade earlier. In spite of the attempt to relate spending to available resources by planning ahead for five years – the central recommendation of the Plowden Report in 1961 – expenditure did rise sharply in the prelude to the 1964 election.[16] Yet for a variety of reasons, this phase of policy was set against an increasingly troubled background. In the first place, as the Financial Secretary to the Treasury, Edward Boyle, told colleagues, the party's ability to offer both tax cuts and good social services had relied on special one-off factors in the 1950s that no longer applied, such as improved terms of trade and scope for large-scale savings in areas such as defence, housing and food subsidies.[17] Minister of Health Enoch Powell hinted at a second difficulty: he noted the urgent need after ten years in power to come up with fresh ideas, yet admitted that in his own field of responsibility 'he had little or nothing to suggest'.[18] The government also left itself open to the opposition charge that, having been 'unable to find an extra sixpence for nurses' – as James Callaghan claimed – it was suddenly engaged on a reckless pre-election spending spree that threatened rampant inflation. All of this took its toll, with Party Chairman Iain Macleod conceding that 'although the aims of the Party had not changed, the impression in the country that "Conservatives Care" had recently been weakened'.[19] As we can see by looking at a range of social policy issues, from 1961 onwards the government found itself ever more vulnerable to relentless Labour attacks.

Social Security and Health

The two areas that caused least political controversy after 1951 were those that dealt with the 'security' aspects of the welfare state: national insurance and health. In spite of major reviews, the structures established by Labour in the late 1940s survived in both cases, though unforeseen difficulties increasingly made themselves felt. In the wake of the Beveridge reforms, it was widely believed that the worst features of pre-war poverty had been eradicated, especially when employment levels remained high for much of the 1950s. Yet Tory ministers did face the task of how to improve provision for pensioners and others in need at a time of rising prices, without either increasing Treasury subsidies or raising the flat-rate contributions upon which the Beveridge system was based. Indeed, this dilemma grew more acute as a million extra claimants qualified for means-tested national assistance in the period 1948–54. The Conservative response was to uprate periodically the level of insurance and assistance benefits, especially in the run-up to elections. Longer-term plans, however, were slow in developing. By 1959 Labour was appealing to the growing army of older voters by proposing 'earnings-related pensions', intended as a means of bridging the gap between those with occupational cover and those struggling on the state pension. Ministers had earlier endorsed the findings of the Phillips Report, claiming that to provide all pensioners with a subsistence-level pension was an 'extravagent use of the community's resources'. In 1959 John Boyd-Carpenter, the Minister of Pensions, attacked Labour's plan as inflationary and offered the more limited idea of 'graduated pensions'. By encouraging those with occupational pensions to opt-out of the state system, Tories found a way of circumventing the Beveridge principle of universalism. 'Statutory minimum provision', concludes Peter Baldwin, 'embellished with voluntary supplements, had been and remained the party's goal.'[20]

In the 1964 election campaign the Conservatives put up a strong defence of their record. Pre-election increases meant that the retirement pension and other benefits for married couples were at a higher percentage of average earnings than in 1948. National assistance benefits, when measured against the retail price index, were also worth almost half as much again as in 1948.[21] Set against this, various types of entitlement – such as sickness and unemployment benefit – were still lower in relation to average earnings than before the war. Any pretence, moreover, that every family's needs might be met without recourse to supplementation by a means-tested addition had quietly been abandoned. National assistance was based on an extremely frugal way of life, especially for the elderly population found to be in need of social-work care as much as higher levels of benefit. It was also the case that not all those in need were eligible for benefit, for example men in full-time work at rates of pay lower than the level of national assistance. Many claimants were also prevented from receiving the full level of entitlement by the so-called 'wage-stop' rule, which prevented an unemployed claimant from receiving more than 85 per cent of his previous take-home earnings.[22] Hence by the early 1960s the idealism that came with the establishment of the Beveridge reforms had evaporated. Voter enthusiasm for social security was dwindling, along with confidence about the eradication of poverty. Much, it was found, depended upon definitions of hardship. While pre-war 'absolute poverty' was on the way out, the concept of 'relative poverty' pointed in the opposite direction. In 1965 Brian Abel-Smith and Peter Townsend, basing their findings on national assistance levels, changed the basis of academic and political debate by calculating that between 1954 and 1960 the number of people who lived in poverty had increased from 8 to 14 per cent of the population. The largest group suffering from the new poverty, it

was found, were not the elderly but those 'working poor' whose pay
was insufficient to meet basic needs.[23]

If public support for national insurance waned, the same could not
be said of the National Health Service. In the minds of many voters,
the NHS *was* the welfare state; its popularity the product both of
removing the pre-war fear of being unable to pay for medical
treatment and of providing a wide range of services from hospital
to GP and maternity care. Charles Webster's history of the emerging
health service has stressed the importance of conflict rather than
consensus in the late 1940s, between the parties and within the
medical profession. At the time of the 1950 and 1951 elections,
Gallup found voters still perceiving important differences between
the parties on this issue. Public dislike of the modest charges on
prescriptions, dental treatment and spectacles proposed by Labour in
1951 – combined with the narrowness of Churchill's election victory
– ensured that Conservative governments worked hard to counter
accusations that they would dismantle the NHS. As one leading Tory
said, it was feasible to cut defence spending or even allow a 'dose of
unemployment. But meddle with National Health? That's political
suicide.'[24] By the end of the 1950s, as the main features of the service
introduced in 1948 were slowly developed, the public were persuaded that party political differences had subsided. This did not
mean, however, that Conservatives were happy with all aspects of a
tax-financed system, or that the NHS was given the same attention it
might have received from Labour, suffering as it did like other
services from the priority given to housing in the early 1950s.
Churchill's first Minister of Health, Harry Crookshank, soon became
bogged down over the imposition of charges and a large pay
settlement for doctors. His main critics were those Tory MPs who
wanted a tougher approach to spending, thereby confirming what
they saw as the extravagance of Bevan's NHS.[25]

Crookshank's younger successor, Iain Macleod, grasped the importance of stronger rhetorical support for health, but in May 1953
he agreed to establish a committee of inquiry into NHS funding,
chaired by the Cambridge economist C. W. Guillebaud. Far from
endorsing Tory concerns about waste, the Guillebaud committee –
relying heavily on research by LSE academics Abel-Smith and
Richard Titmuss – eventually concluded in 1956 that the service
was highly cost-effective. It was pointed out that the 'real terms'
increase in NHS funding since 1948 was small and that net costs had

EMERGENCY
WARD Nº 10
TO-DAY'S
OPERATION:
MAJOR ASSAULT
ON THE
WELFARE
STATE

"RIGHT, PROFESSOR POWELL, YOU START CUTTING AND I COME
LATER WITH THE BROMIDES...."

fallen as a proportion of GNP. Guillebaud went on to call for additional funding, noting that capital investment had been higher before the war and that hospital buildings – nearly half of which were built before 1890 – were in urgent need of repair.[26] Those Tories critical of both the structure and cost of the NHS were aghast – 'now our hands are very largely tied' was a common reaction.[27] After 1956 radical plans for reform, such as Macmillan's desire to pay for health by insurance contributions rather than taxation (thereby instilling 'new responsibility' in doctors and patients alike), struggled to see the light of day. If those who could not afford contributions were denied medical care, ministers conceded there would be an outcry against abandoning the idea of free access.[28] Health debates thus returned to a familiar pattern of Labour attacks on Tory 'cuts', as when Enoch Powell doubled prescription charges in 1961, followed by government measures to regain the initiative. In 1962 Powell announced an ambitious ten-year programme to build 90 new hospitals at a cost of £500 million; his detractors pointed out that in the first decade of its existence not one new NHS hospital had been built, and that growing centres of population such as the 14 new towns boasted 'not a hospital between them'.[29]

The absence of organisational reform helped to ensure an unequal distribution of resources. Hospital, GP and local authority services were each administered separately, thereby causing unnecessary duplication, and with money being allocated to regional boards in line with previous spending, pre-1948 inequalities tended to be exacerbated. Access to health care continued to depend upon where in the country patients lived, and studies in the 1950s found disparities also existed in terms of class, gender and ethnic origin. While a mainly free service brought great benefits for working-class families, especially children and women hitherto excluded from health insurance, it would be misleading to think in terms of a great leap forward in improved health. One study of industrial workers in Wallsend during the early 1950s found that while full employment provided reasonable security, everyday working conditions continued to be characterised by dirt, fumes, noise and damp – all of which contributed to poor health. Similarly, while women benefited from state provision such as family allowances, those who went out work were still expected to take responsibility for running the home, including care of elderly relatives where necessary. Easily accessible health centres were slow to develop, as doctors feared they might become centres of local authority power, and older women in particular suffered from the lack of adequate hospital provision for the chronically sick. New drugs helped to combat diseases such as TB, but hopes of providing equal access for every citizen often reflected 'the triumph of hope over experience'.[30] Charles Webster's official history of the NHS acknowledged that the post-war generation could be thankful for steady rather than spectacular improvements in provision. 'In the atmosphere of retrenchment dominant in the 1950s,' he concluded, 'the idea of a comprehensive health service was consigned to the realm of utopian dreams.'[31]

Housing

Party differences were most acute in two further areas of welfare provision: housing and education. Attlee's housing policy had been much criticised; delays in rebuilding after the devastation of war provided the Tories with a potent electoral issue in 1950–1. For some Labour activists, it was a matter of regret that ministers had retreated from radical wartime talk of land nationalisation. Yet housing policy had demonstrated an ideological cutting edge, with the pre-war roles of the public and private sectors being reversed. Four out of five homes completed under Labour were local authority built. The proportion of those living in council housing rose from 12 per cent in 1945 to 18 per cent in 1951, with the new properties being built to improved standards of specification and design. This approach was in stark contrast to the Conservative commitment to owner occupation, confirmed by Eden's claim in 1946 that the party sought a 'nation-wide property-owning democracy'. After Churchill's return to power, state control of scarce building resources went out of vogue; the term 'planning' was dropped from the title of the renamed Ministry of Housing and Local Government. Although an alternative Tory agenda took time to implement, home ownership was continually lauded as a means of promoting independence and allowing market forces free rein. 'We believe in a property-owning democracy with a decent home for every man,' wrote a member of the Research Department in 1958, 'whereas our opponents pin their faith to a regimented council house monopoly.'[32] On a range of other issues – such as the control of rents and the purpose and aim of council housing – Conservative housing policy after 1951 proved to be both contentious and partisan.

In keeping with the cautious domestic policy of the early 1950s – and with Harold Macmillan's political showmanship – pragmatism was initially the order of the day. As minister responsible for meeting the party's election promise to build 300,000 dwellings per year, Macmillan used a mixture of administrative skill and hints of resignation to secure 'more than my fair share' of resources.[33] Subsidies to local authorities were temporarily raised in order to boost council house completions, thereby enabling Macmillan to claim a political triumph during 1953–4. As his opponents pointed out, this success came at a price. More houses were built because room sizes were reduced and installations kept to a minimum. The policy equally had little effect on those living in the worst conditions. Ramshackle tenement blocks, cramped and damp flats and back-to-backs were still commonplace. One third of homes still had no bath, and in 1954 an estimated 43 per cent of houses in Liverpool and 32 per cent in Manchester were said to be unfit for human habitation.[34] Nor was Macmillan's approach uncontroversial among colleagues. In addition to Treasury demands for a slowdown while the economy remained fragile – resisted by Macmillan with Churchill's backing – Woolton as Party Chairman was alarmed by a strategy that herded together 'more people into these huge County Council housing areas, which become predominately Socialist in political outlook'.[35] Pressure built up for a new approach that ceased to privilege housing investment over other priority areas. By 1953 Macmillan was reassuring the Chancellor that the number of new houses would be scaled down in future, 'in order to make way for repairs, improvements, conversions, slum clearance and the rest', as well as encouraging private enterprise to build and sell.[36]

Here then was the basis for a government White Paper, *Houses: The Next Step*, and for a strategy carried forward by Macmillan's successors after 1954, Duncan Sandys, Henry Brooke, Charles Hill and Keith Joseph.[37] Three key elements of Tory policy began to emerge. The first was the encouragement of private enterprise. Controls on the licensing system for private-house building used by Labour were eased and then abolished in 1954. The development charge on new building introduced in 1947 was abolished; stamp duty on houses under £3000 was reduced; and owner-occupiers were made exempt from 'Schedule A' income tax in the early 1960s. In consequence, private-sector completions rose dramatically, such as to increase owner occupation from 29 per cent of households in 1951 to over 45 per cent by 1964. The second strand of policy was to use council housing increasingly for residual needs, catering only for those who could not afford to buy their own home. After the abolition of the 'general needs' sudsidy in 1956, local authorities had little choice but to turn their attention to slum clearance and rehousing. Further pressure on council housing resulted from the insistence that local authorities raise money not, as in the past, from a centrally funded Public Works Loan Board, but on the open markets. This meant higher rates of interest repayment, which local authorities could only meet by increased rents or further reductions in standards. Council house completions fell sharply from the peak of the mid-1950s, especially when the 'September measures' of 1957 bit deep into housing expenditure. By 1959 the annual total number of newly completed council houses had fallen to 100,000 from the earlier peak of well over 300,000.[38]

The third element in Tory policy was a concerted effort to revive the private rented sector. Wartime rent controls had been maintained by Labour after 1945 and, as part of the drive for decontrol, the Conservatives introduced legislation in 1954 permitting rent rises subject to expenditure on necessary repairs. This measure, though, proved too complex to succeed, and in 1957 a further Rent Act was passed enabling rent increases in all properties of a given rateable value; landlords below the threshold were also allowed to raise rents upon a change of tenancy. The 1957 Act occasioned bitter party controversy in parliament. Tory MPs supported reform as a way of expanding the supply of rented accommodation, while Labour backbenchers complained that rents for the poor would rise, which they did quite steeply after 1957. Any public outcry was muted, for many decontrolled properties were sold rather than being re-let, though the Conservatives were pushed on the defensive sufficiently to rule out any further decontrol in their 1959 manifesto. In the early 1960s the downside of decontrol attracted greater publicity, as stories circulated of landlords using intimidation to evict tenants before pushing up rents. 'Rachmanism' came into common usage following revelations that Rachman – a Polish immigrant and owner of a thousand London properties – had used unscrupulous methods to bully poor and elderly tenants, including lifting the roof off one property when the occupants refused to move. Ministers, anxious to avoid making matters worse in the private rented sector, were powerless to prevent a tide of adverse publicity. Rachman was said to have kept photographs of Brooke and Joseph on his wall as the men who kept him in business.[39]

By the end of its period in office, the government was facing criticism in all areas of housing policy. Henry Brooke was forced to concede that the private–public balance had been pushed too far in one direction. He told colleagues that the nation would resent any further cuts in local authority budgets while owner-occupation proceeded unchecked. Private building, he noted, was three times greater in the south east than north east, thereby giving credence to claims that 'two nations' were emerging in the early 1960s.[40] Council housing was consequently encouraged again, with a reintroduced subsidy for 'general needs' allowing completions to climb up to 125,000 by 1964. But the complicated formula this time used favoured rural authorities rather than large urban areas with the most pressing housing problems. The latter were forced to resort increasingly to building cheaper tower blocks which quickly became associated with isolation and vandalism. By 1960 cases were emerging of new flats in Liverpool being subject to blackouts and flooding as children sabotaged electrical and fire-fighting equipment. Residents were quick to complain about notorious design faults, as in the case of the Glasgow tower blocks that had lifts too small for either stretchers or coffins. Contrary to original expectations, high-rise flats were soon being used to house 'problem families' and those with young children, so helping to stigmatise the whole concept of council housing.[41] In 1962 the Research Department admitted in private that problems with the Rent Act, private landlords, mortgages and a feeling that house building was not meeting present requirements all contributed to 'the Conservatives . . . tending to lose the initiative on the housing front'.[42]

The contrast between the early and later years of Tory administration was therefore striking. Macmillan's housing success had helped to ensure the party's re-election in 1955; but by 1964 Wilson had seized the upper hand as on so many other issues. Ministers defended themselves by noting that private-sector completions had risen from less than 25,000 in 1951 to over 150,000 in 1964. At the same time, local authorities had made progress with clearing slums, and improvement grants enabled much necessary repair work to be carried out. But Labour propagandists had several targets to aim at, pointing out that if 'young marrieds' were rightly upset about mortgage costs then the poor were the real victims of Tory housing policy. Not only had security of tenure been undermined, but private rented property was much harder to find. The number of private landlord dwellings had continued to fall, from some 6 million in 1953 to 4.5 million in 1961. Taken together, the contraction of private rented outlets and the slowdown in council house completions created acute difficulty for those unable to buy their own property. Almost three million people were still living in slum accommodation and homelessness was becoming an established feature in larger conurbations, especially London. Council housing, while superior to pre-war provision, had suffered from cost-cutting and stigmatisation, being regarded by Conservatives as suitable only for those unable to compete in market conditions. With expenditure as a proportion of GDP falling across the 1951–64 period, it was not surprising that housing policy remained vulnerable to shifts in popular opinion. Surveys in the 1950s suggesting this was the only area of the welfare state subject to widespread criticism were reinforced by later tales of corruption and high-rise misery. Housing touched a raw nerve in the 1964 election just as it did in 1951, on both occasions rebounding against the government of the day.[43]

Education

The major concern in education during the early 1950s was with rebuilding a system still recovering from war. Oversize classes and inadequate school buildings were commonplace, and the raising of the school-leaving age from 14 to 15 under the 1944 Education Act made it imperative to find places for thousands of extra pupils. But if the government's programme was largely predetermined, its sense of urgency left much to be desired. Education, like other social services, found itself the victim of the high priority given by Churchill to housing. The new minister, Florence Horsburgh, was denied a place in Cabinet for nearly two years, and education officials conceded that the Ministry was proceeding with 'a bare minimum programme' of school building compared with Macmillan's 'triumph as a builder of suburbs'.[44] Rab Butler, the architect of the 1944 Act, ironically launched as Chancellor a series of assaults on education spending, demanding that Horsburgh consider cuts by shortening compulsory attendance 'at both ends' and aiming to reintroduce fee paying in secondary schools.[45] Horsburgh's successor in 1954, David Eccles, proved more resistant to Treasury intimidation, but for several years the ritual continued of education ministers fighting a rearguard action. In 1957 Geoffrey Lloyd said that the Treasury's latest demands for reductions in investment 'will revive doubts about the sincerity of the Conservative Party with regard to education that were so widespread during the years immediately after 1951'.[46] It was only after 1959 that Macmillan considered the possibility of education playing the same role as housing in the early 1950s; expenditure on schools, colleges and universities began to grow sufficiently to rival the Health Service as the second highest area of spending after social security.

What marked out education as an area of strong party disagreement was the question of secondary school organisation. The 1944 Act had opened the way for the development of three types of state secondary school: grammar schools, secondary moderns and technical schools. Horsburgh's wait-and-see attitude was spelt out soon after she came to office: 'We have the tripartite scheme. Cannot we try that out and see whether it succeeds?'[47] At the same time she was prepared to allow on an experimental basis the development of comprehensives schools, approving 32 out of 36 Local Education Authority (LEA) proposals. This pragmatic approach offended many within her party who felt that allowing children in any locality no option other than a single comprehensive school ignored 'vital differences' among pupils. Controversy slowly developed over two features of the evolving secondary system. One was that the accuracy of 'eleven-plus' tests to determine selection by aptitude and ability was increasingly criticised in an important minority of cases. Secondly, it was difficult to see how the 1944 ambition of 'parity of esteem' between different types of secondary school was to be achieved. Technical schools were expensive and slow to develop; in the meantime secondary moderns were considered inferior to prestigious grammar schools by parents, children and teachers alike. These twin difficulties encouraged the view among Labour activists that the only equitable answer was a complete reorganisation along comprehensive lines; only if selection at eleven was abandoned could all children be guaranteed equality of opportunity.[48]

Party policies on education were thus presented in highly adversarial terms. Tory conferences in the early 1950s emphasised the government's determination to develop tripartitism, and condemned 'Socialist policies for destroying the grammar schools'. Many within Labour ranks, including party leaders, were in reality still supporters of an educational 'ladder' that allowed bright working-class children to aspire to grammar schools. But opposition advocacy of speeding up the spread of comprehensives was a theme Tory ministers were keen to exploit. Horsburgh's successor David Eccles, aware that much of the educational 'establishment' favoured caution, was quick to declare that he would 'never agree to the assassination of the grammar schools'. To sweep away existing grammar schools in order to introduce comprehensives, he said, would be 'an absurd extra-vagance'.[49] In the run-up to the 1955 election, Labour were kept on the defensive. Eccles conceded privately that with 75 per cent of children in secondary moderns, parity of esteem 'has not yet hap-pened, and resentment [of those excluded from grammar schools] appears to be growing'. But he sensed that, providing secondary moderns were made more attractive to parents, public opinion would continue to back selection for everybody – 'the right policy' – rather than selection for nobody.[50] Eden's victory in 1955 appeared to have settled the question for the foreseeable future. Shortly after becoming Prime Minister, he confirmed that Tory policy was to continue encouraging variety (including a few comprehensives, for example in scattered rural communities), while underlining the intention to preserve and strenghten both secondary moderns and grammar schools.[51]

Yet in the second half of the 1950s criticism of tripartitism intensified. One reason for this was growing evidence that at least 10 per cent of children were misallocated owing to the shortcomings of eleven-plus testing methods. Press stories frequently appeared highlighting examples of 'coaching' and 'late developers' who bene-fited or suffered arbitrarily. Concern also developed over whether 'parity' could ever be achieved under the tripartite system. Sociol-ogists of education produced a mass of new evidence embarrassing to grammar-school apologists. In the first place there were gross disparities within and between local authorities. In Westmorland 42 per cent of secondary places were found in grammar schools; across in Gateshead the corresponding figure was 9 per cent. Children in Northern Welsh counties were 20 times more likely to achieve a grammar school place than those born in East or West Ham.[52] Prospects of reaching the grammar school varied not only region by region but were also heavily influenced by a child's background. In spite of greater opportunities under the 1944 Act, it was clear that 'a boy has a greater chance of entering a grammar school if he comes from a middle class rather than a working class home'.[53] One study in Birmingham found children in middle-class outer wards of the city five times as likely as those from inner city wards to secure a grammar school place. Another concluded that far from there being parity of esteem, there was 'a strongly established hierarchy, corresponding closely to the hierarchy of social classes'. Whereas many middle-class parents saw failure to reach the grammar school as a 'social disgrace', working-class children who did pass the eleven-plus were far less likely to stay for a full five-year course.[54]

In response to these findings, the terms of political debate shifted. Geoffrey Lloyd, successor to Eccles, told Macmillan that the government was cast in a 'defensive role' as champion of the status quo; attacks on the eleven-plus would grow unless 'we can find enough money quickly to improve the secondary modern schools'.[55] Gaitskell, however, found it difficult to exploit the situation. He welcomed the way local autonomy was used in London to develop comprehensives that appeared to be free of selection problems and capable of academic success; elsewhere he could claim that the needs of all children were not being met. But stung by its failure in 1955, the party was reluctant to give more hostages to fortune. Hence Gaitskell put the emphasis on securing greater flexibility in selection procedures, and rejected charges that Labour would compel all children across the country to attend large, allegedly impersonal comprehensives. With the Prime Minister's backing, Lloyd found a way of counter-attacking. In 1958 he was able to publish a White Paper, *Secondary Education for All: A New Drive*, announcing a five-year multimillion building programme. Far from retreating in the face of criticism, this aimed to make secondary moderns more credible by allowing greater scope for examinations and building up courses for those remaining in school beyond the age of 15.[56] In private, the education minister admitted that the policy was heavily influenced by political calculations. There would, he noted, have to be an expansion of secondary school places to meet demographic needs over the next few years. Why not then take the opportunity to smash the bogey of the eleven-plus by improving secondary moderns to the point where parents would regard them as equal yet different? This would also dish Labour by removing once and for all calls to abolish selection. Macmillan was duly impressed, and in the optimistic mood of 1959 was found claiming: 'We can do with Education what we did with Housing.'[57]

The stepping-up of school-building did little to prevent ever greater unease about the eleven-plus in the early 1960s. Evidence confirming the unfairness of the system continued to pile up. The Ministry of Education's own statistics confirmed that the social class gradient in educational opportunity was still unmistakable; survey research elaborated on this by demonstrating how working-class children were disadvantaged in eleven-plus tests by poor housing and parental indifference or hostility to staying on at school.[58] At the same time efforts to raise the status of secondary moderns proved unconvincing. A report in 1963 concluded that, according to the Ministry's own defined standards, two thirds were overcrowded, 45 per cent lacked a dining room and only a minority had adequate library or science facilities.[59] Many local authorities, concerned by disquiet about the eleven-plus, were moving to the view that new building should be in the form of comprehensives. Between 1960 and 1964 about a quarter made major changes to their selection procedures, and larger city authorities especially put forward plans to build new comprehensives alongside existing tripartite provision. Pressure intensified on Tory ministers to change the 1950s policy of allowing strictly limited numbers of comprehensives. Edward Boyle, one of the younger ministers promoted by Macmillan after the 'Night of the long knives' in 1962, began to use language alien to his predecessors. He publicly questioned whether children could be sharply differentiated into various types at 11 and agreed that tripartitism need not be seen as the 'normal way of organising secondary education'. As a result he encouraged a move away from simply tolerating a few comprehensives to encouraging their growth where the case was strong, especially in rural areas. Boyle presented himself as advocate of 'voluntary' comprehensives.[60]

Yet any shift in Tory policy was rhetorical as much as practical. In other speeches Boyle said he still regarded comprehensives as experimental, unproven either academically or socially. While he was prepared to see the adoption of new selection methods, such as teachers' reports instead of formal intelligence tests, he was keen to emphasise that existing grammar schools should not be endangered. Many onlookers were left confused. Boyle's own parliamentary secretary later wrote:

His cautious and apparently agnostic position did not win him many plaudits. The supporters of reorganisation were unimpressed by his hesitancy, while the defenders of the grammar schools had the distinct impression that a pass was about to be sold.[61]

Certainly Boyle stirred unease among Tory MPs, some of whom founded the '61 society' as a means of resisting the gathering pace of change 'from the tripartite system to comprehensive education without any proper research'.[62] Unwilling to align himself fully on either side in an increasingly polarised debate, Boyle left himself open to Harold Wilson's drive for greater fairness in education, skilfully woven into his 1963 conference speech. In the late 1950s Gallup found education to be low among public priorities. But by 1964, on the back of several 'state of the nation' critiques, it had become a prime issue of concern. For the first time since 1951, Labour could present itself as the party of reorganisation without incurring voter displeasure. The Conservatives were left to make the vague pledge that opportunities would be provided for 'all children to go forward to the limits of their capacity in good schools of every description'.[63]

Education had echoes of housing policy in the 1951–64 period. Ideological differences between the parties remained strong, and by the early 1960s, as Boyle admitted, 'we are on the defensive' in the face of 'our opponents' attacks'. As also in housing, numerical growth – in terms of school and pupil numbers – at first sight seemed impressive. But most of this expansion took place within the hierarchical tripartite structure. By 1963 there were only 175 comprehensive schools, compared with 1000 grammar schools, 4000 secondary moderns (600 built since 1951), and 200 technical schools.[64] In spite of the expansion promised in the Robbins report, there was still a 'chronic shortage of places' in higher education; selection at eighteen, as at eleven, meant most of those who squeezed through the narrow gateway of opportunity did so by birth.[65] Conservative ministers – who as one admitted had little understanding of the issues 'because so few of them have been involved in the maintained schools' – were 'cautious consolidators' rather than innovators in education.[66] Grammar school excellence was on no account to be diluted, especially not to make way for a new form of school regarded by the likes of the *Times Educational Supplement* as an insidious threat to the English way of life. Those comprehensives that were developed before 1964 tended to be in new suburban areas lacking secondary provision. Here there was found to be middle-class backing for something that avoided the stigma of secondary modern schools. Hence new comprehensives could safely be established, themselves conforming to concern for elitism by streaming pupils on the basis of ability and background. Tory education policy ultimately reinforced rather than challenged Britain's class divisions. New comprehensives, like other schools before 1964, tended to 'confirm their pupils' life chances rather than change them'.[67]

Conclusion

Conservatives stoutly defended their welfare record in the run-up to a general election. Greater numbers of houses built, improved health and increased educational opportunities – all were cited as evidence of solid progress. But privately it was acknowledged that voters were turning to Labour on social policy issues because the government had lost the initiative. None of the Conservatives' favoured slogans was striking a responsive chord. The 'property-owning democracry' had lost its appeal in the face of housing scandals and high mortgages; while the 'opportunity state' appeared to offer advantages to limited groups of key voters. Middle-class families not only had access to speedier medical treatment via private health insurance; they also benefited most from the boom in owner occupation and continued to monopolise the best of the state education system. One Conservative argued in 1961 that the small proportion of working-class children passing the eleven-plus posed a problem because many children from good backgrounds who failed the tests 'would achieve more in grammar schools than the theoretically more able children from poor homes'. Educational inequality was manifest in a system which left the majority of working-class children in schools widely regarded as the 'dump that took the leavings'.[68] Furthermore, growing prosperity had not disguised a rising number of homeless families and squalor in the housing conditions of lower-paid workers, im-migrant groups and large numbers of pensioners. By abandoning wartime notions of equality in favour of self-help, concludes one study of 1950s housing, Conservative policy promoted 'an ideal society where freedom and social mobility allowed its members an equal opportunity to become unequal'.[69]

Tory difficulties were rooted ultimately in the lack of an agreed framework for running the welfare state. The Research Department's Policy Committee on the Social Services, set up in 1960, began by noting that the development of policy in the 1950s had been pragmatic, and that no wide-ranging exposition of Conservative principles had been attempted. As Chairman, Michael Fraser claimed that the Committee began its work with a bias in favour of radical change – wishing to explore issues such as the nation's capacity to pay, whether benefits went to those in real need, and how to encourage further 'self reliance and individual responsibility'. Yet before long the Committee was conceding that the proportion of national income spent on the social services was 'by no means excessive' compared with other countries. Fraser concluded that no major departures in policy could be agreed upon: the more we looked at 'dramatic proposals' for reform, 'the less we liked them'.[70] Hence Tory attitudes towards the post-war settlement remained ambiguous. During Churchill's premiership in particular, the government – with one eye on its small majority – had accepted the need to maintain both full employment and a wide range of social entitlements. At the same time, many within the party, including those found in the One Nation group, preferred limiting state intervention in order to accommodate tax cuts. With any return to pre-1939 provision politically unacceptable, what followed was a 'middle way', broadly supportive of state action while also seeking to move away where possible from Labour's 'fair shares' ethos. But as the economy faltered in the early 1960s, ministers found themselves caught between two stools: unwilling to cut back welfare services for fear of incurring unpopularity but unable to develop any coherent alternative based upon first principles.[71]

The central impression in social policy as Macmillan left office was one of drift. This absence of direction – characteristic as we have seen of much government policy – both contributed to Tory electoral difficulties and imperilled longer-term prospects for a sustainable welfare state. As James Cronin has argued, by subordinating economic policy to the dictates of sound finance and lower taxation, Conservative ministers were 'denying the state the policy devices that might have been used to guarantee fulfilment of the commitments taken on between 1945 and 1955'. There was, in other words, a steadily widening gap between demands placed on the state and the means available to meet such demands. Public opinion favoured expanding social services, yet this had to be achieved without raising taxes.[72] Here was a circle that was ever more difficult to square, especially for a party that could never bring itself to embrace fully the inheritance of 1951. Whereas Attlee's government had actively sought to convince voters that social services were not 'free' but could only be paid for by an improving economy, Tory administrations largely abandoned 'public education' as too expensive, thereby contributing to negative notions of dependency rather than building a more constructive view of the welfare state. In the words of Rodney Lowe, the experience of the Social Services Committee under Eden pinpointed the 'serious limitations of post-war consensus':

> The mid-1950s was a period when, following the immediate post-war traumas, long-term reforms should have been effected. The Civil Service should have developed the requisite managerial skills to discharge permanently increased responsibilities; the public should have been made to recognise the cost as well as the benefits of the welfare state; and politicians should have accepted responsibility to take a long-term view. That all three challenges were evaded meant that . . . it was not the construction but the destruction of the welfare state that was, in Britain, to become the object of 'conviction' politics.[73]

7 The Affluent Society: Popular Politics and Voting Patterns

Introduction

By the early 1960s, as we have seen in the previous three chapters, Conservatism was in retreat. Macmillan's government was vilified for its handling of the economy and pilloried as part of an outdated 'Establishment' that prevented Britain from engaging in a process of modernisation. Ministers responsible for social policy were assailed for their half-hearted endorsement of the welfare state. What this left as the one apparently indisputable success of the Tory years was a steady improvement in living standards. Economic growth and low unemployment in the 1950s were the twin engines of a sustained consumer boom which saw expenditure rising sharply on a range of goods: from cars and motorcycles to furniture, television sets and electrical goods. The era of abundance owed much to American methods and companies, and in 1958 it was the Harvard economist J. K. Galbraith who found a name to reflect developments across the western world in his work *The Affluent Society*.[1] This label was in turn readily attached by historians to the 'never had it so good' ethos of Macmillan's Britain:

> It is said that Lord Poole, one of Macmillan's most astute and influential party managers, used to drive on a Saturday from his country home to nearby Watford. Here he observed the changing moods of the suburbs by watching people shopping in the new supermarkets, enjoying the opportunities they had never had before, absorbed in the rickety world of hire-purchase, intent on becoming owners of a television or a cut-price (imported) washing machine. If these were their desires and what they demanded with their votes, is it fair to blame the Governments of Churchill, Eden, Macmillan and Home for providing them so generously?[2]

Certainly, explanations of Tory success at the polls in the 1950s have traditionally focused on the theme of affluence. This was believed to have a particularly telling effect among sections of the working-class. Successive Conservative victories were said to be the product of new-found prosperity; as a result many 'affluent workers' were beginning to adopt middle-class values and voting habits. From the mid-1950s onwards, press commentators and writers frequently connected the greater availability of consumer goods with apparently related social changes: widespread migration to more fluid suburbs and new towns, for example, and the numerical decline of blue-collar employment at the expense of white-collar work. Shortly before Galbraith published *The Affluent Society*, an American journalist, Drew Middleton, spoke of the 'new' manual worker in Britain, better housed and more securely employed than his parents could have imagined possible:

> He moved to a New Town or a housing estate from a slum or near-slum. . . . He is living in what to him is comparative luxury: a living-room, a clean and, by British standards, modern kitchen. There is a bedroom for the children and a modern bath and toilet. He can walk or cycle to work and, if the weather is fine, he comes home for lunch. In the evening there is the 'telly' or the football pools form to be filled in. . . . It is a quiet life, but to our subject a satisfactory one.[3]

In the aftermath of Macmillan's 1959 triumph, the theory of 'embourgeoisement' gained currency among writers from across academic disciplines. The assumption of a levelling process within British society influenced the Nuffield election studies pioneered by political scientists. Social change, it was said, had weakened traditional working-class loyalties and made discussion of British politics in terms of class divisions less meaningful. 'With the disappearance of the most overt distinctions between middle and working-class,' argued David Butler, 'the sense of class conflict has been much reduced.'[4] From the realm of sociology Ferdinand Zweig wrote of a 'deep transformation of values', such that working-class life 'finds itself on the move towards new middle-class values and middle-class existence'.[5] Popular histories told the same story. According to Harry Hopkins, changing consumption patterns, dress styles and voting behaviour were all part of the same process: a progressive erosion of class barriers and the growth of the 'Endless Middle'. Throughout the length and breadth of Britain, noted Hopkins, 'on council estates as in Acacia Avenue, Sunday morning was devoted to the ritual laving of the car'.[6] In reassessing the popular politics of the period, this chapter will suggest that the relationship between prosperity and voting preference must be approached with caution. Affluence, it will be shown here, was not as widespread as many assumed; and its impact varied according to time and place. The importance attached to the 'affluent worker' has been exaggerated by contemporary observers and this has helped to obscure other significant movements of opinion, such as a drift of middle-class voters away from Conservatism. Far from withering away, as we shall see, class divisions remained at the heart of popular politics.

Social Class and Social Change

Any discussion of affluence and popular politics must first consider the nature and extent of social progress in the 1950s. On all sides it was agreed that prosperity had outwardly transformed living standards. In the words of Mark Abrams, one of the pioneers of survey research:

> Much more money is now being spent on household goods. The proportion of families with a vacuum cleaner has doubled, ownership of refrigerators has trebled, owners of washing machines have increased tenfold; we have stocked our homes with vastly more furniture, radiograms, carpets, space heaters, water heaters, armchairs, light fittings, lawn mowers, television sets . . . and film projectors . . . And all this means that for the first time in modern British history the working-class home, as well as the middle-class home, has become a place that is . . . pleasant to live in.[7]

But three qualifications must immediately be added. In the first place, it would be wrong to exaggerate the speed at which consumption standards were changing. While a majority possessed television sets, in 1960 only one in five working-class families owned a car; one third had washing machines and only 13 per cent refrigerators.[8] Secondly, there were important regional variations. Much of the discussion about affluence centred on prosperous industries or new estates and satellite towns, often in southern England. Visitors to, say, Tyneside were struck by a very different picture: of 'the musty taint of poverty', for the north-east has 'more places in it which look as if they are wasting away than anywhere else in the country'.[9] Related to regional variations was a third qualification. 1950s affluence had little impact on the poorest groups in society, for example the growing number of coloured immigrants struggling in run-down inner-city accommodation. London had a homeless population of over 5000 in the early 1960s. Figures collected by the Ministry of Labour suggested that those living below the poverty line were increasing not decreasing, owing to longer life-spans and larger family sizes. Scraping a living was an everyday reality for the 3,000,000 members of families whose head was in work, 2,500,000 pensioners, the 1,500,000 families of unemployed fathers, and over 1,000,000 families whose head was either deceased or chronically ill.[10]

At the same time, it should not be assumed that rising living standards easily eroded class identities and voting preferences. Nancy Mitford's attempt in 1955 to define differences between 'U' and 'non-U' speech (the upper classes would always used a napkin not a serviette) pointed to the survival of an aristocracy that retained political influence and 'social position through the Queen'.[11] In a survey of 6000 people carried out during the mid-1950s, less than 1 per cent of those questioned refused to place themselves in an identifiable social bracket. 'Unquestionably,' wrote Mark Abrams, the author of the survey, 'we are divided into groups with distinctive ways of life; people are aware of these divisions and they do rank some as carrying more prestige than others.'[12] Abrams, like most contemporaries, categorised voters according to their occupational ranking within the class system. For the growing band of polling organisations, the British electorate could be divided into two: middle-class professionals and white-collar workers (social groups A, B and C1), making up one third of voters; and the working-classes, ranging from skilled artisans to the poor (groups C2, D and E), comprising about two thirds of the total electorate. This categorisation was far from ideal, taking little account of the voting preference of women, for example, or different age groups within the electorate.[13] It did nevertheless point to the strongest determinant of voting behaviour. Both major parties, in order to secure a parliamentary majority, had to appeal across class boundaries. But at every election since the war, certainly through to 1959, a broad pattern had been evident: whereas some three-quarters of middle-class voters supported the Conservatives, nearly two-thirds of the working-classes backed Labour.

Underpinning such allegiances were class barriers that remained more stubborn than many have recognised. In spite of a 10 per cent improvement in living standards per head of the population between 1938 and 1958, the relative income of middle and working-classes as a whole remained almost unchanged.[14] What had occurred was the reduction of earlier gross inequalities. Differences in income never-theless remained, and were reinforced by contrasts in numbers of hours worked and conditions of work. Segregation at the workplace was still commonplace: 'the cotton millhand does not yet sip martinis from his lunchbox'.[15] Aside from consumer spending and a more home-centred life style, there was little evidence of manual workers adopting middle-class modes of behaviour, such as formal entertain-ment or involvement in community work. Drew Middleton found that workers' deep-rooted attachment to collective action was re-flected in the absence of any desire to establish their own small businesses.[16] Other local studies suggested that as equalisation occurred in terms of consumption, so the middle-classes became more liable to pull themselves apart by exaggerating cultural differences – in speech, social manners and patterns of leisure activity. In the London suburb of Woodford, most working-class inhabitants lived in particular enclaves. Those that lived in mixed areas found integration difficult. 'Those people from the East End are good-hearted folk, but you couldn't make friends of them', commented one resident. 'Sounds a bit snobbish . . . but we've got nothing in common with them.' This was reciprocated by incomers to the district, such as the docker from Poplar who complained that the stand-offishness of neighbours made it impossible to make friends. 'Inside people's minds . . . the boundaries of class are still closely drawn', concluded the authors. 'There were still two Woodfords in 1959, and few meeting points between them.'[17]

It was the case that a sizeable minority of skilled workers, when asked, were describing themselves as middle-class. This reflected a blurring of the most obvious distinctions between affluent workers and the lower middle-class. Income, though, was only one of the economic aspects of class: job security and prospects for advancement still pointed up the differences between the teacher and the engineer.[18] Similarly, changes were taking place which promised greater social mobility. Unlike the pre-war period a steadily increasing number of children from working-class families were gaining access to state-funded grammar schools. But progress was painfully slow. There was widespread disdain among working-class parents for a boy 'stuffing 'is head with a lot of nonsense 'e'll never use' by staying on at school.[19] Children from middle-class families still made up nearly 90 per cent of those attending grammar schools or continuing in full-time education beyond the age of nineteen.[20] Instead of a drive towards the 'endless Middle', the 1950s primarily witnessed new ways – in changing circumstances – of being working-class. Workers might be enjoying more leisure, but holiday camps were far removed from 'private' holidays for the middle-classes; pop music appeared to have a universal appeal, but on closer inspection showed strong class patterning.[21]

There were, of course, major differences *within* working-class communities. 'Roughs' and 'respectables' were often found to have little in common, and the new towns around London were a world away from the industrial heartlands of northern England and Scotland, where miners, dockers and shipyard workers continued to live in densely populated areas of terraced housing: 'a world of tough, hard-drinking men, clearly demarcated conjugal roles and a class imagery which sharply divided the world into "Them" and "Us"'.[22] Yet it was not difficult to find evidence from all parts of the country to indicate that – whatever new opportunities were arising in education, employment or housing – class consciousness remained acute. The Dean of Balliol College, Oxford, was scornful of 'inky fingered grammar school boys' and maintained that only those with independent means should be entitled to higher education. In the same city middle-class residents erected a wall in the 1950s to prevent council tenants from walking past their houses on the way to the shops. In the early 1960s one London commuter complained that he paid 'God knows how much in income tax and . . . I go home from the station past a council housing estate full of tv aerials with Consuls outside the doors . . . yet I have to subsidise their rents'.[23] British people on the whole were less impressed by social change than historians have been looking back with the benefit of hindsight. A majority of those questioned by Gallup thought living standards had not improved but rather 'stayed the same' in the 1950s, and shortly

before the 1964 election more voters agreed than disagreed with the
view that 'there is a class struggle in this country'.[24]

Working-class Voting Patterns

At the beginning of the period it was not, therefore, surprising to find
a close alignment between social class and party preference. Labour
took comfort from the 1951 election as a 'victory in votes but defeat
in terms of seats'. The highest ever vote hitherto polled by a party in
British politics (nearly fourteen million) derived from Labour piling
up huge majorities in working-class industrial strongholds. Churchill's slim majority was primarily the result of reduced Liberal
intervention compared with 1950; the Conservatives won support
among erstwhile middle-class Liberals especially, winning seats such
as Buckingham, King's Lynn and Yarmouth.[25] Although there had
been a small but uniform swing across the country, the Nuffield
election study calculated that on balance only 'a handful of former
Labour supporters' switched allegiance between 1950 and 1951.[26]
Pioneering sample surveys of individual constituencies confirmed
that 'social class . . . is the chief determinant of political behaviour'.[27]
In Bristol North East Labour supporters were found to be mainly
male, working-class and young; Tory backing was concentrated
among women, the middle-classes and older voters.[28] It was true
that the minority of workers supporting Churchill was much greater
than the minority of middle-class Labour voters. Yet there was no
suggestion that the former were guided primarily by material considerations. In areas of relatively weak support for Labour among
industrial workers, such as the High Peak town of Glossop, working-
class Toryism was associated with the Anglican Church.[29] In Banbury, where only a fraction of Labour's support earned more than
£500 per year, nearly 30 per cent of manual workers backed the
Conservatives on the basis of 'traditionalism', identifying with the
town's native community against incomers over recent decades.[30]
   Eden's election victory in 1955, though based upon a prosperity
ticket, produced surprisingly little evidence of a shift in working-class
voting patterns. Shortly before polling day one newspaper reported
that 'it is strangely difficult to discover candidates or agents who
claim to have unearthed any appreciable number of voters who have
changed their allegiance since the election of 1951'.[31] This was borne

out when a steep fall in the Labour vote was not matched by a corresponding Tory increase. Labour leaders agreed with newspaper commentators that apathy was the prime cause of an increased Tory majority. Labour had polled well in close fights, but elsewhere large numbers of former supporters had stayed at home. As Morgan Phillips observed, some voters may have changed sides, but more important was 'comparative "prosperity" which has lulled many of our supporters into inactivity'.[32] In Bristol North East over eight out of ten people voted the same way as in 1951. The main source of a small swing in Bristol was confirmed to be Labour abstentionism; economic stability had eroded the party's association with full employment.[33] Tory strategists developed the same theme, questioning why the government had not managed to win more votes in such favourable circumstances. Many within the lower social groupings, it was conceded – while disillusioned with Labour – still harboured a prejudice against voting Conservative.[34] According to one of the party's candidates, 'they weren't listening because emotionally they are incapable of giving the Tories a fair hearing. This is not just the old class war game. Rather it is an underlying suspicion of Conservative intentions as being interested in successful and established interests.' The task for the parliament ahead was to win not just the approval of such voters but also their hearts and consciences.[35]

This was exactly what Central Office sought to do in the years that followed. Before 1955 neither party had systematically engaged in market research. But in 1956–7 the Tory Chairman Oliver Poole, looking for ways to counter government unpopularity, gave the go-ahead for an advertising agency to undertake survey research into voter attitudes. This and findings from opinion pollsters appeared to highlight an important social development. Younger manual workers and their wives, it was found, those earning reasonably high wages and buying their own homes, were keen to dissociate themselves from outdated notions of working-class life. Hence skilled workers and white-collar clerical staff were made the target of concerted Tory propaganda in the run-up to the 1959 election. By contrast, apart from minor experimental surveys, Labour relied on no polling evidence other than what could be gleaned from newspapers.[36] Within Labour ranks there was much residual hostility both to new marketing techniques and to outright pandering to material interests. As one MP put it: 'What man eating cornflakes wanted to be in danger of swallowing a toy submarine?'[37] There was similar ambivalence towards home ownership, which many activists saw as a solely middle-class aspiration and a distraction from the preferred policy of producing more municipal housing for rent.[38] Macmillan's 'never had it so good' triumph in 1959 thus had an element of self-fulfilling prophecy. Conservative rhetoric was said to be more in tune with the wishes of the young and upwardly mobile; a larger proportion of skilled manual workers voted Tory than at any election since 1935. *Tribune*, meanwhile, was left to lament that Macmillan had received a mandate for 'the unjust society, the casino society, the ugly society'.[39]

Inquests by both main parties appeared to confirm the arrival of the 'affluent worker' as a potent electoral force, at least in the southern half of England. The Conservative Research Department believed there was more evidence than in 1955 that removal of working-class voters from city centres to new towns and housing estates 'tends in some cases to change their political allegiance from Socialist to Conservative'.[40] Labour's National Executive Committee was told that for the first time since the war there had been a significant movement of voters away from the party. Young married couples in their twenties, especially if both were in employment, were said to be particularly reluctant to vote Labour. Workers living on newly established housing estates were deemed to be immune from older forms of collective loyalty, choosing instead more privatised and home-based life styles revolving around the garden and the television set. One candidate defeated in a London suburb said in his home 'the Red Flag, the Co-op, the trade union, are things that get an answer in the tingling of my blood. They get no answer in tingling blood in the suburbs of London'.[41] In the new towns Labour hoped that the movement of workers out of London would push up its level of support. But in Horsham, Hemel Hempstead, Epping, Basildon and Hitchin – all with electorates expanded by over 10,000 – Tory majorities were increased. A post-election survey in Stevenage new town (part of the Hitchin seat) revealed considerable support for the Conservatives among working-class incomers in the electronics and aerospace industries, several of whom expressed the view that 'I voted for them this time because the standard of living of the working-classes has gone up'.[42]

In the months following Macmillan's triumph, the affluent worker became an object of fascination. Polling companies commissioned research which found that whereas manual workers supported

Labour by 2:1, the Tories held a narrow lead among non-manual workers in the C2D class. 'It is no exaggeration to say that the Conservatives govern by permission of the working-class and in particular of the lower paid non-manual worker'.[43] In the spring of 1960, Mark Abrams and Richard Rose carried out a survey of 500 working-class voters, later published as *Must Labour Lose?*, which found found that Labour was suffering among groups of voters most susceptible to the appeals of affluence, especially women and the young.[44] This study also reinforced the idea that those workers who labelled themselves 'middle-class' were more likely to vote Tory (see Figure 1):

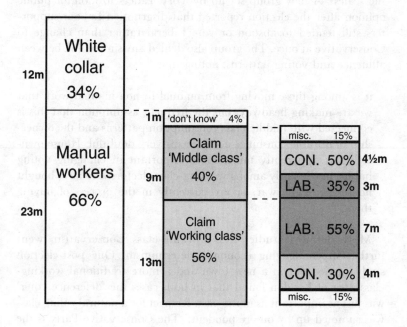

Figure 1   The British electorate, 1960

SOURCE: M. Abrams, 'Social Class and British Politics', *Public Opinion Quarterly*, XXV: 3 (1961), p. 343.

At the time, though, there was as much scepticism as support for the affluent worker thesis. Although bitterly disappointed, Gaitskell was right to question the scale of his election reversal: only three voters in every 200 had switched sides. Moreover, the changing allegiance of skilled workers was not the only electoral movement of note in 1959. Gallup polls indicated that equally significant was Labour's loss of middle-class backing since 1955. At the same time, promises to pensioners had produced stronger support among the elderly and the poor, sufficient to deny the Conservatives many more seats. This was off-set by a modest swing from Labour, mainly to the Liberals and non-voting, in the lower-middle/working-classes. Although the movement here was slight, because these voters made up the great majority of the adult population, it was 'sufficient to tip the scales'. A new group set up by Tory leaders to monitor public opinion after the election reported that disgruntled Labour supporters still tended to abstain or vote Liberal rather than change to Conservative at once. The group also denied any simple link between affluence and voting patterns, noting that:

> it is among those moving from manual to non-manual work that we are making headway, but the frequent assumption that this is connected with middle-class consumption patterns and the ownership of durable consumer goods seems very doubtful. House ownership is apparently much more important in changing voting habits, particularly among working-class electors who have bought houses since the war, or are currently in the process of buying them.[45]

More detailed studies into working-class Conservatism went further in challenging economic determinism. One post-election study carried out in a new town and a more traditional working-class area of London found that in both cases the 'deference voter' was just as important as in the past. Respect for a natural ruling class was summed up by one respondent: 'The Conservative Party is the gentleman's Party. . . . I always vote for them. I'm only a working man and they're my guv'nors.'[46] A larger survey undertaken in the early 1960s also found that personal income was not the key to voting behaviour: the proportion of those workers voting Tory was the same in a range of income groups. The importance of middle-class identification was reaffirmed, as was 'deference', though an equally large number were guided by 'secular objectives': the Conservatives were regarded as best at maximising personal well-being, especially in relation to the economy, whereas many Labour sympathisers defined their vote largely in terms of satisfying class interests.[47] Central to studies of this type was the finding that workers could be swayed by their sense of satisfaction or dissatisfaction with the government of the day. 'Floating' voters could not be relied upon by either main party.[48]

It follows that the Conservatives, in spite of a large majority in 1959, would be at the mercy of unfolding events. The authors of *Must Labour Lose?* concluded that the question could not be answered with certainty in 1960 because 'politics is continually in a state of flux'. Although loyalty to Labour had been weakening, Tory popularity could easily be dented if the economy slumped or if expectations of prosperity – fed by 1959 style rhetoric – proved impossible to fulfil.[49] This prophecy was rapidly borne out; indeed the major shortcoming of the affluent worker theory was its failure to last the test of time. Labour's recovery from 1961 onwards, at local and by-elections as well as in opinion polls, cast doubt on the notion that aspiring workers were being irretrievably lost to Conservatism. Hard empirical evidence was also provided by a survey of several hundred factory workers in Luton, carried out in 1963. The survey revealed a consistently high level of support for Labour among manual workers in the car, chemical and ball-bearing industries, with no evidence of a long-term shift towards the Conservatives. The small number of Tory supporters among the sample were characterised not by higher standards of living, but by larger numbers of white-collar workers among their kin. On this basis, it was concluded that what distinguished 'new' from 'traditional' working-class communities was that the former were more volatile and 'instrumental' in their support for Labour. Home-centred life-styles in Luton were a far cry from the collective solidarity of the coal-mining districts. As a result, affluent workers supported the party less through instinct than through the calculation that Labour could best serve their economic interests.[50]

This debunking of the affluent worker thesis, published in full by a team of sociologists in the late 1960s, was itself later challenged. The Luton sample did not, for example, allow comparisons to be made between small- and large-scale enterprises.[51] Other social scientists such as Ivor Crewe pointed out that the Luton study was carried out at a single point in time when Labour was riding high, and yet there was no evidence of *increased* support as might be expected. There was little solid basis, other than guesswork, for the alternative theory of 'instrumentalism'; and there was no analysis of 'traditional' workers or of other 'affluent' constituencies. Ivor Crewe's own wider examination of 15 seats, carried out in 1970, showed modest backing for the idea of embourgeoisement but none for instrumentalism as a guide to voting patterns.[52] Yet as far as the early 1960s were concerned, it was clear old habits died hard. By the time Harold Macmillan resigned, Conservatives were sensing that the 'prosperity ticket' had backfired, especially among those who had reached the shores of affluence in 1959 and had passed on to a stage of disillusionment. Any change in working-class voting behaviour was therefore a protracted and uneven process. Harold Wilson was able to command the loyalty of working-class voters in all regions and occupations, whether 'traditional' or 'new'. A majority of the Luton sample questioned in 1963 explained their allegiance to Labour in terms more readily associated with a past age or with workers in heavy industry. Labour, said one respondent, 'are always inclined to do that bit more for the working man. My opinion of Tory government is that they're for the capitalists'.[53]

The Middle-class Vote

What then of middle-class voters? As this report from one of the polling companies shows, white-collar workers – like the working-classes – varied considerably in terms of income and lifestyle:

Group A   Upper Middle-class
Professional workers, Company Directors, Professors, Doctors, Dentists, Headmasters of large schools, Editors, High Local Officials such as Town Clerks, High Civil Servants, High-ranking Army or Police Officers, Farmers of large farms. . . .
   Nearly all people in this class will probably have a telephone and a car, employ servants and live in large detached houses or expensive flats.

Probable income: Over £1,750.

Group B   Middle-class
Junior Executives, Managers of middle sized shops, workers in
Insurance or Banks . . . with responsibility for department, Head
Librarians, Lecturers, medium-ranking Army or Police officers . . .
Headmasters of smaller sized schools. . . .

Many of these people will have telephones and cars and many
employ part-time domestic help. Their houses will not be as
luxurious or as large as Group A but will still be pleasant,
probably semi-detached houses in the suburbs. . . .

Probable income: £950–£1,750.

Group C1   Lower-Middle-class
Primary or Secondary School Teachers, Nurses, Bank Clerks,
Junior Lecturers, Junior Civil Servants, Managers of small shops,
Shop Assistants with high responsibilities or training. Typists,
Laboratory Assistants, Junior Army Officers, Police Sergeants. . . .

Probable income: £950.[54]

This list was by no means exhaustive. Several groups might be
added for a more complete picture: those, for example, with private
incomes; wives and dependants; and pensioners who before retirement were engaged in business or white-collar employment. The
ranks of the middle-class were also being swelled in the 1950s by
newly emerging professionals, such as television producers and
market-research consultants. However, a definition of middle-class
voters could not be based on occupation alone. A minority of those
engaged in manual employment, as we have seen, insisted on
defining themselves when asked as middle-class. Nevertheless the
middle-classes remained broadly recognisable. They were, according
to *The Times*, all those people who 'do not clock in and out'.[55]
Middle-class voters were also relatively stable in terms of political
allegiance. Between the wars they helped to bolster the Conservative/
National governments of Baldwin and Chamberlain. A central
feature of 'safety first' Conservatism was its opposition to higher
taxation – the antithesis in middle-class eyes of individual initiative
and business risk-taking. This tradition of anti-socialism was interrupted briefly in 1945, when Labour captured the likes of Chisle-
hurst, Wimbledon and Winchester as part of its election landslide.

But flirtation with the left proved short-lived. Dalton's maintenance of high wartime taxes and privations associated with Crippsian austerity soon hardened attitudes. Echoing events just after the First World War, a Middle-class Union was formed and tales abounded of 'bishops' wives scrubbing floors'.[56] This provided the backcloth for a Conservative revival that served to reinforce the class basis of party alignment.

In 1945, middle-class voters were estimated to have backed the Tories by 2:1. In 1950 this ratio was 3:1 and by 1951, when Churchill defeated Attlee to secure a narrow majority, it had risen to 3.5:1. Whereas Labour secured a higher total vote by winning the support of two-thirds of working-class electors, the Conservatives relied for more seats on two-thirds of the middle-class vote. The narrow margin of victory posed an electoral dilemma for the new government. On the one hand, Labour had been defeated in part by raising the expectations of middle-class voters: Churchill's pledge was to 'set Britain free' by attacking bureaucracy, controls and high taxes. On the other hand, the Tories could ill afford to alienate working-class support. In the circumstances bequeathed by the out-going administration – of progressive taxation helping to finance an extensive welfare system – any return to 1930s-style minimalist government geared to middle-class concerns was out of the question. Yet by a mixture of skill and good fortune Churchill succeeded in the delicate task of maintaining a broad electoral coalition. Expanding world trade helped to ensure the maintenance of full employment, and moves to free up the economy – through limited denationalisation, the ending of controls and rationing, and reduced income tax – all won plaudits among business and middle-class interests. In the spring of 1955 the Chancellor, Rab Butler, decided to cut income tax further from 9s to 8s 6d in the pound. A month later the government comfortably secured re-election, its cross-class appeal remaining undiminished. In the months that followed, however, during the troubled premiership of Anthony Eden, the alliance between the government and its middle-class supporters came under intense strain. Indeed for much of the mid-1950s there was talk of a 'middle-class revolt'.

The primary cause of discontent was the prolonged economic downturn that followed the 1955 election. As memories of the early-1950s boom receded, middle-class grievances became a prime concern for press editorials. *The Times* underlined how far inflation had eroded favourable pre-war conditions: it estimated that someone earning £400 a year in 1935 might now receive £1000 per annum, but would be over ten per cent worse off in terms of income tax. For the upper middle-class the position was worse still. A top civil servant would find his income 'worth only 44 per cent of what it was then'.[57] Newspaper columns began to fill up with case studies of those who complained about life as 'hardly interrupted drudgery' on £2600 a year. One lamented that instead of two living in staff, he could only afford 'a part-time daily woman', with the result that an 'increasing burden of cooking, cleaning and mending has been assumed by my wife'. Another complained that his family had 'not had an hotel holiday for six years;. . .[we have] no TV and we think twice about going to the theatre or buying a bottle of sherry'.[58] While newly emerging professional workers might not hark back to a pre-war golden age, they often shared anxieties about social status. Central to much middle-class disaffection was the language of class rivalry. While the thrifty suffered, it was alleged, ministers spent too much time 'coddling the workers', either by giving in to high wage demands or through welfare handouts. According to the *Sunday Times*, the middle-classes were the cinderellas of the economic system. 'They have no trade unions to keep them, like a skilled surf-rider, on the foamy crest of the inflationary wave, but have been doused and buffeted in its trough.'[59] What was worse, tax rises imposed in the emergency budget of 1955 looked like 'Socialist egalitarianism under a Conservative administration', and were said to have left a feeling of hopelessness among the middle-classes. If relief from 'monstrously' high tax rates 'is not given by a Conservative Government, will it ever be given?'[60]

Disquiet amounted to more than individual complaints taken up in sympathetic newspapers. Other manifestations of middle-class revolt were evident more broadly in popular politics. The first was voter disenchantment with Eden's government. After the Tories came close to losing the Tonbridge by-election in June 1956, one angry supporter, Mrs Beryl Platts, wrote to *The Times* to say that the government must act upon middle-class grievances or face the consequences:

> The Conservative agents who describe the result as due to apathy delude themselves. It is a wonderfully encouraging gesture from a class which . . . refuses to be exterminated. For – and let the Conservative headquarters be under no misapprehension about

this – if we refuse to vote and thereby admit the Socialists to power, we allow a period of Socialist legislation which can later be revoked. If we permit the Conservatives to frame Socialist measures in their ill-considered bid for left-wing support, we are saddled with such measures for ever. Which is the greater evil?[61]

A second example of discontent, mentioned in an earlier chapter, was the emergence of new pressure groups, notably the People's League for the Defence of Freedom (PLDF) and the Middle-class Alliance. The fears of Tory leaders about these nascent groups should not be exaggerated. Neither was taken very seriously by the national press, and no attempt was made to co-ordinate protest action against the government. Both groups lost momentum when the Suez crisis became a test of national loyalty. But if new fringe movements caused concern rather than alarm, the underlying causes of middle-class disquiet had yet to be addressed. Inflation continued to rise and those attracted by the People's League were dismayed to see that Eden shied away from any legislative reform of trade unionism. The abrupt resignation of Eden left the Tories facing an unresolved electoral conundrum: how to maintain the balance between the thirteeen million who voted Conservative and the vocal middle-class groups which include 'so many of the Party's zealots'.[62]

Between 1957 and 1959 the tide of middle-class disquiet slowly receded. Indeed, the Middle Class Alliance was quickly wound up altogether, the victim of internal wrangling. However, it would be wrong to assume that tension disappeared overnight. In his first year as Prime Minister, Eden's successor Macmillan was forced to tighten the deflationary belt further and faced the resignation of his entire Treasury team. In these circumstances further Liberal advances, for example at the Ipswich by-election, were seen by local Tories as 'evidence that the middle-classes, by abstaining or supporting the third party, are still registering a vote on censure on the Government, in particular over its failure to check the ever-rising cost of living'.[63] The first signs of a turnaround came with the London bus strike in May 1958, which at last saw the government taking an anti-union line that satisfied middle-class sentiment. Macleod, the Minister of Labour, told colleagues that legislation on the closed shop or sympathetic strike action 'would be extremely popular within the Party and attract the Liberal vote more than almost anything else'. Any such change though, he added, might 'frighten the trade union world more

than it would bring in the Liberal vote'.[64] Macleod recognised that
the best way of securing cross-class support – vital to a third election
victory – was to ensure a flourishing economy that benefited all
sections of the community. 1958, as we have seen, brought a change of
fortune for the government on this front. The combination of an
imporving economy and a triumph over the unions had a discernible
impact on middle-class voters. By-elections in June 1958 witnessed a
recovery attributed by commentators to the reputation of union
leaders as bully boys in the eyes of the middle-classes.[65]

By the time of the general election in 1959 the government had
behind it the advantage of a budget that gave full rein to Macmillan's expansionary instincts. Supermac's triumph swept out of sight
mid-terms blues; the bark of 'disgusted of Tonbridge' turned out to
be worse than the bite. Aside from a strong showing among skilled
workers, the Conservatives had maintained a strong lead over
Labour in all sections of the middle-class. Among the upper middle-class (socio-economic group A), this was by as much as 85.5 to
5.7 per cent. Within the middle and lower middle-class (groups B
and C1) the lead was an impressive 66.3 to 17.4 per cent.[66] But the
Tories had not entirely won back their traditional supporters.
Labour had lost ground among the middle-classes since 1955, but
so too, according to Gallup, had the Tories, with a movement among
the upper middle-classes especially towards the Liberals (and to
abstentionism) in 1959. As senior Conservatives recognised, the
Liberals had stopped the inexorable decline evident earlier in the
decade by doubling their vote to one and a half million, and had
done so primarily at the expense of Tory candidates.[67] The middle-
class revolt of the mid-1950s thus had more lasting significance than
was evident in the wake of a third election victory. The party's bond
with the middle-classes had been growing stronger at every election
since 1945; this trend, if not reversed, had been checked in 1959.
Middle-class doubters who had returned to the fold were won over
ultimately by an expansionary economic policy that on past experience would prove difficult to sustain. Neither could it be taken for
granted that the Labour opposition would forever be shackled by its
image as a party for the working-classes. Loyalty among the middle-
classes, in other words, was becoming conditional – just as it was for
affluent workers – on the government 'delivering the goods'.

Indeed the drift of the middle-class vote away from the Conservatives accelerated during the early 1960s when Macmillan again ran

into economic difficulties. The Liberals once more benefited. In September 1959 there were just 475 local Liberal councillors; by May 1962 this figure had more than trebled. Success was mainly evident in suburbia and 'resort' towns such as Bath, Harrogate and Eastbourne.[68] Growing support for the Liberals in by-elections culminated in the resounding triumph at Orpington in 1962, explained by Macmillan in his diary as a 'conjunction of a spiritual vacuum and a vague feeling in the middle-classes that all they had striven for was turning to dead sea fruit'.[69] As long as the Liberals were the main beneficiaries of protest voting, the Prime Minister could hope that the pattern of 1956–8 might be repeated. But the differences with the previous parliament were as striking as the similarities. After eleven years in power, Macmillan conceded, voters 'really are tired of us', and the 'second middle-class revolt' was different from its predecessor in nature and scope. Many of the 'new' middle-class were young couples migrating from areas of heavy industry to rapidly expanding suburbs, especially around London. For these aspiring families, high mortgage costs and commuter charges were major grievances. 'This', claimed *The Economist*, rather than the retired brigadiers and fixed-income widows, is the pressured middle-class that Mr Macleod has to deal with now.' It followed that this new class was less certain of its political identity: while the Liberals had been quick off the mark in recruiting support, allegiances were there for the taking among what amounted to the largest available 'pool of floating voters'.[70]

What made matters worse for Macmillan was the growing appeal of Labour among such voters. By the time Liberal popularity peaked in the summer of 1962, Labour had re-emerged as a credible alternative government, maintaining a clear poll lead and securing three by-election gains from the Tories. The first of these, at Middlesbrough West in June 1962, was described as 'Labour's revenge for Orpington', showing that the party was beating back 'the Liberal effort to sweep up Labour's share of the white-collar, suburbanite vote'.[71] This transformation resulted partly from government failures and partly from determined efforts to reshape Labour's image. Party leaders were firmly told after 1959 that an attempt had to be made to appeal to the rapidly expanding sector of administrative, technical and clerical workers, which had grown from 16.5 to 21 per cent of the workforce over the past decade. The pay pause was regarded as a prime opportunity to win over those who had hitherto been hostile or indifferent.[72] With this in mind, Labour for the first time used new advertising techniques to underline its support for the material ambitions of the aspiring classes. This process was enhanced, if not initiated, by the arrival of Harold Wilson as opposition leader in 1963. His emphasis on technology was designed not only to contrast his Kennedy-style vision with Macmillan's allegedly outdated appeal. It also aimed – via its promise to liberate the talents of the ambitious – at reducing middle-class fears about the prospect of a Labour government. 'I am', Wilson remarked, 'making myself acceptable to the suburbs.'[73] His claim was soon to be put to the test.

Conclusion

Continuity rather than change was the prime hallmark of voting patterns in the 1950s. The link between social class and party preference remained more enduring than was acknowledged by those who played up the importance of the 'middle-classation' of British society. In circumstances where, as we have seen, fundamental class differences survived greater affluence, it was no surprise that the major parties relied upon traditional sources of support. In Bristol North East the archetypal Conservative voter was found to be a retired middle-class teacher, a lay-reader in the Church of England; he had always supported the Tories as they stood for the 'general well-being of the people'. By contrast, the working-class lorry driver was a trade union member and regular Labour voter: he was unswerving in his support because Labour stood for 'the average man' and not 'the capitalist class'.[74] At every election since 1945, three quarters of the middle-class had backed the Conservatives, whereas more than half the working-classes supported Labour. But the class–party axis had never been complete, and electoral success depended, as it had in the past, on appealing across the class divide. Senior Tories were aware that the pace of social change could be easily exaggerated, and even after a third successive victory in 1959, the importance of maintaining a broad electoral coalition was regarded as vital:

It is a striking fact that though the divisions between the classes have narrowed, people are voting more by class than before the war. The rise in the number of white-collar workers and the fall in the number of manual workers has favoured us. . . . . Nevertheless, it must be remembered that the tendency towards a more middle-class society has a long way to go yet, and it is still from the working-class two thirds that we get more than half our votes – and have to if we are to win an Election.[75]

What had occurred during the 1950s was that Churchill and his successors proved more adept at attracting that significant minority of the electorate – found in all social classes – whose loyalty was not unswerving: the floating voter. As seen in previous chapters, this had as much to do with everyday politics as it did with long-term societal change. To take one example, in 1951 Labour comfortably held all three seats in Coventry, home of the thriving motor industry, where two constituencies had among the highest proportion of 'affluent worker' home and car owners in the country. The loss of Coventry South in 1959, according to recent research, resulted not so much from 'middle-classation' as from Labour simply losing touch with young voters and new home-owners; the earnest 'moralism' of party workers and their distaste for naked materialism did little to help.[76] The picture from Coventry, as elsewhere, was not one of disintegration or irretrievable loss; in 1959 nine out of ten of those who backed one of the main parties in 1955 voted the same way as before. There was, in other words, no burgeoning army of Tory-inclined affluent workers, as became clear in the early 1960s when it was the government's turn to suffer from political failings and changing perceptions of its image and leadership. As consumer purchasing power dwindled, confidence in Conservative economic policy slumped, both among manual workers who had been promised rising living standards and among professionals who were suffering from high mortgages. When Macmillan left office in 1963, a private poll of 7500 voters confirmed that the Tories had lost ground among all social groupings; while some suburban protest voters were turning to the Liberals, others were finding Wilson's Labour party once more attractive. Social change had not then fundamentally altered the basis of voting behaviour. Rather, in the words of one observer, it was thanks to events in the world of politics that there was 'a general fed-upness with the Government, the feeling that it has been there too long, that Ministers are old and tired – summed up in a frequent reply to the polls: "We could do with a change" '.[77]

8 Smart Alec vs Dull Alec, 1963–4

Introduction

All the tensions and frustrations of Britain in the early 1960s came together at the 1964 general election. This was the first occasion – apart from the exceptional wartime circumstances of 1945 – that Labour removed the Tories from power with a majority over all other parties combined, albeit narrowly. The whole of Macmillan's 1959 majority of 100 parliamentary seats was wiped out. Both the national swing against the government, averaging 3.2 per cent, and the fall in the Conservative share of the vote (down from 49.4 per cent to 43.4 per cent) were the largest since the war. How, then, should the outcome of the 1964 election be explained? Historians have tended to present Labour's victory as a truimph of Harold Wilson's persona and politics: the grammar schoolboy made good managed to persuade voters that Labour would create a modernised, technologically advanced 'New Britain'.[1] Here it will be argued that the 1964 result owed less to endorsement of Labour values than to a desire to punish the incumbent government. Not since 1906 had a peacetime Tory administration been ousted by a government capable of commanding an outright majority in the Commons. Yet the Conservative share of the vote now slumped far more than Labour's had in 1950–1; indeed, the fall was greater than any between successive elections in the twentieth century other than in 1931.

Part of the explanation for this lay in factors already touched upon in earlier chapters: Macmillan's faltering leadership after 1959; the anti-establishment mood of the early 1960s; concern about unequal provision in welfare services; and disillusionment about promises of ever greater affluence. Wilson's victory, this chapter suggests, also owed much to events in the final year of the 1959 parliament. This period was vital not because, as is often claimed, the dynamic leader of the opposition faced a new Prime Minister whose aristocratic background, aloofness and 'matchstick' grasp of economics made him an easy target. According to *That Was the Week That Was*, the television satire programme, 'Dull Alec', Lord Home, was no match for Labour's 'Smart Alec', Harold Wilson. Yet Tory fortunes were to revive under Lord Home, to the point where victory was almost snatched from the jaws of defeat. More critical was the extraordinary leadership contest in October 1963 which saw Home emerge as the compromise choice after a mysterious 'process of consultation'. The aftertaste of bitterness left some leading Tories openly claiming that Macmillan's long-time deputy, Rab Butler, had been cheated of his rightful inheritance. 'I do profoundly hope', Macmillan wrote in his diary, 'that the *image* of the Party is not injured by all this public disputing.'[2] Yet this was precisely what did happen: of all the blows to Tory morale and prestige during the period, the legacy of an undignified struggle for the party leadership was to prove one of the most damaging and difficult to shake off.

The Blackpool 'Beauty Contest', October 1963

Macmillan's decision to resign was followed by the most disputed Tory succession since the 1920s, making Churchill's handover to Eden in 1955 appear far smoother than it had been at the time and causing much greater bitterness than Macmillan's triumph over Butler in 1957. Several factors complicated the whole process. The first was the lack of an obvious successor. Butler's unrivalled experience made him favourite, and he was widely regarded as the most obvious figurehead to appeal to middle-of-the-road voters. Macmillan though had grave doubts about Butler's suitability, and had tried – without success – to bring on one of several younger possibilities such as Macleod, Maudling or Heath. Linked to this was the coincidental passage earlier in 1963 of a measure allowing hereditary peerages to be disclaimed. This had the effect of broadening the field of contenders further, bringing pledges first from Lord Hailsham and then Lord Home to renounce their titles and sit in the House of Commons. The part played by the outgoing Prime Minister also complicated the plot. Having agreed to go on medical grounds, Macmillan delayed his actual resignation until he was in a position to advise the Queen about a successor; instead of leaving the monarch's advisers to take private soundings, he seemed determined to act as both judge and kingmaker. Plotting and intrigue were inevitable as everything had to wait upon Macmillan's recovery from his opera-

tion in King Edward VII hospital. What was more, because the
Prime Minister was struck down in the middle of party conference
week, Tory activists were drawn into the process in an unprecedented way. When 4000 shocked delegates at Blackpool were told
that Macmillan was unable to lead them into the next election,
intense speculation about the succession immediately developed. In
the full glare of media publicity, the race for the leadership became a
'seaside beauty contest'.[3]

As Macmillan underwent surgery, three names were the talk of the
Imperial Hotel. In the words of one MP, the choice was clear:
'Butler, donnish, dignified and dull; Maudling, matey, manly and
moneywise; Hailsham, ebullient, erudite and erratic'.[4] Maudling's
star had waned since the summer; he had little appeal for many of
the party's traditionalists and was held to be out of the running after
a poor conference speech. As a result, most delegates spent their time
aligning themselves into Butler and Hailsham camps, each determined to outmanoeuvre the other. But the main protagonists failed
to live up to expectations. Hailsham, buoyed up by earlier assurances
that he was Macmillan's preferred successor, overplayed his hand by
immediately announcing his intention to renounce his peerage. As
Hailsham went off to a Young Conservative dance to receive a
rapturous welcome, more detached observers saw him as 'a man in
the grip of suppressed hysteria, smirking and protesting loyalty to
Macmillan'.[5] Within the party establishment, Hailsham's unseemly
haste and the vulgarity of his supporters provoked a backlash; the
Chief Whip later noted that for Hailsham 'the cork had popped too
soon . . . his was a spent force after that night'.[6] At the other
extreme, Butler went out of his way not to abuse his position as
acting head of government. To the disappointment of his supporters,
Rab's speech on the final day of the conference failed to impress and
he spent much of the time in his hotel room trying to avoid 'creating
the wrong impression'.[7] In the meantime, pressure was being applied
on the Foreign Secretary, Lord Home, to put himself forward as an
alternative to both Hailsham and Butler. Reluctantly he agreed if
there was evidence of the 'draft Home movement' gathering momentum, though he was still considered an outside bet as delegates
made their way home from Blackpool.

As Macmillan slowly emerged from sedation he thus found the
party in some disarray. If he had hoped that Hailsham's popularity
with the rank-and-file would decisively undermine Butler's prospects,

then post-conference it was difficult to see what advice he might offer
the Queen. With remarkable tenacity for someone emerging from
major surgery, Macmillan took two decisive steps. In the first place,
in the words of Nigel Birch, 'he switched peers in midstream',[8]
abandoning Hailsham and finally persuading Home that he must
come forward as a candidate in the interests of party unity. Secondly,
he dictated the terms on which the party might be consulted about
the succession. Far from being 'customary processes', Macmillan
insisted that broader soundings than ever before should be carried
out: by the Lord Chancellor, Lord Dilhorne, within the Cabinet; by
Martin Redmayne, the Chief Whip, among MPs; by Lord St
Aldwyn in the House of Lords; and by Oliver Poole among activists
outside Westminster. Butler, although·he harboured suspicions that
the 'Great Urgency movement' was designed to damage his own
chances, secured the unanimous backing of the Cabinet for this
procedure on Tuesday, 15 October. Over the next two days, leading
Tories were confronted with a series of questions: who should
succeed?; who should be the second choice?; and who was least
suited to the leadership? On Thursday Macmillan's emissaries told
him that Home was the preferred choice of about half the Cabinet;
Home also held a narrow lead among MPs and was favoured 2:1 by
Conservative peers. Macmillan summed up that there were strong
feelings for and against both Butler and Hailsham; though activists
were said to favour Hailsham, it was believed 'everyone would rally
round Home'.[9] Macmillan's final act as Prime Minister was to
compile a memorandum incorporating these findings, which he then
presented to the Queen on the morning of Friday, 18 October. In
resigning he advised Queen Elizabeth to send for Lord Home.

The drama begun at Blackpool and continued in the King Edward
Hospital had one further sting in the tail. As news of the likely
outcome leaked out on Thursday evening, efforts to thwart Home
were set in motion. Enoch Powell organised a late-night meeting of
the disaffected, including Macleod and Maudling, and Hailsham
openly told Home that the outcome was 'disreputable'.[10] Macmillan
was quickly informed about 'the revolt in the night', which he
understood to be:

an organised revolt by all the *unsuccessful* candidates – Butler,
Hailsham, Maudling and Macleod – against Home . . . Home
rang up and felt aggrieved. He had only been asked to come

forward as a compromise candidate, from unity. He felt like
withdrawing. I urged him not to do so. If we gave in to this
intrigue, there would be chaos. Butler would fail to form a
Government; even if given another chance (for Queen might then
send for Wilson) no one else would succeed. We should have a
Wilson Government; or dissolution; and our Party without even a
nominal leader.[11]

By the time Butler, Hailsham and Maudling met on Friday morning
to sink their differences, Home was already on his way to the Palace.
He agreed to return after attempting to form an administration: an
undertaking that required awkward meetings with colleagues who
initially reserved their positions. On Friday evening the disappointed
trio went to No. 10, where Hailsham was the first to give way.
'Quintin, having started the day by buzzing about like a fly in a
bottle', Maudling recalled, 'simply capitulated', agreeing to continue
as Minister of Science.[12] The following morning, Butler agreed in the
interests of party unity to serve as Foreign Secretary. Maudling
continued as Chancellor and by the time Home returned to Buckingham Palace to accept formally the royal commission, it was clear
there would be only two defectors from the Cabinet – Powell and
Macleod, both of whom told the Prime Minister they believed his
background was an insuperable barrier to winning an election.[13]

   Three months later it was Macleod who helped to ensure that the
leadership contest would scar the party for a generation to come.
Incensed by the imminent publication of Randolph Churchill's
version of events, which he described as 'the trailer for the screenplay'
of Macmillan's memoirs, Macleod launched a blistering attack on the
'magic circle' of Etonians he believed had manipulated the process to
deny Butler the succession. 'The truth is', Macleod bluntly claimed,
'that . . . from the first day of his premiership to the last, Macmillan
was determined that Butler, although incomparably the best qualified of the contenders, should not succeed him.'[14] In reflecting on the
events of October 1963, recent historical accounts have followed Tory
leaders at the time in suggesting that Macleod overstepped the mark.
Vernon Bogdanor, for example, argues that Macmillan was no more
important in determining the outcome than senior backbenchers
such as John Morrison, Chairman of the 1922 Committee, who
several months earlier had told Butler that 'the chaps won't have
you'. Butler's chances were blighted, in other words, by the so-called

'Blue Blood and Thunder' brigade, a group of 30–40 right-wing MPs who hated Rab for his 'equivocation, his sly jokes' and, since the time of Suez, for his lack of the 'soldierly virtues'.[15] Bogdanor concedes that the selection procedure was not as open as it might have been. As Home was not initially believed to be a candidate, he was not scrutinised in the same way as his opponents, and there was little opportunity for a 'stop Home' movement to develop. But the outcome of the consultation exercise can be used to conclude that there was no serious misrepresentation of party opinion. As in 1957, Butler may have been outmanoeuvred, but there was no evidence that he commanded more support than Home.[16]

Yet Macmillan himself provided such evidence, writing in his diary after the Blackpool conference (in an entry not reproduced in his memoirs) that 'the party in the country wants Hogg; the Parliamentary Party wants Maudling or Butler; the Cabinet wants Butler. The last 10 days have not altered this fundamental fact.'[17] It was immediately after this that Macmillan devised a form of consultation which, by emphasising second-choice preferences and opposition to particular individuals, greatly enhanced the prospects of Home as a compromise or 'unity' candidate. Any doubts that this was the intention were removed by the way in which the Prime Minister's emissaries carried out their task. 'What do you think of Alec Home?' was a question introduced into conversation when ministers made no mention of his name. Macmillan himself, when told by Edward Boyle of his support for Rab, replied 'I can quite see that you would like someone like Alec or Rab'.[18] Backbenchers, anxious not to jeopardise future prospects of advancement, were under even greater pressure from the Chief Whip. One MP said that when Redmayne asked if their order of preference would be different if Home appeared most likely to unite the party, some colleagues changed their votes. Behind the scenes works by the whips office, and by Macmillan's former chief whip Edward Heath, helps to explain why the parliamentary party gave the answer Macmillan was hoping to hear.[19] Similar pressures were at work in the sounding of opinion within the Cabinet. Enoch Powell noted on the morning of 18 October that seven ministers declared their willingness to serve under Butler and would not serve under Home unless Rab first agreed. This was echoed by a more impartial senior figure with contacts on all sides, Lord Swinton, thus casting grave doubt on how the Queen came to be advised that Cabinet opinion favoured Home.[20]

It was not only the operation of the consultation exercise which suggested that Macmillan was as ruthless in quitting the party leadership as he had been in acquiring it. In later years, after recovering from his illness, Macmillan was to deny charges that his purpose was to 'down' Butler. His diary again suggested otherwise. As the dust was settling, he justified the choice of Home to himself by writing (in a further entry that found no place in his memoirs) that Rab 'has no strength of character or purpose and for this reason should *not* be P. M. '.[21] From start to finish there were indications that Macmillan was determined to avoid any such outcome. In spite of his role as acting head of government, Butler was allowed to play no part in determining the nature and timing of Macmillan's statement to conference. He argued with Redmayne that such precipitate action closed off the possibility either of Macmillan recovering or of a more dispassionate contest; starting the contest in the atmosphere of an American-style convention looked certain to favour Hailsham, whereas waiting for the reconvening of parliament might undermine the prospects of candidates from the House of Lords. Even before Hailsham ruined his own prospects, Macmillan was known to be pressing Home to put himself forward, and Macleod was not alone in questioning the power of the 'magic circle' to influence events behind closed doors. Another Cabinet minister records how at Blackpool – before Home was known to be in the running – he attended a function at which his wife was interrupted over dinner by a local MP, Colonel 'Juby' Lancaster, 'saying with some suggestion of surprise that she didn't know, that it was of course Alec Home who would be chosen'.[22] What was certain was that Macmillan acted decisively at the climax of the struggle, refusing requests to call a full Cabinet meeting and hastening his resignation early on the Friday morning so that Home could be called to the Palace. As Nigel Fisher concludes: 'From his hospital bed, sick as he was, the Prime Minister controlled the situation through Dilhorne, Redmayne, St Aldwyn and Poole.'[23]

Why though was Macmillan able to triumph from his sick-bed? The answer to this lay not only with those prepared to do his bidding, but in the part played by senior ministers. In Lord Home the Prime Minister had an ally prepared to act with much greater cunning than later accounts of his reluctant emergence suggest. As Butler pointed out, it was Home who visited Macmillan in hospital and insisted on an early statement of his intentions; a review of the facts could not 'stress too strongly that Alec Home obtained this and

himself read it out'.[24] One of those urging Home forward at Blackpool was Lord Dilhorne, the figure charged with the task of
impartially sounding out Cabinet preferences; other associates of
the Prime Minister such as Redmayne were frequently seen visiting
the Foreign Office during the week that followed, whereas Butler
remained on the sidelines in spite of his official status.[25] Home was
sufficiently confident to publicly rebuke Hailsham for his behaviour
at conference, and he showed himself willing to tough it out with
rivals once invited to the Palace. When Maudling openly told him
that his preference was for Butler, Home replied that because
opposition to Rab was so strong, Maudling himself might have to
come forward. Here he was clearly repeating, as a device to bring
Maudling on board, Macmillan's spectre of the Tories being unable
to form an administration, thereby letting Labour in.[26] Divisions
among other leading ministers also played into Macmillan's hands.
In the week after Blackpool, the Hailsham and Butler camps spent
most of the time 'eyeball to eyeball, refusing to blink'. Similarly the
'revolt in the night' of 17–18 October came too late. Macleod had
hitherto supported Maudling, believing that the idea of Home was
'bloody ridiculous'.[27] By the time it became clear who was to be
summoned to the Palace, there was much less prospect of stopping
the Home bandwagon, especially as Butler was reluctant to align
himself fully with the Cabinet dissenters.

The role played by Macmillan's deputy throughout his premiership was, in the final analysis, pivotal in explaining Home's triumph.
Those who agree with the view of one MP that 'the whole thing has
been cooked up . . . to keep Rab out' often add that Butler himself
threw away his chance. Yet the trickiness of the task facing Rab was
greater than often assumed. Before the night of 17 October he could
not do what Churchill had done in 1940 – make it clear he would not
serve under a rival – because this would open him to charges of
sabotage and further harden the resolve of those who wanted 'anybody but Butler'. Hailsham later spoke of presenting the succession
'on a plate' by agreeing on the Friday morning to serve under Butler,
but this was only if Home proved unable to form a government.[28]
Once Home had been to the Palace, Butler had to face the fact that
he would only succeed at the risk of defying the consultation process
and splitting the party with a general election on the horizon. If he
became the second minister unable to form an administraion, there
was the further prospect of an early dissolution. It should therefore

come as no surprise that Butler refused to fire what Enoch Powell
called the 'loaded revolver'. He felt himself to be up against a 'terrific
gent' and not, as he later said, some 'ghastly walrus' – clearly a
sideswipe at Macmillan, who had always possessed a more ruthless
streak.[29] And as one Cabinet colleague put it, the Prime Minister
'knew his Butler, knew he was temperamentally incapable of aggra-
vating a crisis by refusing to serve and allowing his many Cabinet
friends to join him in refusing'.[30] The manner in which Home's
succession had been engineered, and Rab's inability to prevent it,
was best summed up by Butler himself:

> The Chief Whip said to me later that it would have been possible
> to alter the whole decision in my favour, but that he thought I
> would never have been happy again if I had done so. With this
> diagnosis I agree . . . One cannot alter one's nature. I had always
> worked for the unity of the party and I did so on this occasion.[31]

Sir Alec Douglas-Home as Prime Minister

News of Home's appointment as Prime Minister caused incredulity
in many quarters. Several newspapers took the view that he would be
'too nice, too slow, too gentle' to take on Labour's confident new
leader; those who conceded that he might develop into a tough if
reserved leader like Attlee added that it was a strange choice for a
party trying to portray itself as youthful and forward-looking. In this
the press reflected public opinion polls, which indicated that barely
one in ten Tory voters favoured Home, compared with overwhelming support for Butler.[32] The priority accorded to party unity over
public reaction was a common complaint among disappointed backbenchers. Butler's PPS, Paul Channon, consoled his chief with the
words: 'How we can be expected in 1964 to go forward to victory
under the 14th Earl of Home passes all understanding.'[33] The
outcome of the leadership struggle was certainly greeted with
satisfaction and relief by opposition leaders. Wilson had feared that
a younger Prime Minister might persuade voters that a change of
government had taken place, but with so many familiar faces in
charge he was able to continue his attacks on the 'old guard'. Tony
Benn wrote in his diary that Maudling and Macleod were much

feared, whereas Home will be 'a dud when it comes to exciting the electorate and Wilson will run rings round him'.[34] With the benefit of hindsight, these snap judgements on Home found their way into the history textbooks. Home's privileged background, as the owner of thousands of acres of land in Scotland, together with political experience mostly confined to foreign affairs, were said to make him anachronistic:

> His grouse-moor image stood out rather awkwardly against the background of modern Britain and his aristocratic origins and education – Eton, Christ Church, the fourteenth earldom of Home – served to emphasise his almost total lack of experience in British domestic politics.[35]

In the event, Home's leadership proved to be more effective than many predicted or have subsequently allowed. Sir Alec Douglas-Home, as he was known after renouncing his peerage, made an unimpressive start in the House of Commons, but was soon restoring the morale of party activists by attacking Wilson as the 'slick salesman of synthetic science'. By Christmas he could claim support from the 'overwhelming mass' of Tory MPs, and though far from being master of the House, he had in no way been 'cut to pieces by Wilson'.[36] Home's difficulties stemmed not so much, as was later suggested, from an absence of political acumen. Rather he faced three intractable problems. In the first place, unlike Macmillan in 1957, he had only a very short time – a year at most – in which to convince voters about his own authority and identity. This explains the large number of public-speaking engagements he took on, leaving him vulnerable to the counter-charge of not getting on with the job of government; he was also found to be more uncomfortable with voters in industrial constituencies than in the old-world farming community of Kinross and West Perthshire.[37] Secondly, though an acceptable compromise for most Conservatives, it was difficult for Home to conceal that the party was less united than when Macmillan came to power. Macleod not only refused to join the Cabinet and reopened wounds by publicly claiming that Macmillan manipulated the succession; he also re-signed as Party Chairman. This made it necessary to bring in a less experienced and charismatic successor, John Hare, formerly Minister of Labour, who as Viscount Blakenham combined the Chairmanship with Chancellorship of the Duchy of Lancaster. Although the party organisation remained steadily competent in terms of money raising and publicity, Central Office missed Macleod's acute tactical sense.[38] Arising out of the legacy of the leadership struggle was a third difficulty, namely that Home needed his Cabinet colleagues more than they needed him; early in 1964 it became apparent that the Prime Minister could not stand out against determined ministers for fear of re-igniting smouldering party divisions.

At the heart of the new dispute, ironically, was the colleague promoted by Home to signal the government's continuing commitment to modernisation. Edward Heath's appointment as Secretary for Trade, Industry and Development, in addition to the Presidency of the Board of Trade, was trumpeted by the press as a prelude to a concerted assault on outdated working practices in British industry. Few envisaged the storm that would blow up when Heath proposed to remove restrictions on competition by abolishing Resale Price Maintenance (RPM), a system that allowed manufacturers to enforce by law the price of goods leaving their outlets. Small traders and shopkeepers, many stalwarts of local Conservative associations, were outraged by a plan which many believed would put them out of business. These concerns were taken up by backbenchers and ministers, but after heated Cabinet exchanges, 'eyeball to eyeball' with his critics, Heath secured permission to go ahead. The Chief Whip among others argued that, whatever the merits of the case, 'delaying tactics' were the best course with an election so close.[39] Heath prevailed, however, after threatening to resign, confident that the Prime Minister could not contemplate a major ministerial departure within weeks of coming to power, especially one that would destroy the modernisation strategy.[40] Once the Cabinet had given the go ahead, there was no choice but to face down over 40 MPs who either voted against the measure or abstained: the largest revolt by Tory backbenchers since the fall of Neville Chamberlain. Heath narrowly won the day, but at a heavy price. He not only acquired a reputation for inflexibility and arrogance, but also prevented the party directing its full attention to the opposition. In the words of one Labour leader, the importance of RPM was that it kept normally right-wing newspapers 'in anti-Tory mood in the months running up to the election'.[41]

Ministerial emphasis on modernisation was gradually downplayed in 1964. Although the government could point to forward-looking policies, such as endorsement of the call by the Robbins Committee for greatly expanded higher education, Wilson's 'New Britain' rhetoric made it difficult to proclaim a distinctive approach even before the RPM episode unfolded. From the spring of 1964 onwards Conservative propaganda switched to proclaiming the virtues of an improving economy. The Chancellor's 'dash for growth' gave every appearance of paying off. Export order books were full as production rose sharply, unemployment had stabilised and Maudling was confident of meeting the NEDC's growth target of 4 per cent per annum for the 1961–6 period. But there was a downside: once again a rapidly deteriorating balance of payments position. In order to avoid overheating, the Chancellor felt there was no option but to introduce mild restraint in his 1964 budget, raising taxes by a modest £100 million through duties on tobacco and drink. This was a far cry from the tax-cutting budgets that preceded the last two elections, and some commentators spoke of 'political and economic unimaginativeness' in a 'fag-end of a budget at what looks like the probable fag-end of a decade and a half of Tory rule'.[42] In the summer Maudling looked to have made a judicious assessment as production levelled off, though behind the scenes ministers were anxious to conceal their fear that rising costs, combined with buoyant consumer demand, was placing such strain on the economy that 'sterling may come under heavy pressure'.[43] By early autumn signs that something was badly amiss with the balance of payments left Maudling open to inevitable Labour accusations that he was deliberately concealing and underrating an imminent crisis for electoral reasons.[44]

Although the Chancellor came under heavy opposition attack, not least for failing to produce an agreed incomes policy with the trade unions, he could claim some of the credit for bringing the government back from what looked like a hopeless electoral position. By-elections during 1963 had shown an average swing towards Labour of 7.5 per cent, enough to deliver a parliamentary majority of 100 seats. In the spring of 1964 Labour swept the board in local elections, thereby justifying the advice of Blakenham not to gamble on a general election in June. But over the summer a government advertising campaign on improving living standards appeared to produce results. Conservative support in the opinion polls began to rise, first at the expense of the Liberals. Signs of inroads into Labour support were particularly welcome, and by August the party was clawing back to equality in terms of which party the voters felt would win the election.[45] Grumbling about Wilson's tendency to operate as

THE ECONOMIC SITUATION IS MORE PROMISING THAN AT ANY TIME SINCE THE MIDDLE OF 1959.
—F.B.I. Report

ELECTION BOOM

ELECTION BOOM

DEPARTMENT OF FUNNY COINCIDENCE

a 'one-man show' developed in Labour ranks; and his critics waited in anticipation. If Labour lost, he would have thrown away Gaitskell's victory; if it won, 'he would have stolen it'.[46] In the meantime Home's mastery of foreign affairs won plaudits and he was credited with transforming party morale and unity by his own example of honesty and integrity.[47] The Prime Minister could take comfort from one or two improved by-election performances, notably at Devizes, and could hope that a blazing summer – as in 1959 – would further take the edge off anti-government sentiment. Labour, he knew, had never won an autumn election, whereas the Conservatives had triumphed in all five October elections held since 1900.[48] By September the average of public opinion polls put the Labour lead at only 2–3 per cent, within the margin of error and sufficient if accurate to produce only a narrow majority. Far from being the easy Labour victory that had been predicted for the past three years, only one thing now seemed certain as the election campaign finally got under way: it would be a close run thing.

Labour Returns to Power: the 1964 Election

Harold Wilson opened the campaign by echoing the message of Labour's manifesto, *The New Britain*: 'Those who are satisfied should stay with the Tories. We need men with fire in their bellies and humanity in their hearts.'[49] But many voters appeared to lack 'fire in the belly'. One effect of delaying the election until the last possible moment was that most of the arguments had been fully rehearsed. In the early stages, neither party appeared to make headway with their chosen themes. Labour gave prominence to growth and scientific change: new ministries of Economic Affairs and Technology were intended to show planning rather than nationalisation as the way forward. The Conservative manifesto was called *Prosperity with a Purpose*, perhaps acknowledging that Macmillan's campaign in 1959 had smacked too much of 'prosperity without a purpose'. Promises for a fourth term of Tory rule included a review of trade unions, action on monopolies and mergers, rating reform and a new house-building programme. Yet it was not obvious which issues had most resonance with the electorate. Home tried to highlight Labour 'ambiguity' about British retention of nuclear weapons, but found defence did not figure prominently among voters' priorities. Whereas land and house prices were frequently mentioned in the south of England, elsewhere pensions were said to be of greater interest on the doorstep.[50] As the campaign progressed, attention focused increasingly on rival claims about the economy. The Prime Minister dubbed Labour's manifesto a 'menu without prices', and his attacks on opposition inexperience appeared to be paying off when Wilson inferred that strikes were deliberately fomented at election time in the Conservative interest. Publication of poor trade figures, however, allowed Labour to return to the offensive, claiming that the Tories were trying to conceal an impending economic crisis.[51] Wilson's poise returned. Thereafter he gave a virtuoso performance, shrugging off claims in the final days before polling that a Labour government would mean more nationalisation and higher taxation.

Tension was intensified on election night as early declarations pointed to a close outcome. It was not until Friday afternoon that victory in Brecon and Radnor confirmed Labour's victory. Although the electorate had increased in size by half a million since 1959, the Labour vote was down by 11,000 compared with the previous election. What made all the difference was that the Conservative vote had dropped by nearly 1.75 million since 1959 – the largest fall for any party since Churchill's humiliation at the end of the war. The Liberal share of the vote, meanwhile, had doubled, leaving party leader Jo Grimond close to holding the balance of power (see Table 4).

Perhaps the most striking individual result was one which went against the tide: Labour's Patrick Gordon-Walker was defeated at

Table 4 *General Election of 15 October 1964*

Party	Votes	MPs	Share of vote	Change since 1959
Conservative	12,001,396	304	43.4%	−6.0%
Labour	12,205,814	317	44.1%	+0.3%
Liberal	3,092,878	9	11.2%	+5.3%
Others	347,905	0	1.3%	+0.4%
Labour majority:	4			

Smethwick, where the Tory candidate had shamelessly told voters: 'If you want a nigger for a neighbour, vote Labour.' All told, Labour lost five seats, though this was more than compensated for by over sixty gains. These came in all parts of the country, including twenty in the south-east, thirteen in the north-west and nine in the Midlands. Compared with what could have been expected on the basis of the local elections, over a million voters had moved away from Labour since the spring. But Wilson's achievement confounded overnight those who believed that in an affluent society Labour 'must lose'.

A test of 'affluent worker' seats points to the resilience of Labour's working-class support in 1964. Of the fifteen constituencies identified as containing the highest proportion of affluent workers (based on home and car ownership) – all in the southern half of England – the average swing at 3.6 per cent was above the national average. Four of the eleven Labour-held seats in this category were won from the Tories at the election.[52] An alternative group of the twelve most 'affluent council tenant' constituencies experienced a mean swing of only 2.2 per cent. But half of this group were located in the Midlands; the remainder were again above the national average.[53] Any erosion of class ties as a result of affluence was thus a protracted and uneven process. Conservatives had to concede that 'the never had it so good' rhetoric of 1959 had misfired badly. Economic difficulties over recent years had helped to lose votes particularly among 'those sections of the working-classes who had reached the shores of affluence in 1959 and had now passed on to a stage of disillusionment'.[54] Other influences that operated beyond day-to-day political events also played a limited part in explaining the outcome in 1964. With many Labour strongholds declining in population, through slum clearance and migration to the suburbs, it was assumed that demographic change was damaging the Conservatives. Yet only one of seventeen seats with the largest increase in population since 1959 actually changed hands; two others in this category were marginals retained by the Tories.[55] At the same time there was little evidence that abstentions or much increased Liberal intervention held the key to Labour's success. Non-voting affected Labour areas as much as Tory marginals, while in most areas Liberal support was drawn fairly evenly from the two main parties, helping to account for Labour's failure to increase its total vote.[56]

In spite of unevenness in certain parts of the country, it was still the case that a strong movement of opinion had taken place from

Tory to Labour since 1959, best explained by a combination of policy questions, party images and perceptions of leadership. More extensive questioning than in the past, notably the interviewing of 2000 voters in what became known as the British Election Survey, confirmed what had long been suspected: that economic well-being was critical to voting intention, and that rising unemployment especially was a prime cause of government unpopularity in the early 1960s. Those who saw their economic position deteriorating showed a stronger than average trend away from the Tories, whereas those who believed things were improving showed a preference for the government. Herein lay the key to Home's recovery in the polls in 1964, as he was able to claim that unemployment was falling and disposable incomes steadily rising.[57] The economy was not the only policy area that worked to Labour's advantage. When asked what were the most important problems facing the nation, respondents often mentioned social welfare and housing ahead of economic concerns. This again pushed the Conservatives on the defensive. There was strong public support for Labour's pledge to increase old-age pensions, and firm backing for controls over the price of building land. The number of those who wanted to see the social services expanded and saw Labour as better able to do so greatly exceeded the minority who favoured restrictions on welfare spending.[58]

Key political issues such as the economy and social policy were not the only short-term forces that facilitated a movement of opinion to Labour. Equally important, and closely related, were the changing images of the parties held by voters. In the 1950s, as we have seen, the Conservatives had successfully identified themselves with rising living standards. But the Tory reputation for economic competence was not only undermined in the early 1960s; it was also overlaid by a more debilitating trend. In spite of ministerial pronouncements about modernisation, the Conservatives widely became seen as being out of date. The party's own research brutally concluded early in 1964 that it was seen as 'less exciting, young and modern' than the opposition.[59] Conversely, Labour had managed to shake off some of its own old-fashioned image of 1959. Much of the credit for this went to Gaitskell's period of leadership. By the time of his death, unity had been restored to Labour ranks and the party's programme carried far fewer hostages to fortune. Gaitskell also initiated publicity campaigns aimed at associating Labour in voters' minds with increased opportunities for the aspiring classes. Although some complained that 'working-class solidarity' was being replaced by 'petty bourgeois wine bibbing', the effect was to help transform Labour's reputation among key groups of voters.[60] As *The Economist* observed, by 1964 Labour's association with extremism, disunity and irresponsibility had been superseded by 'Mr Wilson's capture of the more positive image of the white laboratory coat'.[61]

Wilson's skilful handling of 'scientific socialism' clearly enhanced his party's image. But in doing so he only built on earlier trends: this appeal should not therefore be regarded as the key to the lead which Labour had in the 'presidential' contest between the respective party leaders. More important here was Wilson's exploitation of his own persona and background. Sir Alec, though highly regarded by Tory activists, had a consistently lower popularity rating than his predecessor, and was condemned in survey research for things as diverse as his looks, his 'weakness' and his speaking manner.[62] By contrast, Wilson was given high ratings as a leader of his party. Both by accident and design, he was better suited than Gaitskell to embarrassing his opponents across the despatch box. Propelled unexpectedly into the leadership, Wilson's freshness enabled him to take up the so-called 'Kennedy theme' of progressive-inspired national renewal. His lower middle-class background also allowed him – unlike Gaitskell – to point an accusing finger at the upper class of Etonians and land speculators. What followed was a message that combined simplicity with plausibility: the reason Britain was not moving forward like the United States was that all top positions still went to an old-fashioned and unrepresentative elite. Nowhere was this message more convincingly conveyed than on television, which gave Wilson the opportunity to present himself as relaxed and confident. Although Home worked hard to develop his own style, his inexperience in front of the cameras told when he attempted to cancel out hecklers at a meeting in Birmingham by shouting at the top of his voice. The sight of a Prime Minister unable to control events, Home later asserted, was a humiliation from the Conservative campaign never recovered.[63]

Conclusion

The 1964 election victory was a personal triumph for Harold Wilson. He had made very few mistakes since assuming the Labour leadership. In parliament, he had outshone his Tory adversaries. His

194   *Retreat from New Jerusalem*

adeptness as a party manager had been seen to its best effect at the
Scarborough conference, and his shrewdness as a tactician was
manifest in the way he seized and held the initiative in the 1964
campaign. Wilson's rapport with the public centred, above all, on his
association with the anti-establishment mood of the day. His was a
social identity very different from the narrow exclusiveness of Macmillan and Home: 'Yorkshire, meritocratic, anti-metropolitan, and
anti-glamour'.[64] Traditional Labour supporters and middle-class
converts alike were susceptible to this appeal, with its promise of a
more dynamic, classless society. However, it does not follow that
1964 should be judged solely or even mainly in terms of Wilson's
personal popularity. As we have seen, Gaitskell had already made
substantial progress in leaving behind the party's reputation for
fostering out-dated class warfare. Wilson's white-heat strategy continued down the same path; its potency as a vote winner in its own
right offset by the attention ministers themselves gave to modernising
rhetoric. Similarly, the real damage to the government's popularity
came in the middle of the electoral cycle, before Wilson became party
leader. As Conservatives themselves admitted: 'We forfeited public
confidence during the period between the crisis "little budget" of
July, 1961, and the unemployment peak of February 1963, as a result
of the misguided economic policies of the Selwyn Lloyd era.'[65]

Nor should we forget that, for all his brilliance as opposition
leader, Wilson only just scraped home in 1964. In the event, Home
came within a whisker of securing a fourth successive Tory victory –
a feat achieved by no party since the 1860s. The Tory leader later
claimed that the result could have been different but for isolated
misfortunes: notably the disloyalty shown by Macleod and the mid-
campaign publication of adverse trade figures.[66] It might be an
exaggeration to conclude, as some have, that Home lacked nothing
more as Prime Minister than loyalty and time to establish himself.[67]
But he does deserve credit for restoring hope to what looked like a
lost cause. By delaying the election until the last possible moment, he
allowed some of the pain inflicted during 1962–63 to recede in
people's memories. In its place, he sought to encourage renewed
confidence in Tory economic management. If a tiny number of extra
voters had remained loyal, Home would have been cast in the role of
saviour, whereas Wilson's leadership would have been cast in an
altogether different light. For all his qualities, Wilson was unable to
improve upon the total number of votes gained by Gaitskell in 1959.

Indeed the number of those backing Labour had fallen at every election since the high point of 1951. Although sceptics who claimed that Labour had no future had been confounded, there was little evidence that a secure long-term platform had been established. The NEC was told that:

> the result is not altogether satisfactory. The relatively low poll, combined with massive Tory abstentions, shows that, while we have succeeded in eroding many voters' faith in Conservative policies, much remains to be done to convince the majority of the electorate of the ability of the Labour Party to govern.[68]

1964 therefore needs to be explained primarily in terms of disillusionment with a government felt to be in power too long. The Conservatives lost overnight all the ground made up since the end of the war; the party's total vote in 1964 fell below that of 1950, despite a greatly expanded electorate. Most damaging of all was the way in which the traumas of 1962–3 alienated lifelong Tory voters. Many were thoroughly disenchanted with those in charge, as was made clear in the complaint to Central Office of a 44-year-old industrial manager:

> We are sick of seeing old men dressed in flat caps and bedraggled tweeds strolling with a 12 bore. For God's sake, what is your campaign manager doing? These photographs of Macmillan's ghost with Home's face date about 1912.[69]

The party's own research among a cross-section of voters underlined the point. Conservative leaders seemed ill-equipped for modern industrial management, and were suited only to governing an empire that no longer existed. Disaffection was such that it was no longer a case of finding policies that might persuade deserters or waverers to come back to the fold. 'Rather, the problem is a major crisis of confidence, in which it is conceivable that the number of Conservative voters may shrink to its hard core.'[70]

Although this fear had not been borne out in October 1964, there was nevertheless a widespread feeling that after thirteen years it was time for a change. This was perhaps the overriding cause of Labour's victory, though like all the other factors outlined above, it could not alone determine the election outcome. In order to have its full effect, two further conditions needed to be met. The first was that the opposition had to be trusted. Gaitskell and Wilson had managed this, though not to the same extent as Attlee and Bevin when Labour last ousted the Tories in 1945. Secondly, Conservative leaders had to miss what opportunities they had to counteract the desire of voters for change. Harold Macmillan was certainly conscious of the need for a forward-looking strategy in the early 1960s, but found that policy failures and security scandals left him incapable of making up lost ground. What was worse, he bungled efforts to convince voters that change was occurring in terms of personalities if not policies. Macmillan miscalculated badly with his Cabinet purge of 1962; this was compounded by his handling of the succession crisis in 1963, which failed to give the impression of renewal from within – of the government providing a new leader who deserved a chance in his own right. Home did his best to revive Tory fortunes, but was too closely associated with the 'old gang' to represent a decisive break with past failures. It was once said it was not Churchill who lost the 1945 election for the Tories; it was the 'ghost of Neville Chamberlain' and his discredited associates. By the same token, it was not Sir Alec Douglas-Home who lost the 1964 contest; it was the 'ghost' of Harold Macmillan.

Conclusion

The record of Conservative governments after 1951, as presented in this account, was mixed at best. Sympathisers point to a strong economic performance, with total industrial production rising by 40 per cent between 1951 and 1964. Yet as we have seen, satisfaction with improving world trade quickly turned to anxiety that Britain was failing to keep pace with its main competitors. As Macmillan's popularity slumped, Tory 'modernisation' was criticised as too little, too late. Unlike the 1940s, a mood of national introspection and heightened awareness of the need for fundamental reform took hold. Yet the chance to tackle structural weaknesses in the economy or to overhaul outdated, status-ridden institutions was missed. Defenders of the Conservative regime often point to progress in social policy: Britain was better educated, better housed and better cared for in old age than ever before. Here it has been argued that hard electoral realities – with Labour capturing over 40 per cent of votes cast even in defeat – made any direct challenge to the welfare state unthinkable. As one Tory MP said, 'no one shoots Santa Claus'.[1] However, efforts were made to refashion welfare provision by reducing the role of the state, especially in housing. In education inequality remained deeply embedded: while a few from modest backgrounds reached the prestigious grammar schools, the majority of working-class children languished in secondary moderns. Class awareness contined to act as the main determinant of voting behaviour and underpinned cultural developments such as the 'angry young men' literature of the period. Entrenched class divisions survived what has widely been regarded as the one unqualified success of the Tory years: increased affluence. Even allowing for inflation, there had been a 30 per cent rise in the average standard of living, thereby feeding a rapid rise in consumerism and a threefold increase in the number of foreign holidays. But levels of prosperity, we have noted, varied greatly according to locality, age and ethnic background. Poverty may have been 'rediscovered' in the 1960s; it had not gone away in the 1950s.

There was, moreover, no unanimity on the question of whether material progress was entirely beneficial. While many were gratified to see advances denied to previous generations, concern was voiced about what was being lost in the process. At Labour's conference in 1959, Aneurin Bevan described the emerging affluent society as 'ugly'; a society 'in which priorities have gone all wrong'. The task of socialists, he argued, was to fight against the complacency that had descended since 1951 and to restore the ethics of service and community. As we have seen, anti-materialist sentiment was deep-rooted in Labour thinking, and helped to pave the way for Macmillan's 1959 election triumph. Bevan's views have often been regarded as isolated and anachronistic, kicking against an irreversible trend; yet his critique was shared by a surprisingly wide range of opinion, well beyond the confines of the Labour left. In 1960 Edward Boyle told Rab Butler that journalists had asked him if recent ministerial speeches emphasising 'work' and 'duty' were meant to imply a departure from the philosophy of 'never had it so good'. He replied that there was no inconsistency: to aim for economic expansion was not counter to the values of service and self-discipline. Higher living standards, Boyle underlined, ensured that millions of people could aspire to lives freer than ever before – hence there was nothing unworthy about the government's desire to improve material conditions. 'I only mention this', he concluded, 'because . . . too many people seem to associate the Tory programme of prosperity and expansion, quite unfairly, with selfishness and complacency.'[2] Yet charges of 'complacency' found support in both the decline in turnout at general elections since 1951 and the falling membership of both major parties. References to apathy were becoming commonplace, and were couched in terms of politics being unable to compete with the rival attractions of home and garden, as well as the failure of politicians to develop a language suitable for the times: 'have the political parties nothing to say to Angry Young Men and Teddy Boys?' One study carried out at the time of the 1959 election found only 15 per cent of respondents who were 'very interested in politics'; one in five were unable to name a single major political figure.[3]

Equally, concern about 'selfishness' was not limited to opposition ranks; it also found expression in various quarters. In 1960 the Archbishop of Canterbury, Geoffrey Fisher, spoke of how the nation, having secured freedom by surviving its greatest peril in wartime, ran the risk of forgetting 'what it is for'. He went on to attack that 'dreadful' phrase 'We've never had it so good', claiming it was used to justify 'a smug contentment which ignores the perils of our own situation and the appalling conditions of people in other countries'. Ministers insisted attention was paid to spiritual as well as material matters. Macmillan responded by publicly emphasising Christian values, but Fisher returned to the fray, telling the Prime Minister that 'much is yet to be done here at home before society can regard itself as [one] in which advancement in political power or money power depends on individual merit and individual merit alone'.[4] Here the Archbishop was echoing the claims of 'state of England' writers, whose concern was that affluence had been allowed to eclipse values such as 'work' and 'duty' by being narrowly defined in terms of private rather than public good. 'We are now madly rushing ahead with motor cars and television', noted Nicholas Davenport, 'before we have even cleared the slums or stamped out poverty'. The stain of continuing class divisions, he added, was the inevitable product of a 'public policy of growth without social direction'.[5] Ministers themselves were finding it difficult to conceal evidence implying that affluence brought dangers as well as rewards. In 1962 a highly publicised report from the Central Statistical Office found that growing personal incomes contributed to greatly increasing debt levels and to an 'alarming development of crime amongst young men and boys'.[6]

The feeling that genuine opportunities for economic and social renewal had been missed was reinforced by comparisons with what was referred to at the beginning of this work as the 'hope and public purpose' of the 1940s. Again it was not simply socialist writers such as Richard Hoggart and Raymond Williams who lamented the disappearance of community structures and the primacy given to private, home-centred activities. Among the broad swathe of professionals involved in housing and town planning, the high idealism of the previous decade – the belief that a New Jerusalem could physically be created out of the rubble of war – contrasted with the 1950s reality of housing as a symbol of the 're-emergence of a divided society', deeply fragmented along lines of class and region.[7] Much of the newspaper press, including those titles traditionally supportive of the Conservative cause, could not resist contrasting the 'flagging economy' and the unseemly scandals of 1963 with wartime values. 'Popularity by affluence is about played out, especially when it rests on so insecure a basis', *The Times* asserted, calling for a return to the virtues of 'blood, sweat and tears'.[8] By this time some Conservative activists were also becoming fearful that more than defeat at the polls beckoned. A Tory pamphlet in 1963 acknowledged that an excessive concentration on personal prosperity might endanger the democratic process by undermining any concept of active citizenship. The nation had discovered what it called the 'fallacy' behind the slogan 'never had it so good'. Outward prosperity 'still needed ideals to give it body', and yet younger voters in particular were found to be 'tired of naked materialism, of cynicism, of expediency'. Unless dynamic leadership and fresh remedies were found quickly, Britain was likely to suffer from more of what it had been experiencing in the past few years: 'drift without ideas or purpose'.[9] The retreat from New Jerusalem was a complex, multi-faceted process taking place at many different levels; in some respects the process accelerated when Harold Wilson subsequently disappointed hopes that he would bring dynamic leadership and fresh remedies. But there was no doubt when the rot set in: it was during the 1950s.

Notes

Notes to the Introduction

1. K. O. Morgan, *Labour in Power, 1945–1951* (Oxford, 1984); H. Pelling, *The Labour Governments, 1945–51* (London, 1984); A. Cairncross, *Years of Recovery: British Economic Policy, 1945–51* (London, 1985); P. Hennessy, *Never Again: Britain, 1945–1951* (London, 1992).
2. J. Saville, *The Labour Movement in Britain* (London, 1988); J. Fyrth (ed.), *Labour's High Noon: The Government and the Economy, 1945–51* (London, 1993).
3. C. Barnett, *The Audit of War: The Illusion and Reality of Britain as a Great Nation* (London, 1986); *The Lost Victory: British Dreams, British Realities, 1945–1950* (London, 1995).
4. Symposium, 'Britain's Postwar Industrial Decline', *Contemporary Record*, 1: 2 (1987), pp. 11–19; N. Tiratsoo (ed.), *The Attlee Years* (London, 1991).
5. J. Tomlinson, 'Welfare and the Economy: The Economic Impact of the Welfare State, 1945–1951', *Twentieth-Century British History*, 6: 2 (1995), pp. 194–219.
6. Hennessy, *Never Again*, p. 453. See also M. Francis, 'Economics and Ethics: the Nature of Labour's Socialism, 1945–1951', *Twentieth-Century British History*, 6: 2 (1995), pp. 220–43.
7. S. Fielding, P. Thompson and N. Tiratsoo, *'England Arise!' The Labour Party and Popular Politics in 1940s Britain* (Manchester, 1995), pp. 209–18.
8. P. Kellner, 'It Wasn't All Right, Jack', *Sunday Times*, 4 April 1993. See also *The Guardian*, 9 September 1993.
9. For a summary of the claims made by the political parties, see J. Barnes and A. Seldon, '1951–64: 13 Wasted Years?', *Contemporary Record*, 1: 2 (1987).
10. V. Bogdanor and R. Skidelsky (eds), *The Age of Affluence, 1951–1964* (London, 1970); S. Brittan, *Steering the Economy: The Role of the Treasury* (Harmondsworth, 1971).
11. A. Seldon, *Churchill's Indian Summer: The Conservative Government, 1951–55* (London, 1981); R. Lamb, *The Failure of the Eden Government* (London, 1987); *The Macmillan Years, 1957–1963: The Emerging Truth* (London, 1995). There are in addition three chapters on individual parliaments in P. Hennessy and A. Seldon (eds), *Ruling Performance: British Governments from Attlee to Thatcher* (Oxford, 1987). See also

J. Ramsden, *The Age of Churchill and Eden, 1940–57* (London, 1995); *The Winds of Change: Macmillan to Heath, 1957–75* (London, 1996).

12. E.g. D. Carlton, *Anthony Eden* (London, 1981); R. Rhodes James, *Anthony Eden* (London, 1986); A. Horne, *Macmillan*, vol. I: *1894–1956* (London, 1988) and vol. II: *1957–1986* (London, 1989); J. Turner, *Macmillan* (London, 1994); P. Williams, *Hugh Gaitskell* (Oxford, 1982 edn); B. Pimlott, *Harold Wilson* (London, 1992).

13. E.g. R. Lowe, *The Welfare State in Britain since 1945* (London, 1993); H. Glennerster, *British Social Policy since 1945* (Oxford, 1995); N. Timmins, *The Five Giants: A Biography of the Welfare State* (London, 1995); N. F. R. Crafts, B. Duckham and N. Woodward (eds), *The British Economy since 1945* (Oxford, 1991).

14. Bogdanor and Skidelsky (eds), *Age of Affluence*, p. 10. See also D. Kavanagh and P. Morris, *Consensus Politics from Attlee to Thatcher* (Oxford, 1989); D. Dutton, *British Politics since 1945: The Rise and Fall of Consensus* (Oxford, 1991).

15. K. O. Morgan, *The People's Peace: British History, 1945–1989* (Oxford, 1990), p. 137.

16. Harriet Jones, 'New Tricks for an Old Dog? The Conservatives and Social Policy, 1951–55', in A. Gorst, L. Johnman and W. Scott Lucas (eds), *Contemporary British History, 1931–61: Politics and the Limits of Policy* (London, 1991), pp. 33–43; N. Rollings, ' "Poor Mr Butskell: A Short Life, Wrecked by Schizophrenia"?', *Twentieth-Century British History*, 5: 2 (1994), pp. 183–205.

17. Owing to limitations of space other key issues in these years, for example immigration, are only touched upon briefly.

18. *Guardian*, 25 April 1995: comments by Elizabeth Young, reviewing Peter Vansittart's book *In the Fifties* (London, 1995).

19. Michael Shanks, *The Stagnant Society: A Warning* (Harmondsworth, 1961), pp. 173–4.

Notes to Chapter 1: Setting Britain Free, 1951–5

1. D. E. Butler, *The British General Election of 1955* (London, 1955), p. 15.

2. A. Seldon, 'The Churchill Administration, 1951–1955', in Hennessy and Seldon (eds), *Ruling Performance*, pp. 65–7. For a similar emphasis, see Kavanagh and Morris, *Consensus Politics from Attlee to Thatcher*, and Dutton, *British Politics since 1945*.

3. A. Seldon, 'Conservative Century', in A. Seldon and S. Ball (eds), *Conservative Century: The Conservative Party since 1900* (Oxford, 1994), p. 46. See also the fullest account of this period to date, Seldon's work *Churchill's Indian Summer*.

4. See D. E. Butler, *The British General Election of 1951* (London, 1952).

5. M. Kandiah, 'Lord Woolton's Chairmanship of the Conservative Party 1946–1951', unpublished Exeter University PhD thesis (1992), pp. 214–26.

6. B. Pimlott (ed.), *The Political Diary of Hugh Dalton, 1918–40, 1945–60* (London, 1986): diary entry for 'End of October' 1951, p. 567. Herbert Morrison wrote a more sober assessment, saying that policy making was more difficult than in 1945 and that Labour now had to find a formula 'which will not only inspire convinced Socialists but which the electorate will, on the whole, find acceptable': Labour Party National Executive Committee (NEC) Minutes, 26 February 1952.

7. Butler, *1951 Election*, pp. 239–42; Ramsden, *Age of Churchill and Eden*, p. 231.

8. Harold Macmillan, *Tides of Fortune, 1945–55* (London, 1969): diary entry 28 October 1951, p. 362.

9. Ramsden, *Age of Churchill and Eden*, p. 239; Viscount Chandos, *The Memoirs of Lord Chandos* (London, 1962), p. 341.

10. Cited in Butler, *1951 Election*, p. 244.

11. Macmillan, *Tides of Fortune*: diary entry for 21 September 1951, p. 355.

12. Colonel J. R. Hutchinson MP to R. A. Butler, 21 November 1951: R. A. Butler Papers, Trinity College, Cambridge, B17, f. 153.

13. 'Our Conservative Crusade', notes drafted by Conservative Research Department (CRD), 27 December 1951: Conservative Central Office (CCO) Papers, Conservative Party Archive (CPA), Bodleian Library, Oxford, CCO 4/4/237.

14. *Chandos Memoirs*, p. 344.

15. Geoffrey Lloyd MP to Sydney Butler, 28 October 1951: Butler Papers, B17, f. 180.

16. N. Fisher, *Harold Macmillan: A Biography* (London, 1982), p. 136; Horne, *Macmillan*, vol. I, p. 333.

17. Macmillan, *Tides of Fortune*, p. 363; Lord Birkenhead, *Walter Monckton: The Life of Viscount Monckton of Brenchley* (London, 1969), p. 276.

18. Lord Birkenhead, *The Prof in Two Worlds: The Official Life of Professor F. A. Lindemann, Viscount Cherwell* (London, 1961), pp. 280–1. Churchill admitted his need for assistance in this area, confessing to one colleague: 'I was Chancellor of the Exchequer for five years but, you know, I never understood it!' (see John Boyd-Carpenter, *Way of Life* (London, 1980), p. 87).

19. Macmillan, *Tides of Fortune*: diary, 28 October 1951, p. 365.

20. *The Economist*, 3 November 1951.

21. R. Shepherd, *Iain Macleod* (London, 1994), pp. 73–8. In the course of six minor reshuffles and one major reconstruction of the government that followed, places were however found for several younger ministers.

22. G. N. Worswick and P. Ady (eds), *The British Economy in the Nineteen-Fifties* (Oxford, 1962), pp. 15–16.

23. John Colville, *The Fringes of Power: Downing Street Diaries, 1939–1955* (London, 1985), p. 635.

24. A. Cairncross (ed.), *The Robert Hall Diaries, 1947–53* (London, 1989): diary entry for 29 October 1951, p. 176.

25. Macmillan, *Tides of Fortune*, pp. 366 and 384.

204   *Notes*

26. 'The Economic Position: Analysis and Remedies', memorandum by the Chancellor of the Exchequer, 31 October 1951: Public Record Office (PRO), Prime Minister's Papers (PREM), 11/132; 'The Economic Situation', CRD memorandum, 7 November 1951: CPA, CRD 2/9/5.

27. R. Cockett (ed.), *My Dear Max: The Letters of Brendan Bracken to Lord Beaverbrook, 1925–1958* (London, 1990): letter dated 15 January 1952, p. 129.

28. Edwin Plowden, *An Industrialist in the Treasury: The Post-War Years* (London, 1989), p. 140. Plowden, head of the economic planning staff at the Treasury, did not identify the minister.

29. Cockett (ed.), *My Dear Max*: Bracken to Beaverbrook, 15 January 1952, p. 129.

30. The three main advocates were Leslie **Ro**wan, George **B**olton and **Ot**to Clarke.

31. 'External Action', memorandum by the Chancellor of the Exchequer, 21 February 1952, PRO PREM 11/140.

32. Churchill to Eden, 21 February 1952, PRO PREM 11/138.

33. Donald MacDougall, *'Don and Mandarin': Memoirs of an Economist* (London, 1987), p. 90.

34. Cherwell to Churchill, 26 February 1952, PRO PREM 11/140.

35. Arthur Salter, *Slave of the Lamp: A Public Servant's Notebook* (London, 1967), pp. 222–3.

36. MacDougall, *'Don and Mandarin'*, pp. 98–9, notes that Butler was backed by Lyttelton, Swinton and Crookshank; opponents included Churchill, Eden, Salisbury, Maxwell-Fyfe and Macmillan.

37. Cairncross (ed.), *Hall Diaries*: 4 March 1952, p. 206.

38. Birkenhead, *The Prof*, p. 285.

39. Cited in Lord Butler, *The Art of the Possible* (London, 1971), p. 160. Lyttelton added: 'They prefer a genteel bankruptcy, *force majeure* being the plea'.

40. Plowden, *Industrialist in the Treasury*, p. 156; *Hall Diaries*: 4 March 1952, p. 206.

41. Morgan, *The People's Peace*, pp. 120–2.

42. 'Setting the Pound Free', memorandum by Lord Cherwell, 18 March 1952, PRO PREM 11/137; Salter, *Slave of the Lamp*, p. 221.

43. A. Howard, *RAB: The Life of R. A. Butler* (London, 1987), pp. 187–8.

44. Butler, *Art of the Possible*, pp. 158–9.

45. *Hall Diaries*: 18 March 1952, p. 211.

46. *The Economist*, 12 April and 17 May 1952.

47. Minute to the Prime Minister from the Chief Whip, 23 November 1951, PRO PREM 11/136.

48. Mr Jack Binns and twelve other signatories to Churchill, 11 June 1952, PRO PREM 11/136.

49. *Hall Diaries:* 10 April 1952, p. 217.

50. Salisbury to Churchill, 12 May 1952, PRO PREM 11/213; Colville, *Fringes of Power*: 16 May 1952, p. 647; Churchill to Eden, 9 August 1952, PRO PREM 11/654.

51. Cockett (ed.), *My Dear Max*: Bracken to Beaverbrook, 25 April 1952 and 7 January 1953, pp. 130 and 135.

52. Lord Moran, *Winston Churchill: The Struggle for Survival, 1940–1965* (London, 1965): diary entry for 20 June 1952, p. 417; *Manchester Guardian*, 19–20 June 1952.

53. *Hall Diaries:* 25 April 1952, p. 221; Assheton to Butler, 30 May 1952, Butler Papers G24, f. 45.

54. Butler to Churchill, mid-August 1952, Butler Papers, G24, ff. 60–2.

55. 'Government Publicity', memorandum by David Gammans MP, 30 May 1952: Walter Monckton Papers, Bodleian Library, Dep. Monckton 2, ff. 226–30.

56. J. C. R. Dow, *The Management of the British Economy, 1945–60* (Cambridge, 1964), pp. 73–5.

57. *The Economist*, 11 October 1952.

58. J. Morgan (ed.), *The Backbench Diaries of Richard Crossman, 1951–64* (London, 1981): diary entry for 6 November 1951, p. 31.

59. A comment attributed to Tom Driberg MP, cited in J. Campbell, *Nye Bevan and the Mirage of British Socialism* (London, 1987), p. 273. See also M. Jenkins, *Bevanism: Labour's High Tide* (Nottingham, 1979).

60. K. Harris, *Attlee* (London, 1982), p. 499.

61. Douglas Jay, *Change and Fortune: A Political Record* (London, 1980), p. 223.

62. Ian Mikardo, *Back-Bencher* (London, 1988), p. 127.

63. Pimlott (ed.), *Dalton Diary*: 24–8 October 1952, p. 601; *Tribune*, 16 January 1953; NEC Minutes, 28 January 1953.

64. Jay, *Change and Fortune*, p. 221.

65. 'Budget Proposals', memorandum by the Chancellor of the Exchequer, 19 March 1953, PRO PREM 11/410.

66. Churchill to Butler, 27 September 1952, PRO PREM 11/29.

67. Chief Whip to Prime Minister, 14 April 1953, PRO PREM 11/410.

68. *The Times*, 15–16 April 1953; *The Economist*, 18 April 1953.

69. *The Economist*, 8 August 1953.

70. *My Dear Max*: Bracken to Beaverbrook, 7 January 1953, p. 133.

71. NEC Minutes, 24 June 1953.

72. A. Potts, 'The Sunderland South By-Election of 13 May 1953 in the Context of Conservative Recovery', *Durham University Journal*, 84 (1992), pp. 191–200.

73. 'By-Election Swing', memorandum from Mr Cohen to Mr Watson, 3 July 1953, CCO 4/5/9.

74. 'Civil Supply 1954–55', memorandum by the Chancellor, 16 December 1953, PRO PREM 11/658; *My Dear Max*: Bracken to Beaverbrook, 30 December 1953, p. 153.

75. Colville, *Fringes of Power*, pp. 667–71; *My Dear Max*: Bracken to Beaverbrook, 14 August 1953, pp. 148–9.

76. Letters to Butler from Bill Anstruther-Grey MP and Ralph Rayner MP, 7 July and 12 July 1953, Butler Papers, G26, ff. 62–4; Colville, *Fringes of Power*: diary, 19 July 1953, p. 671.

77. Moran, *Winston Churchill*: diary, 11 October 1953, pp. 509–10, citing a conversation with Colville.
78. Woolton diary, 1 October 1953: Woolton Papers, Bodleian Library, MS Woolton 3, f. 115.
79. *The Economist*, 2 January 1954. Frustrated by finding himself in a minority of one, Bevan was soon to resign from the Shadow Cabinet.
80. 'Government Methods of Financing and Effects of Taxation', memorandum by the Chancellor, 2 March 1954, PRO PREM 11/653; Woolton diary, 6 April 1954, ff. 122–5.
81. *The Economist*, 3 July 1954.
82. *The Observer*, 17 January 1954, cited in Seldon, 'Churchill Administration', p. 84.
83. *The Economist*, 3 July 1954.
84. Butler to Eden, 17 February 1955, PRO Treasury (T) papers, 172/2126.
85. Cabinet Minutes, 23 and 24 February 1955, PRO Cabinet (CAB) papers, 128/28.
86. 'Summary of Public Opinion Reports up to 16 October 1954': copy in Anthony Eden Papers, Birmingham University Library, AP11/10/222.
87. *My Dear Max*: Bracken to Beaverbrook, 17 January 1955, p. 171: 'The middle classes here are bitterly disillusioned. They are the victims of an ever increasing cost of living but they have none of the power of the TUC or the FBI to compensate themselves for the ravages of inflation'.
88. Macmillan, *Tides of Fortune*: 22 September and 19 November 1954, pp. 543 and 548.
89. Harry Crookshank diary, 22 March 1954: Bodleian Library, MS. Eng. Hist. d. 361; 'Note of talk with PM', 11 March 1954, Butler Papers, G27, f.18.
90. Woolton diary, 6 April 1954, ff. 123–4; Macmillan diary, July 1954, cited in Horne, *Macmillan*, p. 353: 'We must have a completely new Cabinet and Government, representative of the party. The present Cabinet does *not* represent the party.'
91. Colville, *Fringes of Power*, p. 703: Churchill tried to give an impression of freshness by moving ministers such as Macmillan (to Defence) while promoting younger hopefuls such as Sandys (to Housing).
92. Crookshank diary, 8 September 1954, MS. Eng. Hist. d. 361.
93. Woolton diary, 22 December 1954 and 11 March 1955, ff. 134 and 142–5.
94. Macmillan, *Tides of Fortune*: 4 April 1955, p. 556.
95. Cited in Butler, *Art of the Possible*, p. 173.
96. *New Statesman*, 3 April 1954.
97. *The Economist*, 25 July 1953.
98. Edward Boyle, cited in A. Thompson, *The Day Before Yesterday: An Illustrated History of Britain from Attlee to Macmillan* (London, 1971), p. 95.

99. N. Rollings, ' "Poor Mr Butskell" ', *Twentieth-Century British History*, pp. 183–205.
100. 'Note on Taxation', Norman Brook [Cabinet Secretary] to Churchill, 2 March 1954, PRO PREM 11/653.
101. *The Economist*, 27 February 1954.
102. J. Cronin, *The Politics of State Expansion: War, State and Society in Twentieth-Century Britain* (London, 1991), p. 184.
103. *New Statesman*, 3 April 1954.

Notes to Chapter 2: 'The best Prime Minister we have', 1955–7

1. *The Yorkshire Post*, 7 April 1955.
2. *Daily Telegraph*, 21 April 1955.
3. Michael Fraser to Butler, 10 October 1955: Butler Papers, H36, f. 120.
4. Sir Anthony Eden, *Full Circle* (London, 1960), p. 272.
5. Lord Woolton, *The Memoirs of the Rt Hon. Earl of Woolton* (London, 1959), p. 419.
6. Eden to Churchill, 8 April 1955, PRO PREM 11/864.
7. Brittan, *Steering the Economy*, p. 201.
8. Eden, *Full Circle*, pp. 277–8.
9. Cairncross (ed.), *Hall Diaries:* 7 April 1955, p. 31. See also R. Rose and T. Karran, *Taxation by Political Inertia* (London, 1987), p. 170.
10. Conservative Party, *United for Peace and Progress* (London, 1955), p. 7.
11. Pimlott (ed.), *Dalton Diary*: 26 May 1955, p. 671.
12. Butler, *Election of 1955*, pp. 67–92.
13. *The Economist*, 4 June 1955: e.g. at Faversham in Kent, the Labour majority of 562 was reduced to 59 (swing 0.04 per cent); but in the neighbouring Maidstone seat, the Tory majority was increased from 6447 to 7406 (swing 1.25 per cent).
14. *New Statesman*, 4 June 1955; *Reynolds News*, 29 May 1955.
15. *Manchester Guardian*, 28 May 1955; *The Times*, 28 May 1955.
16. CRD, 'Report on General Election 1955', June 1955, CRD 2/48/54.
17. *Daily Mirror*, 28 May 1955.
18. *The Observer*, 29 May 1955.
19. CRD, 'Report on General Election p. 55', CRD 2/48/54.
20. 'Rab notes on relations with WSC, and . . . succession from WSC to Eden', n.d. (1957), Butler Papers, G31, ff. 92–5.
21. Pimlott (ed.), *Dalton Diary*: 1 April 1955, p. 658.
22. Boyd-Carpenter, *Way of Life*, p. 123; Woolton diary, 6 April 1955, ff. 123–4. Butler once said that 'Anthony's father was a mad baronet and his mother a very beautiful woman. That's Anthony – half mad baronet, half beautiful woman' – cited in P. Cosgrave, *R. A. Butler* (London, 1981), p. 12.
23. Horne, *Macmillan*, vol. I, p. 376.

24.   Lord Kilmuir, *Political Adventure: The Memoirs of the Earl of Kilmuir* (London, 1964), p. 308.

25.   Nigel Nicolson MP, cited in Thompson, *Day Before Yesterday*, p. 121.

26.   Eden diary, 24 and 26 August 1955: Avon Papers, AP20/1/31.

27.   Cabinet Minutes, 21 September, 4 and 25 October 1955, PRO CAB 128/29.

28.   Lamb, *Failure of Eden Government*, pp. 15–24.

29.   Cabinet Minutes, 7 June 1955, PRO CAB 128/29.

30.   Memorandum by the Minister of Labour, 22 July 1955, PRO PREM 11/1402.

31.   See comments by Harold Watkinson, Monckton's deputy, in *Turning Points: A Record of Our Times* (Salisbury, 1986), p. 59; Eden, *Full Circle*, pp. 286–7.

32.   Eden diary, 2 October 1955, Avon Papers, AP20/1/31.

33.   Butler, *Art of the Possible*, p. 181.

34.   Fraser to Butler, 1 December 1955, Butler Papers, G28, ff. 81–5.

35.   Macmillan, *Tides of Fortune*, pp. 658–92.

36.   J. Barnes, 'From Eden to Macmillan, 1955–1959', in Hennessy and Seldon (eds), *Ruling Performance*, p. 109.

37.   *The Economist*, 24 December 1955.

38.   Bracken to Beaverbrook, 17 January 1955, cited in Carlton, *Eden*, p. 389; Kilmuir, *Political Adventure*, p. 256.

39.   Handwritten notes by Rab, n.d., Butler Papers, G31, f. 89.

40.   Cited in Gilbert, *Churchill*, vol. VIII, p. 1164.

41.   L. Hunter, *The Road to Brighton Pier* (London, 1959), p. 222.

42.   Cited in B. Pimlott, *Hugh Dalton* (London, 1985), pp. 622–3.

43.   Jay, *Change and Fortune*, p. 247.

44.   Denis Healey, *The Time of My Life* (London, 1989), p. 154.

45.   C. A. R. Crosland, *The Future of Socialism* (London, 1956) pp. 102ff.

46.   Cited in Campbell, *Nye Bevan*, p. 312.

47.   *Daily Telegraph*, 3 January 1956.

48.   *Manchester Guardian*, 9 January 1956.

49.   *The Times*, 19 January 1956; 'Notes of Prime Minister's Meeting with Newspaper Editors', 23 January 1956, PRO PREM 11/1539.

50.   Randolph Churchill, *The Rise and Fall of Sir Anthony Eden* (London, 1959), p. 10.

51.   *Sunday Times*, 22 January 1956.

52.   Eden diary, 3 January 1956, Avon Papers, AP20/1/32.

53.   *The Economist*, 14 January 1956.

54.   Donald MacLachlan, cited in Thompson, *Day Before Yesterday*, p. 122.

55.   Diary entry for 30 December 1955, cited in Horne, *Macmillan*, vol. I, p. 378.

56.   Macmillan to Eden, 11 February 1956, PRO PREM 11/1324.

57.   Bracken to Beaverbrook, 17 February 1956, cited in Carlton, *Eden*, pp. 396–7. At this time, according to Eden's Press Secretary, Macmillan was said to have wondered 'whether Anthony can stay in the saddle' (William Clark, *From Three Worlds: Memoirs* (London, 1986), p. 155).

58. Minute from Macmillan to Eden, 5 April 1956, PRO PREM 11/1326.
59. Cairncross (ed.), *Hall Diaries:* 28 March 1956, p. 65.
60. 'Notes for the PM at the 1922 Committee', 26 July 1956, Avon Papers, AP20/19/65.
61. 'Note to PM from Chloe Otto', 20 February 1956, Avon Papers, AP11/9/7.
62. *Manchester Guardian*, 11 June 1956.
63. Ramsden, *Age of Churchill and Eden*, pp. 294–303. See also Chapter 7 of this book for a detailed assessment of middle-class voters.
64. Drew Middleton (*New York Times*) to Winthrop Aldrich, 9 March 1956, cited in Carlton, *Eden*, p. 399.
65. Hubert Ashton to Butler, 8 March 1956, Butler Papers, A178; Howard, *RAB*, pp. 224–9.
66. Nigel Nicolson (ed.), *Harold Nicolson: Diaries and Letters*, vol. III, *1945–62* (London, 1968): diary entry for 26 July 1956, p. 305.
67. The Melton by-election of December 1956 produced a swing of 7.6 per cent to Labour, in line with Tonbridge.
68. *The Economist*, 8 December 1956.
69. Cited in Rhodes James, *Eden*, p. 567.
70. Butler, *Art of the Possible*, p. 194; diary notes, n.d. (1957), Butler Papers, G31, ff. 96–100.
71. L. Johnman, 'Defending the Pound: the Economics of the Suez Crisis, 1956', in T. Gorst, L. Johnman and W. S. Lucas (eds), *Postwar Britain 1945–64: Themes and Perspectives* (London, 1989), pp. 126–9.
72. Cited in Cosgrave, *Butler*, p. 119.
73. Nigel Birch MP: see Horne, *Macmillan*, vol. I, p. 453.
74. Enoch Powell, cited in Howard, *RAB*, pp. 240–1.
75. Bracken to Beaverbrook, 7 December 1956, cited in Carlton, *Eden*, p. 463.
76. Cited in Thompson, *Day Before Yesterday*, p. 160.
77. Ibid., p. 145.
78. K. Kyle, *Suez* (London, 1991), pp. 532–3.
79. V. Rothwell, *Anthony Eden* (Manchester, 1992), p. 245.
80. Bracken to Beaverbrook, 23 January 1957, cited in Carlton, *Eden*, pp. 463–4.
81. Bracken to Beaverbrook, 4 February 1957: Carlton, *Eden*, p. 465.
82. Cited in Horne, *Macmillan*, vol. I, p. 376.
83. Tony Lambton MP to Selwyn Lloyd, 22 November 1956: Selwyn Lloyd Papers, Churchill College, Cambridge, SELO 1/88.
84. Ramsden, *Age of Churchill and Eden*, pp. 318–19.
85. Edward Boyle to Hugh Trevor-Roper, 20 November 1956: Edward Boyle Papers, University of Leeds, MS 660/3871.
86. Pinto-Duschinsky, 'Bread and Circuses?', in Bogdanor and Skidelsky (eds), *Age of Affluence*, pp. 68–9.

Notes to Chapter 3: 'Never had it so good', 1957–9

1. *The Economist*, 20 July 1957.
2. Nicolson (ed.), *Harold Nicolson*: Nicolson to Vita Sackville-West, 26 June 1957, p. 335.
3. Kilmuir, *Political Adventure*, p. 285.
4. Butler, *Art of the Possible*, p. 195.
5. Harold Macmillan, *Riding the Storm, 1956–59* (London, 1971), pp. 184–5.
6. Foreign Secretary Selwyn Lloyd refused to give an opinion; Enoch Powell – a Butler supporter – said he was not asked (see A. Roth, *Enoch Powell: Tory Tribune* (London, 1970), p. 159).
7. E. Hughes, *Macmillan* (London, 1962), pp. 126–36; G. Sparrow, *RAB: Study of a Statesman* (London, 1965), pp. 138–48.
8. Macmillan, *Riding the Storm*, p. 184.
9. Kyle, *Suez*, p. 533.
10. Butler's diary account of the succession, February 1957, Butler Papers, G31, ff. 70–3. Kilmuir's diary for 9 January 1957 notes that the Chief Whip thought 'that the whole party would follow H[arold] while some might not follow R[ab]' (Kilmuir Papers, Churchill College, Cambridge, 1/5).
11. Memorandum of 'confidential exchange with Chief Whip', 21 February 1957, Butler Papers, G31, f. 76.
12. Henry Fairlie, *The Life of Politics* (London, 1968), p. 61.
13. D. R. Thorpe, *The Uncrowned Prime Ministers* (London, 1980), p. 209.
14. Rab note on relations with WSC, March 1957, Butler Papers, G31, ff. 89–91.
15. *The Economist*, 12 January 1957. Ramsden, *Age of Churchill and Eden*, p. 322, notes that the collective mood of the party post-Suez was that 'it was better to have tried and failed than not to have tried at all'.
16. Butler's diary account, February 1957, Butler Papers, G31, ff. 70–3. Butler also told a colleague he had not 'got it' because 'Cabinet were against' and because of the influence of the 'society and press network' (note by Patrick Buchan-Hepburn, 10 January 1957: Lord Hailes Papers, Churchill College, Cambridge, 4/12).
17. Fairlie, *Life of Politics*, p. 61. One MP wrote that there was a feeling before Christmas that Macmillan was 'playing a political game'. Withdrawal from Suez would make Eden's position impossible and it 'may be that HM . . . fancies himself as the chief salvager of the moment' (Lambton to Selwyn Lloyd, 2 December 1956: Lloyd Papers, SELO 1/88).
18. Cited in Horne, *Macmillan*, vol. II, p. 7. Horne adds (p. 8) that by keeping on his close ally Selwyn Lloyd, Macmillan hoped to maintain control of foreign policy.
19. Lord Hill, *Both Sides of the Hill* (London, 1964), p. 235.
20. Earl of Swinton, *Sixty Years of Power: Some Memories of the Men who Wielded It* (London, 1966), p. 172.

21. Macmillan, *Riding the Storm*, pp. 185 and 198–200.
22. Hugh Massingham, *The Observer*, 12 May 1957.
23. Cited in J. Ramsden, 'From Churchill to Heath', in Lord Butler (ed.), *The Conservatives* (London, 1977), p. 449.
24. *The Times*, 22 July 1957.
25. Cabinet Minutes, 31 January 1957, PRO CAB 128/31.
26. 'Memorandum by the Chancellor of the Exchequer', 30 April 1957, PRO CAB 128/31.
27. Macmillan, *Riding the Storm*: diary entry for 15 March 1957, p. 346.
28. Cabinet Minutes, 14 March 1957, PRO CAB 128/31.
29. Cabinet Minutes, 1 August 1957, PRO CAB 128/31.
30. Brittan, *Steering the Economy*, pp. 209–12.
31. Cabinet Minutes, 12 September 1957, PRO CAB 128/31.
32. 'Copy of Statement by Mr Harold Wilson on ITV News on Friday 20th September 1957', Labour Party Parliamentary Committee Minutes, 23 September 1957.
33. S. Haseler, *The Gaitskellites: Revisionism in the British Labour Party* (London, 1969), pp. 99–111.
34. *The Economist*, 20 April 1957.
35. Comments by Charles Hill, Chancellor of the Duchy of Lancaster: Minutes of the 3rd Meeting of the Policy Study Group, 1 April 1957, CRD 2/53/24.
36. Fisher, *Macmillan*, p. 196.
37. 'Some Notes on the Present Situation', memorandum by Michael Fraser, 20 September 1957, PRO PREM 11/2248.
38. Thorneycroft to Macmillan, 8 December 1957, PRO PREM 11/2306.
39. Thorneycroft to Macmillan, 19 December 1957, PRO PREM 11/2306.
40. Cited in Macmillan, *Riding the Storm*, p. 363.
41. Cabinet Minutes, 31 December 1957, PRO CAB 128/31.
42. Cabinet Minutes, 3 January 1958, PRO CAB 128/31.
43. Boyd-Carpenter, *Way of Life*, pp. 137–9.
44. Cabinet Minutes, 5 January 1958, PRO CAB 128/31.
45. Macmillan diary, 7 January 1958, cited in Horne, *Macmillan*, vol. II, p. 73.
46. Lord Hailsham, *The Door Wherein I Went* (London, 1975), p. 163.
47. Speech notes on after-effects of Chancellor's resignation, n.d., Butler Papers, G32, f. 63; *The Sunday Times*, 12 January 1958.
48. PLP Minutes, 22 January 1958; *The Times*, 20 January 1958.
49. Butler to Macmillan, 14 February 1958, PRO PREM 11/2227.
50. *The Economist*, 15 February 1958.
51. Diary, 31 January 1958, cited in Horne, *Macmillan*, vol. II, p. 78.
52. Cited in G. Hutchinson, *The Last Edwardian at No. 10* (London, 1980), p. 69.
53. *The Economist*, 11 and 18 January 1958.
54. Nigel Birch, cited in Thompson, *Day Before Yesterday*, p. 166.
55. Lord Hailsham, *A Sparrow's Flight: Memoirs* (London, 1990), pp. 318–19.

56. Interview cited in Horne, *Macmillan*, vol. ii, p. 76.
57. 'Draft Report on Rochdale', 28 February 1958, CRD 2/21/4; *The Economist*, 15 February 1958.
58. Lord Boyle, cited in Thompson, *Day Before Yesterday*, p. 169.
59. Cabinet Minutes, 13 May 1958, PRO CAB 128/32.
60. Macmillan diary, 6 May 1958: *Riding the Storm*, p. 713.
61. Cabinet Minutes, 4 June 1958, PRO CAB 128/32; G. Goodman, *The Awkward Warrior. Frank Cousins: His Life and Times* (London, 1979), pp. 183–5.
62. *The Economist*, 28 June 1958.
63. Macmillan to Amory, 5 April 1958, PRO PREM 11/2305; Macmillan diary, 14 March 1958, cited in Horne, *Macmillan*, vol. ii, p. 141.
64. Interview with Amory, cited in Horne, *Macmillan*, vol. ii, p. 141; Prime Minister's Comments on Treasury paper, 23 October 1958, PRO PREM 11/2311.
65. P. M. Williams, *Hugh Gaitskell* (Oxford, 1982 edn), pp. 460–4.
66. PLP Minutes, 13 February 1958.
67. Kilmuir, *Political Adventure*, p. 291.
68. *The Economist*, 19 April, 24 May and 21 June 1958.
69. 'Gallup Polls and the General Election. Regional Analysis', 24 March 1959, CRD 2/21/5.
70. *The Economist*, 11 April 1959.
71. N. Fisher, *Iain Macleod* (London, 1973), p. 133.
72. Hailsham to Macmillan, 15 April 1959, copy in Butler Papers, G34, f. 22.
73. *The Economist*, 25 July 1959.
74. Steering Committee Minutes, 12 March 1958, CRD 2/53/27.
75. Fisher, *Macleod*, p. 136.
76. Williams, *Gaitskell*, p. 489.
77. Horne, *Macmillan*, vol. ii, p. 146.
78. Hailsham, *Sparrow's Flight*, p. 324.
79. 'General Election 1959', Report by National Opinion Polls, CCO 4/8/104.
80. Charles Curran MP, cited in Harold Evans (ed.), *Downing Street Diary: The Macmillan Years, 1957–63* (London, 1981), p. 44.
81. *News Chronicle*, 10 October 1959.
82. CRD, 'Report on General Election 1959', October 1959, CRD 2/48/72.
83. 'General Election 1959. Report of Election Sub-Committee', NEC Minutes, 28 October 1959.
84. D. E. Butler and R. Rose, *The British General Election of 1959* (London, 1960), p. 23.
85. 'General Secretary's Preliminary Report on General Election', NEC Minutes, 28 October 1959.
86. CRD, 'Report on Election', CRD 2/48/72.
87. *Sunday Times*, 11 October 1959; *Sunday Telegraph*, 11 October 1959.
88. *The Times*, 10 October 1959.

89. *The Economist*, 17 October 1959. The resilience of Labour support is
     argued in M. Donnelly, 'Labour Politics and the Affluent Society
     1951–64', unpublished Surrey University PhD (1994), e.g. p. 235,
     which notes that Labour's average share of the vote in 1955 and 1959
     was 45.1 per cent, remarkably high in the context of elections since
     the First World War.
90. Butler to Lord Hailes, 12 May 1958, Butler Papers, G. 32, f. 87;
     Cabinet Minutes, 24 July 1958, PRO CAB 125/32.

Notes to Chapter 4: 'Mac: The End', 1959–63

1. Butler letter to constituency chairmen, 9 December 1959: Butler
    Papers, G34, f. 161.
2. Macmillan to Selwyn Lloyd, 26 September 1960, PRO PREM 11/
    3883.
3. The term 'all-class party' was coined by Butler in an interview with
    the *Yorkshire Post* (Butler Papers, May 1960, G35, ff. 136–45).
4. *The Economist*, 16 April 1960.
5. *The Economist*, 31 October 1959.
6. Howard, *RAB*, p. 278.
7. Selwyn Lloyd diary, 1 November 1959: cited in D. R. Thorpe, *Selwyn
    Lloyd* (London, 1989), p. 296.
8. 'Note for Record of Meeting between Prime Minister and Chancel-
    lor', 1 July 1959, PRO PREM 11/2662; Macmillan to Amory, 27
    February 1960, PRO PREM 11/2962.
9. Butler, handwritten notes, 15 March 1960: Butler Papers, G35, f. 121.
10. Martin Redmayne to Buchan-Hepburn, 25 April 1960, Hailes Papers,
    4/7; *The Times*, 5 April 1960; *The Economist*, 9 April 1960.
11. Macmillan diary, 3 and 27 April 1960: *Pointing the Way, 1959–61*
    (London, 1972), pp. 224 and 226.
12. Minute from Amory to Macmillan, 27 June 1960, PRO PREM 11/
    3291.
13. *The Times*, 28 July 1960; *The Economist*, 30 July 1960. Macmillan
    persuaded a reluctant Selwyn Lloyd to leave the Foreign Office by
    suggesting that the Treasury might be a step towards the party
    leadership: 'he was sure Butler could not lead the party – he would
    not hand over to him'. He also offered the prospect of at least three
    years in the new post (Lloyd diary, 24 May and 10 June 1960: Selwyn
    Lloyd Papers, SELO 4/22).
14. Macmillan diary, 30 July 1960: *Pointing the Way*, p. 234.
15. Jay, *Change and Fortune*, pp. 272–5.
16. R. Winstone (ed.), *Tony Benn. Years of Hope: Diaries, Letters and Papers,
    1940–1962* (London, 1994): 28 November 1959, p. 320.
17. I. McLean, 'Labour since 1945', in C. Cook and J. Ramsden (eds),
    Trends in British Politics since 1945 (London, 1978), p. 48.

18. Jay, *Change and Fortune*, p. 277.

19. S. Crosland, *Tony Crosland* (London, 1982), p. 93.

20. D. Marquand, *The Progressive Dilemma: From Lloyd George to Kinnock* (London, 1991), pp. 133–4.

21. NEC minutes, 22 June 1960.

22. Gaitskell secured 161 votes to Wilson's 88 – see Pimlott, *Wilson*, pp. 240–5.

23. Benn, *Years of Hope*: 3 November 1960, p. 352.

24. NEC Minutes, 13 July 1960, when a gloomy report was presented by Morgan Phillips on 'The State of the Party'.

25. *The Economist*, 25 February 1961.

26. *Daily Mail*, 28 July 1960; *The Economist*, 22 October 1960.

27. *The Times*, 18 April 1961.

28. Evans, *Downing Street Diary*: 29 July 1961, p. 153; *The Economist*, 29 July 1961.

29. Butler to Macmillan, 14 July 1961: Butler Papers, G37, f. 38. See also Macmillan to Lady Ava Waverley, 12 August 1961: Macmillan Papers, Bodleian Library, Oxford, MS. Eng. His. c. 4778, ff. 95–104.

30. Macmillan diary, 16 September and 10 October 1961: *At the End of the Day, 1961–63* (London, 1973), pp. 40–1. Macleod formally entered the Cabinet as Chancellor of the Duchy of Lancaster.

31. Butler to Lord Home, 1 October 1961: Butler Papers, G36, f. 69.

32. Macmillan diary, 20 November and 20 December 1961: *End of the Day*, pp. 45–6.

33. Evans, *Downing Street Diary*, 3 and 4 February 1962, pp. 181–3.

34. Cited in Thorpe, *Lloyd*, p. 334.

35. Macmillan diary, 7 April 1962: cited in Horne, *Macmillan*, vol. ii, p. 338.

36. 'Transcript of Prime Minister's remarks to Cabinet on 28 May 1962', PRO PREM 11/3930.

37. Evans, *Downing Street Diary*: 3 June 1962, p. 199. See also Ramsden, *Winds of Change: Macmillan to Heath*, pp. 163–4.

38. E.g. in London, 50 of 66 net gains came in the area covered by eight parliamentary marginals – 'Local Election Results', NEC Minutes, 4 July 1962.

39. *The Times*, 15 March 1962; Minutes of the Chairman's Committee, 26 March 1962: CPA, CRD 2/52/8.

40. 'The Political Situation, Spring 1962', memorandum by Macleod, 27 April 1962: copy in Butler Papers, H31, ff. 40–50.

41. Macmillan diary, 24 March and 7 April 1962: *End of the Day*, pp. 59 and 63.

42. Paul Channon to Butler, 23 and 24 May 1962: Butler Papers, F96, ff. 1–2.

43. Macmillan diary, 22 June 1962: *End of the Day*, p. 89.

44. Macmillan diary, 8 July 1962: cited in Horne, *Macmillan*, vol. ii, p. 342.

45. Typed account of the events of 12–13 July (written September 1962): Lloyd papers, SELO 4/22.

46. Watkinson, *Turning Points*, p. 162.
47. Handwritten notes by Selwyn Lloyd: Lloyd Papers, SELO 4/22/.
48. Cited in Thorpe, *Lloyd*, p. 353.
49. Benn, *Years of Hope*: July 1962, p. 418.
50. Watkinson, *Turning Points*, p. 161.
51. Macmillan diary, 14 July 1962: *End of the Day*, p. 97.
52. Handwritten notes, 10 January 1963: Butler Papers, G40, ff. 4–5.
53. *Daily Telegraph*, 21 July 1962.
54. Jay, *Change and Fortune*, p. 291. This was echoed by Jeremy Thorpe's jibe that 'Greater love hath no man than that he lay down his friends for his life'.
55. *The Times*, 14 July 1962.
56. K. Alderman, 'Harold Macmillan's "Night of the Long Knives"', *Contemporary Record*, 6: 2 (1992), pp. 261–2.
57. Reginald Bevins, *The Greasy Pole* (London, 1965), p. 138
58. Cited in Thorpe, *Lloyd*, p. 354.
59. Handwritten notes, 10 November 1962: Butler Papers, G38, f. 29.
60. Evans, *Downing Street Diary*: 25 November 1962, p. 230.
61. Handwritten notes, 1 December 1962: Butler Papers, G40, f. 30; Fraser to Butler, 15 January 1963: Butler Papers, H50, ff. 226–7.
62. Maudling to Macmillan, 23 October 1962, PRO PREM 11/3753; comments by William Rees-Mogg and Michael Fraser, Minutes of the Chairman's Committee, 26 November 1962: CPA, CRD 2/52/8.
63. *The Times*, 15 January 1963.
64. Jay, *Change and Fortune*, pp. 287–8.
65. On the first ballot Wilson won 115 votes to Brown's 88 and Callaghan's 41. After Callaghan dropped out, Wilson defeated Brown on the second ballot by 144 to 103.
66. Morgan (ed.), *Crossman Diary*: 5 March 1963, pp. 983–6.
67. Pimlott, *Wilson*, p. 266.
68. Jay, *Change and Fortune*, p. 295; A. Howard and R. West, *The Making of the Prime Minister* (London, 1965), p. 38.
69. Morgan (ed.), *Crossman Diary*: 8 October 1963, p. 1026.
70. D. Butler and A. King, *The British General Election of 1964* (London, 1965), p. 79; Minute to officials from Macmillan on 'Tasks Ahead', 26 December 1962, PRO PREM 11/4412; Macmillan to Maudling, 20 February 1963, PRO PREM 11/4202.
71. Macmillan to Lady Waverley, 28 January 1963, Macmillan Papers, MS. Eng. His. 4779, f. 36; 'Memorandum on Taxation Policy 1963', Taxation Policy Committee, 10 December 1962: CPA, CRD 2/10/19.
72. Evans, *Downing Street Diary*: 7 April 1963, p. 260. *The Economist*, 6 April 1963, summed up that Captain Maudling's motto was 'half-speed ahead'.
73. Handwritten notes, 7 March 1963: Butler Papers, G40.
74. For detailed accounts of the Profumo case, see W. Young, *The Profumo Affair: Aspects of Conservatism* (London, 1963) and C. Irving *et al.*, *Scandal '63: A Study of the Profumo Affair* (London, 1963).

75. Evans, *Downing Street Diary*: 24 March 1963, p. 259; Macmillan diary, 7 July 1963: *End of the Day*, p. 442.
76. *Daily Mirror*, 8 June 1963; *Sunday Times*, 9 June 1963; *The Times*, 11 June 1963.
77. Evans, *Downing Street Diary*: 23 June 1963, p. 279.
78. H. of C. Deb., 5s, vol. 679, c. 99.
79. Macmillan diary, 7 July 1963: *End of the Day*, p. 442.
80. *Daily Mail*, 18 June 1963; *Daily Telegraph*, 18 June 1963.
81. *Guardian*, 18 June 1963; *Private Eye*, June–July 1963.
82. Cited in Thompson, *Day Before Yesterday*, p. 217.
83. Account by Paul Channon of 1922 Committee meeting, 27 June 1963: Butler Papers, G41, ff. 21–4.
84. Shepherd, *Macleod*, p. 298; Macmillan diary, 2 August 1963, cited in Horne, *Macmillan*, vol. II, p. 488. See also Lamb, *The Macmillan Years*, pp. 479–81, which names the Minister of Transport Ernest Marples as the 'important minister', and notes that the Denning Report eventually omitted any reference to these allegations.
85. Evans, *Downing Street Diary*: 23 June 1963, pp. 276–8.
86. *The Times*, 24 June 1963; Reginald Maudling, *Memoirs* (London, 1978), p. 124
87. Confidential typed note, 31 July 1963: Butler Papers, G40.
88. Evans, *Downing Street Diary*: 28 July and 4 August 1963, pp. 284–6.
89. Confidential typed note, 12 July 1963: Butler Papers, G40. The young Labour hopeful Brian Walden wrote to Edward Boyle: 'I think we will win the election, but I do not accept the present state of your party as being likely to last. The mere fact of a dissolution will bring a whole pile of instinctive Conservative voters back to you. . . Many of your present troubles I think can be traced back to the old malady of "too long in office"' (22 June 1963, Boyle Papers, 660/5493).
90. Horne, *Macmillan*, vol. II, pp. 484–94.
91. *The Economist*, 22 June 1963; Herbert Ashton MP to Butler, 19 September 1963: Butler Papers, G40.
92. E.g. *The Times*, 27 September 1963; *Daily Mirror*, 27 September 1963.
93. Evans, *Downing Street Diary*: 29 September and 6 October 1963, pp. 291 and 293; Macmillan diary, 6 October 1963: *End of the Day*, p. 497.
94. Evans, *Downing Street Diary*: 13 October 1963, p. 299.
95. M. Pinto-Duschinsky, 'From Macmillan to Home, 1959–64', in Hennessy and Seldon (eds), *Ruling Performance*, pp. 155–6. Richard Lamb in the *Macmillan Years* argues he was 'by far the best of Britain's post-war Prime Ministers' (p. 15).
96. Turner, *Macmillan*, pp. 250–1 and 273–5.
97. William Rees-Mogg, cited in the Minutes of the Party Chairman's Committee, 4 February 1963: CPA, CRD 2/52/9.
98. Macmillan diary, 16 September 1961, *End of the Day*, p. 39; *Guardian*, 10 January 1962; comment by Lord Carr, former MP: '1961–64: Did the Conservatives Lose Direction?', *Contemporary Record*, 2: 5 (1989), p. 28.

99. Minutes of the Chairman's Committee, 17 July 1962: CPA, CRD 2/52/8.

Notes to Chapter 5: The Stagnant Society

1. *The Economist*, 14 September 1963.
2. S. Newton and D. Porter, *Modernisation Frustrated: The Politics of Industrial Decline in Britain since 1900* (London, 1988), p. 120.
3. Pinto-Duschinsky, 'From Macmillan to Home', in Hennessy and Seldon (eds), *Ruling Performance*, p. 166. The full implication of these last figures was of course only apparent with hindsight.
4. Cited in D. Porter, 'Downhill All the Way: Thirteen Tory Years 1951–64', in R. Coopey, S. Fielding and N. Tiratsoo (eds), *The Wilson Governments, 1964–70* (London, 1993), p. 23.
5. J. W. Durcan, W. E. J. McCarthy and G. P. Redman, *Strikes in Postwar Britain: A Study of Stoppages of Work Due to Industrial Disputes, 1946–73* (London, 1983), Chapters 3 and 4.
6. H. Pelling, *A History of British Trade Unionism* (London, 1987 edn), pp. 243–9.
7. *The Economist*, 24 November 1951 and 15 July 1961.
8. Michael Shanks, *The Stagnant Society*, pp. 53–5.
9. Ibid., p. 67.
10. Ibid., pp. 60–1.
11. Ibid., pp. 78–93.
12. Pelling, *Trade Unionism*, p. 262. See also P. Stead, 'I'm All Right Jack', *History Today*, 46: 1 (1996), pp. 49–54.
13. John Cole, 'The Price of Obstinacy', in Arthur Koestler (ed.), *Suicide of a Nation? An Enquiry into the State of Britain* (London, 1963), pp. 106–7 and 123. The articles in this collection had first appeared in a special edition of *Encounter Magazine* in 1963.
14. Andrew Shonfield, *British Economic Policy since the War* (Harmondsworth, 1958), pp. 276–98.
15. Nicholas Davenport, *The Split Society* (London, 1964), pp. 66–8.
16. Bevins, *Greasy Pole*, p. 148.
17. *The Spectator*, 23 September 1955. The term had first been used by A. J. P. Taylor, who spoke of no other country in Europe having an 'Establishment so clearly defined and so secure' (*New Statesman*, 8 August 1953).
18. Hugh Thomas (ed.), *The Establishment* (London, 1959), pp. 15–20.
19. Ibid., pp. 83–126.
20. Anthony Sampson, *Anatomy of Britain* (London, 1962), pp. xi–21.
21. Ibid., pp. 175–81.
22. Ibid., pp. 195–201.
23. Ibid., pp. 193 and 217.
24. Ibid., pp. 622–4 and 637–8.

25. G. A. Almond and S. Verba, *The Civic Culture: Political Attitudes and Democracy in Five Nations* (New Jersey, 1963), pp. 455–6.

26. BBC2, 'Frost in the Air', documentary transmitted 29 August 1993.

27. Goronwy Rees, 'Amateurs and Gentleman', in Koestler (ed.), *Suicide of a Nation?*, pp. 40–1. Rees disputed the idea of some 'kind of secret society . . . a genteel Mafia', arguing that 'if there were, things might be a good deal better than they are, for it is at least better that a country's affairs should be administered by a secret society than by no one at all'.

28. Shanks, 'The Comforts of Stagnation', in Koestler (ed.), *Suicide of a Nation?*, pp. 66–7.

29. W. L. Guttsman, *The British Political Elite* (London, 1963), p. 388.

30. Autobiographical fragment, n.d.: Monckton Papers, dep. 49.

31. For a hostile view of Tory industrial policy, see A. Roberts, *Eminent Churchillians* (London, 1994), pp. 243–85. See also the perceptive study by R. Taylor, *The Trade Union Question in British Politics: Government and Unions since 1945* (Oxford, 1993), pp. 82–7.

32. K. Middlemas, *Power, Competition and the State*, vol. 1: *Britain in Search of Balance, 1940–61* (London, 1986), pp. 226–46.

33. *The Economic Implications of Full Employment*, Cmd 1417, March 1956, p. 17.

34. Eden minute to Lord Privy Seal, 10 April 1956: Eden Papers, AP20/21/60.

35. Taylor, *Trade Union Question*, pp. 102–6; N. Harris, *Competition and the Corporate Society: British Conservatives, the State and Industry, 1945–1964* (London, 1972), p. 157.

36. 'Note on Trade Unions and Unofficial Strikes', 30 May 1962: CPA, CRD 2/7/4; memo by Bishop to Macmillan, 17 April 1961: PRO PREM 11/3481.

37. 'Transcript of Prime Minister's Remarks to Cabinet', 28 May 1962: PRO PREM 11/3930.

38. CRD Report, 'Policy for Incomes', 17 April 1962: CPA, CRD 2/52/4.

39. Note by T. Bligh to Macmillan, 18 May 1962: PRO PREM 11/4071. See also K. Phillips and M. Wilson, 'The Conservative Party from Macmillan to Thatcher', in N. Nugent and R. King (eds), *The British Right: Conservative and Right-Wing Politics in Britain* (Farnborough, 1977), pp. 50–3.

40. K. Middlemas, *Power, Competition and the State*, vol. 2: *Threats to the Postwar Settlement, 1961–74* (London, 1990), pp. 254–6.

41. Seldon, 'Churchill Administration', in Hennessy and Seldon (eds), *Ruling Performance*, pp. 77–8.

42. P. Hennessy, *Whitehall* (London, 1989), p. 138. Brook, a product of Wolverhampton Grammar School, was an exception in reaching the top of the civil service in the 1950s. Macmillan told Lord Moran he had pure 'inborn judgement because, as I expect you know, he has no background' (Moran, *Churchill*: 3 August 1959, pp. 795–6).

43. Pimlott, *Wilson*, pp. 276–81.

44. Sampson, *Anatomy*, pp. 56–7; Guttsman, *Political Elite*, p. 312; S. E. Finer, H. B. Berrington and D. J. Bartholomew, *Backbench Opinion in the House of Commons, 1955–59* (Oxford, 1961), Chapter 3.
45. R. Samuel, 'The Deference Voter', *New Left Review*, 1 (January–February 1960), pp. 11–13.
46. Porter, 'Downhill', pp. 22–3.
47. *The Economist*, 14 September 1963.
48. Shanks, 'Comforts of Stagnation', p. 59.
49. Shanks, *Stagnant Society*, pp. 173–4.
50. Ramsden, *Winds of Change*, p. 8.
51. Henry Fairlie, 'On the Comforts of Anger', in Koestler (ed.), *Suicide of a Nation?*, pp. 19–28.
52. Sampson, *Anatomy*, p. 633; Graham Hutton, 'The United Kingdom Economy 1951–61: Performance and Retrospect', *Lloyds Bank Review*, (July 1961), pp. 3–4.
53. *The Economist*, 14 September 1963.
54. Koestler (ed.), *Suicide of a Nation?*, pp. 13 and 238; Davenport, *Split Society*, p. 84.
55. A. Gamble, *Britain in Decline: Economic Policy, Political Strategy and the British State* (London, 1985 edn), pp. 116–17; B. Levin, *The Pendulum Years: Britain and the Sixties* (London, 1970), p. 201; Pinto-Duschinsky, 'From Macmillan to Home', pp. 168–9.
56. *The Economist*, 14 September 1963.

Notes to Chapter 6: The Opportunity State

1. Koestler, *Suicide of a Nation?*, p. 239.
2. Kavanagh and Morris, *Consensus Politics from Attlee to Thatcher*. See also Timmins, *The Five Giants*, Chapter 11. Timmins argues that if consensus is defined as meaning unanimity, 'clearly, there was not'; but if the definition 'trend of opinion' is used, 'it can convincingly be argued there was' (*Guardian*, 11 October 1995).
3. B. Pimlott, 'Is Postwar Consensus a Myth?', *Contemporary Record*, 2: 6 (1989), pp. 12–14. See also figures cited in G. C. Peden, *British Economic and Social Policy: Lloyd George to Margaret Thatcher* (Hemel Hempstead, 1991 edn), pp. 178–9.
4. Lowe, *Welfare State*, p. 85.
5. Glennerster, *British Social Policy*, pp. 70–5.
6. Cronin, *State Expansion*, p. 212.
7. Norman Brook to Churchill, 2 February 1953, PRO PREM 11/658.
8. *The Economist*, 29 May 1954.
9. Harriet Jones, 'New Tricks for an Old Dog', in Gorst, Johnman and Scott Lucas (eds), *Contemporary British History*, pp. 35–40.
10. Cronin, *State Expansion*, p. 215.

11. S. Beer, *Modern British Politics* (London, 1982 edn), pp. 355–69.
12. Sir Richard Clarke, *Public Expenditure, Management and Control: The Development of the Public Expenditure Survey Committee (PESC)* (London, 1978), p. 8.
13. Rodney Lowe, 'Resignation at the Treasury: the Social Services Committee and the Failure to Reform the Welfare State, 1955–57', *Journal of Social Policy*, 18: 4 (1989), pp. 505–17.
14. Memo by Butler on the Social Services Committee, June 1956; note by C. G. Thorley, 7 November 1956, PRO T 227/490.
15. Rodney Lowe, 'The Replanning of the Welfare State, 1957–64', in M. Francis *et al.* (eds), *The Conservatives and British Society, 1880–1990* (forthcoming, 1996).
16. Clarke, *Public Expenditure*, pp. 2–3 and 25–38. The rapid growth in the run-up to the election ensured there was a rise in the social spending share of GDP across the 1951–64 period as a whole, from 16.1 per cent to 19.3 per cent (A. Walker (ed.), *Public Expenditure and Social Policy* (London, 1982), p. 28). See also Rodney Lowe, 'Milestone or Millstone? The 1959–61 Plowden Committee and its Impact on British Welfare Policy', *The Historical Journal* (forthcoming, 1997).
17. Minutes of the Research Department Taxation Committee, 15 July 1960: CPA, CRD 2/10/19.
18. Minutes of the Chairman's Committee, 17 July 1962: CPA, CRD 2/52/8.
19. Ibid.
20. P. Baldwin, *The Politics of Social Solidarity: Class Bases of the European Welfare State, 1875–1975* (Cambridge, 1990), p. 240.
21. Peden, *British Economic and Social Policy*, pp. 187–8.
22. Glennerster, *British Social Policy*, pp. 89–90.
23. A. Deacon, 'Spending More to Achieve Less? Social Security since 1945', in D. Gladstone (ed.), *British Social Welfare: Past, Present and Future* (London, 1995), p. 78.
24. C. Webster, *The Health Services since the War*, vol. 1 (London, 1988), pp. 389–93.
25. Ibid., pp. 187–200.
26. Cmd 9663, *Committee of Enquiry into the Cost of the National Health Service* (London, 1956).
27. Harriet Jones, 'The Conservative Party and the Welfare State, 1942–1955', unpublished London University PhD thesis (1992) pp. 319–29.
28. Papers on the insurance basis of NHS funding, PRO CAB 128/30.
29. Timmins, *Five Giants*, pp. 209–10.
30. Helen Jones, *Health and Society in Twentieth-Century Britain* (London, 1994), pp. 117–43.
31. Webster, *Health Services*, p. 399.
32. Paper by J. Udal on Housing, 22 January 1958: CPA, CRD 2/23/24.
33. Macmillan, *Tides of Fortune*, pp. 287–8; Butler, *Art of the Possible*, p. 129.
34. D. Donnison and C. Ungerson, *Housing Policy* (Harmondsworth, 1982), pp. 113–53.

35. Memorandum by Lord Woolton, 20 June 1952, PRO CAB 129/53.
36. Macmillan to Butler, 21 May 1953, PRO Housing and Local Government (HLG) papers 101/433.
37. Cmd 8996, *Houses: The Next Step* (London, 1953).
38. J. R. Short, *Housing in Britain: The Postwar Experience* (London, 1982), pp. 47–52.
39. Timmins, *Five Giants*, pp. 189–90; M. Halcrow, *Keith Joseph: A Single Mind* (London, 1989), p. 31.
40. 'Future Housing Policy', memorandum by Henry Brooke, 25 February 1960, PRO PREM 11/3389.
41. J. Burnett, *A Social History of Housing, 1815–1985* (London, 1986 edn), pp. 301–2.
42. 'Tory Housing Discontents', note for Keith Joseph, 17 July 1962: CPA, CRD 2/23/24.
43. Lowe, *Welfare State*, pp. 235–8.
44. Note by Ministry of Education on Select Committee Report, 23 June 1953, PRO Education (ED) papers 136/853.
45. Roy Lowe, *Education in the Post-War Years: A Social History* (London, 1988), pp. 89–90.
46. 'Reduction of Capital Expenditure for Education', memorandum by Geoffrey Lloyd, 11 October 1957, PRO ED 136/900.
47. Cited in I. G. K. Fenwick, *The Comprehensive School, 1944–70: The Politics of Secondary Reorganisation* (London, 1976), pp. 61–5.
48. Labour Party, *Challenge to Britain* (London, 1953).
49. Report of speech by Eccles in 'Note on Comprehensive Schools for [Conservative] Candidates', 29 April 1955, CPA, CCO 4/6/93.
50. 'Secondary Education', memorandum by Eccles, 20 April 1955, PRO ED 136/861. See also B. Simon, *Education and the Social Order, 1940–1990* (London, 1991), pp. 183–6.
51. Eden to Joint Committee of the Four Secondary Associations, 20 May 1955, PRO ED 147/209.
52. P. E. Vernon (ed.), *Secondary School Selection* (London, 1957), p. 17.
53. A. H. Halsey and L. Gardner, 'Selection for Secondary Education and Achievements in Four Grammar Schools', *British Journal of Sociology*, 4 (1953), p. 74.
54. Lowe, *Education in the Post-War Years*, pp. 108–13. See also J. Floud, A. H. Halsey and E. M. Martin, *Social Class and Educational Opportunity* (London, 1957).
55. Lloyd to Macmillan, 24 December 1957, PRO ED 136/941.
56. Cmnd 604, *Secondary Education For All: A New Drive* (London, 1958)
57. Lloyd to I. D. Hamilton (Kemsley Newspapers), 3 December 1958; Macmillan to Edward Boyle, 14 January 1959, PRO ED 136/942.
58. J. W. B. Douglas, *The Home and the School: A Study of Ability and Attainment in the Primary School* (London, 1964).
59. Lowe, *Education in the Post-War Years*, p. 119.
60. Boyle to Macmillan, 3 July 1963, CPA, CRD 2/29/10; R. Rhodes James, 'In the House of Commons', in A. Gold (ed.), *Edward Boyle: His Life by His Friends* (London, 1991), p. 93.

61. Christopher Chataway, 'At the Education Ministry', in Gold (ed.), *Boyle*, p. 109.
62. C. Knight, *The Making of Tory Education Policy in Post-War Britain* (Brighton, 1990), p. 16.
63. *The Times Educational Supplement*, 18 September 1964.
64. Fenwick, *Comprehensive School*, pp. 93–4.
65. J. Vaizey, 'The Tragedy of Being Clever', in Koestler (ed.), *Suicide of a Nation?*, pp. 220–1.
66. M. Kogan, *The Politics of Education* (Harmondsworth, 1971), p. 90, quoting a view expressed by David Eccles. M. Hill, *The Welfare State in Britain: A Political History since 1945* (Aldershot, 1993), p. 61, employs the term 'cautious consolidators'.
67. Lowe, *Education in the Post-War Years*, p. 148.
68. See comments by Geoffrey Howe and Baroness Wootton, cited in Lowe, *Education in the Post-War Years*, pp. 79 and 119.
69. A. Simmonds, 'Conservative Governments and the Housing Question 1951–59', unpublished Leeds University PhD (1995) p. 20.
70. See minutes, reports and correspondence of the CRD Policy Committee on the Future of the Social Services, 1960–63: CPA, CRD 2/ 29/6–10.
71. R. Cockett, *Thinking the Unthinkable: Think Tanks and the Economic Counter Revolution, 1931–83* (London, 1994), pp. 159–63, notes that the likes of One Nation and the Bow Group were only groping their way towards a coherent Conservative view of welfare. Keith Joseph, who joined shortly after becoming an MP in 1956, said One Nation was 'compatible with Statism but did assert a Conservative emphasis upon private enterprise and voluntary services as essential to prosperity'.
72. Cronin, *State Expansion*, p. 16.
73. Lowe, 'Resignation at the Treasury', pp. 24–5; Lowe, *Welfare State*, p. 94.

Notes to Chapter 7: The Affluent Society

1. J. K. Galbraith, *The Affluent Society* (London, 1958).
2. M. Pinto-Duschinsky, 'Bread and Circuses? The Conservatives in Office, 1951–64', in Bogdanor and Skidelsky (eds), *Age of Affluence*, p. 77.
3. D. Middleton, *The British* (London, 1957), p. 127.
4. Butler and Rose, *General Election of 1959*, p. 15.
5. F. Zweig, *The Worker in an Affluent Society: Family Life and Industry* (London, 1961), p. ix.
6. H. Hopkins, *The New Look: A Social History of the Forties and Fifties in Britain* (London, 1963), pp. 161 and 351.
7. M. Abrams, 'The Home-Centred Society', *The Listener*, 26 November 1959.

8. M. Abrams, writing in *The Observer*, 23 August 1960.

9. G. Moorhouse, *Britain in the Sixties: The Other England* (Harmondsworth, 1964), pp. 164–5. Moorhouse rejected the idea of a simple division between north and south, noting for example the high unemployment rate in Cornwall. He did however (pp. 18–19) endorse the notion of a 'Golden Circle', whose perimeter 'is approximately one hour's travel by fast peak-hour train from the main London termini'.

10. B. Abel-Smith and P. Townsend, *The Poor and the Poorest: A New Analysis of Ministry of Labour's Family Expenditure Surveys* (London, 1965), pp. 65–6.

11. N. Mitford, 'The English Aristocracy', *Encounter*, 24 September 1955, p. 5.

12. M. Abrams, 'Class Distinctions in Britain', in *The Future of the Welfare State* (London, 1958), pp. 61–3.

13. There were several variations on this system of voter classification: many social scientists, for example, used the Registrar-General's multi-occupational grading scheme. In this chapter the A–E social groupings will be used throughout. On the importance of the women's vote, see I. Zweiniger-Bargielowska, 'Explaining the Gender Gap: the Conservative Party and the Women's Vote, 1945–64', in Francis *et al.* (eds), *Conservatives and British Society* (forthcoming, 1996).

14. R. Titmuss, *Income Distribution and Social Change* (London, 1962), p. 21.

15. Cited in J. Ryder and H. Silver, *Modern English Society: History and Structure 1850–1970* (London, 1970), p. 206.

16. Middleton, *The British*, p. 123: 'The ideal seemed to be a community of equals protected from economic dangers by full employment and high wages. . . Everyone earned about the same amount of money, spent it on the same things, and appeared to think and talk alike.'

17. P. Willmott and M. Young, *Family and Class in a London Suburb* (London, 1960), pp. 121–2. These findings were echoed in C. Rosser, *The Family and Social Change: A Study of Family and Kinship in a South Wales Town* (London, 1965), pp. 113–14.

18. J. Goldthorpe and D. Lockwood, 'Affluence and the British Class Structure', *Sociological Review*, II (1963), pp. 133–56.

19. Middleton, *The British*, p. 122.

20. Abrams, 'Class Distinctions', p. 68.

21. N. Tiratsoo, 'Popular Politics, Affluence and the Labour Party in the 1950s', in Gorst, Johnman and Scott Lucas (eds), *Contemporary British History*, p. 50.

22. B. Williamson, *The Temper of the Times: British Society since World War II* (Oxford, 1990), p. 109.

23. J. Bonham, 'The Middle Class Revolt', *Political Quarterly*, 33 (1962), p. 244.

24. G. H. Gallup (ed.), *The Gallup International Public Opinion Polls*, vol. 1 (New York, 1977): October 1959 and August 1964, pp. 544 and 751.

25. 'General Election Campaign 1951', Report by Morgan Phillips, 7 November 1951, NEC Minutes.

26. Butler, *General Election of 1951*, p. 248.

27. M. Benney and P. Geiss, 'Social Class and Politics in Greenwich', *British Journal of Sociology* (December 1950), pp. 326–7; M. Benney, A. P. Gray and R. H. Pear, *How People Vote: A Study of Electoral Behaviour in Greenwich* (London, 1956), pp. 114–20.

28. R. S. Milne and H. C. Mackenzie, *Straight Fight: A Study of Voting Behaviour in the Constituency of Bristol North-East at the General Election of 1951* (London, 1954), pp. 36–50.

29. A. H. Birch, *Small Town Politics: A Study of Political Life in Glossop* (Oxford, 1959), pp. 100–12. The same point was made more tentatively in P. Campbell *et al.*, 'Voting Behaviour in Droylesden in October 1951', *The Manchester School of Economic and Social Studies*, XX (1952), p. 62.

30. M. Stacey, *Tradition and Change: A Study of Banbury* (Oxford, 1960), pp. 41–56.

31. *The Observer*, 22 May 1955.

32. 'The General Election 1955', Report by Morgan Phillips, June 1955, NEC Minutes.

33. R. S. Milne and H. C. Mackenzie, *Marginal Seat: A Study of Voting Behaviour in the Constituency of Bristol North East at the General Election of 1955* (London, 1958), pp. 43, 91–2, 139 and 166.

34. 'Report on General Election 1955', CRD 2/48/54.

35. Ralph Harris, *Onward*, June 1955.

36. M. Abrams, 'Public Opinion Polls and Political Parties', *Public Opinion Quarterly*, XXVII (Spring 1963), pp. 10–18.

37. Cited in Tiratsoo, 'Popular Politics . . . and the Labour Party', p. 54.

38. M. Pawley, *Home Ownership* (London, 1978), pp. 70–2.

39. *Tribune*, 16 October 1959.

40. 'Report on General Election 1959', CRD 2/48/71.

41. Merlyn Rees, cited in S. Fielding, ' "White Heat" and White Collars', in Coopey, Fielding and Tiratsoo (eds), *The Wilson Governments*, p. 32. See also NEC Minutes, 28 October 1959; *Labour Organiser*, October/November 1959, pp. 183–4.

42. Samuel, 'The Deference Voter', *New Left Review*, (1960), p. 10.

43. 'The General Election of 1959', Report by National Opinion Polls (NOP), CCO 4/8/104.

44. M. Abrams and R. Rose, *Must Labour Lose?* (Harmondsworth, 1960), p. 58.

45. Material in this paragraph is taken from Public Opinion Group, 'First Report to the Chairman of the Conservative Party Organisation', Autumn 1960, CRD 2/21/6.

46. Samuel, 'Deference Voter', p. 9.

47. R. McKenzie and A. Silver, *Angels in Marble: Working-Class Conservatives in Urban England* (London, 1968), pp. 83–4 and 246–7.

48. E. Nordlinger, *The Working-Class Conservatives: Authority, Deference and Stable Democracy* (London, 1967), p. 175.

49. Abrams and Rose, *Must Labour Lose?*, pp. 97–8.

50. J. Goldthorpe, D. Lockwood, F. Bechhofer and J. Platt, *The Affluent Worker: Political Attitudes and Behaviour* (Cambridge, 1968), esp. pp. 73–82.
51. G. Mackenzie, 'The "Affluent Worker" Study: An Evaluation and Critique', in F. Parkin (ed.), *The Social Analysis of Class Structure* (London, 1974), pp. 237–52.
52. I. Crewe, 'The Politics of "Affluent" and "Traditional" Workers in Britain: An Aggregate Data Analysis', *British Journal of Political Science*, 3:1 (1973), pp. 29–52.
53. Cited in Goldthorpe *et al.*, *Affluent Worker*, p. 17.
54. 'General Election of 1959', Report by NOP, CC0 4/8/104.
55. *The Times*, 27 February 1956.
56. J. Bonham, *The Middle Class Vote* (London, 1954), pp. 10–19.
57. *The Times*, 27 February 1956.
58. *The Economist*, 28 April 1956.
59. *Sunday Times*, 10 June 1956.
60. *The Times*, 13 and 27 February 1956.
61. *The Times*, 12 June 1956.
62. Michael Fraser to Butler, 10 October 1956: Butler Papers, H36, ff. 120–1.
63. 'Monthly Summary of Reports [from Party Workers] on Public Opinion', November 1957, CC0 4/7/375.
64. Minutes of Conservative Steering Committee, 23 July 1958, CRD 2/53/31.
65. *The Economist*, 19 April, 24 May and 21 June 1956.
66. 'General Election of 1959', Report by NOP, CC0 4/8/104.
67. Memorandum by James Douglas, n.d. (1960): Psephology Group papers, CPA, CRD 2/21/6; 'Report on General Election 1959', CRD 2/48/72.
68. R. H. Pear, 'The Liberal Vote', *Political Quarterly*, 33 (1962), p. 247.
69. Macmillan, *End of the Day*: diary entries, 24–5 March 1962, pp. 58–60.
70. *The Economist*, 14 April 1962.
71. *The Economist*, 9 June 1962.
72. 'Non-Manual Workers and the Labour Party', Report by the Home Policy Committee, NEC Minutes, January 1960.
73. Fielding, '"White Heat" and White Collars' in Coopey, Fielding and Tiratsoo (eds), *Wilson Governments*, p. 39.
74. Milne and Mackenzie, *Marginal Seat*, pp. 169–72.
75. Public Opinion Group, 'First Report', Autumn 1960, CRD 2/21/6.
76. N. Tiratsoo, *Reconstruction, Affluence and Labour Politics: Coventry 1945–60* (London, 1990), pp. 114–20.
77. R. Waller, 'Conservative Electoral Support and Social Class', in Seldon and Ball (eds), *Conservative Century*, p. 596; Bonham, 'Middle-Class Revolt', pp. 240–1.

Notes to Chapter 8: Smart Alec vs Dull Alec, 1963–4

1. Pimlott, *Harold Wilson*, p. 319. See also textbook accounts such as that by A. Sked and C. Cook, *Post-War Britain: A Political History* (Harmondsworth, 1993 edn), pp. 212–15.
2. Macmillan, *End of the Day*: diary entry, 12 October 1963, p. 505.
3. Howard and West, *Making of the Prime Minister*, Chapter 4.
4. Randolph Churchill, *The Fight for the Tory Leadership* (London, 1964), p. 102.
5. Tony Benn, *Out of the Wilderness: Diaries 1963–67* (London, 1991 edn): 9 October 1963, p. 68.
6. Cited in Horne, *Macmillan*, vol. II, p. 549. Randolph Churchill had been seen handing out badges urging support for 'Q' (Quintin Hailsham), and Hailsham himself made much of attempting to feed his young daughter in public. 'Never discount the baby food' one observer recalled – cited in an article by D. R. Thorpe following the death of Douglas Home, *Sunday Telegraph*, 15 October 1995. This provided extracts from Thorpe's biography, *Alec Douglas-Home* (London, 1996), which appeared too late for consideration in this volume.
7. Typed note, c.20 October 1963, Butler Papers, G40.
8. Birch, later Lord Rhyl, cited in Thompson, *Day Before Yesterday*, p. 218.
9. Macmillan, *End of the Day*: diary entry, 17 October 1963, p. 514.
10. Churchill, *Fight for Leadership*, p. 136.
11. Diary entry, 18 October 1963, cited in Horne, *Macmillan*, vol. II, p. 565.
12. Interview with Anthony Howard, 21 November 1963, cited in Howard, *RAB*, p. 399.
13. Lord Home, *The Way the Wind Blows* (London, 1976), p. 185.
14. Iain Macleod, 'The Tory Leadership', *The Spectator*, 17 January 1964.
15. *The Observer*, 20 October 1963.
16. V. Bogdanor, 'The Selection of the Party Leader', in Seldon and Ball (eds), *Conservative Century*, pp. 78–9. For a more sceptical account of Macmillan's behaviour, see Ramsden, *Winds of Change*, pp. 196–208.
17. Diary entry, 14 October 1963, cited in Horne, *Macmillan*, vol. II, p. 556.
18. Bogdanor, 'Selection of Leader', p. 76.
19. Fisher, *Macleod*, p. 239; J. Campbell, *Edward Heath* (London, 1993), pp. 145–6. The Chief Whip conceded that he might have attached more weight to the views of some MPs than others, saying that after counting the votes for the various contenders, 'one then had to consider carefully the shade of opinions expressed . . . and take a certain objective view': 'The Commons in Action', transcript of BBC Radio interview, *The Listener*, 19 December 1963.
20. 'J. Enoch Powell on how Macmillan deceived the Queen', *The Spectator*, 13 October 1973: the seven ministers were named as Macleod, Maudling, Hailsham, Boyd-Carpenter, Errol, Boyle and

Powell. Lord Swinton was told by St Aldwyn on 18 October that 'the Cabinet prefer Rab', and that MPs' views were mixed, 'probably pro-Rab' (Swinton to Lady Swinton, 18 October 1963: Swinton Papers, Churchill College, Cambridge, 174/7/9).

21. Diary entry, 19 October 1963, cited in Horne, *Macmillan*, vol. II, p. 571.

22. Boyd-Carpenter, *Way of Life*, p. 174.

23. Fisher, *Macleod*, p. 243. Macleod in *The Spectator* concluded that 'the decisive roles in the selection of Lord Home as Prime Minister were played by Macmillan and Redmayne'.

24. Typed note, c.20 October 1963, Butler Papers, G40.

25. *Sunday Times*, 20 October 1963.

26. Maudling, *Memoirs*, p. 129. That Home's diffidence was superficial was confirmed in Macmillan's memo to the Queen, where he wrote that Lord Home 'is not ambitious in the sense of wanting to scheme for power, although not foolish enough to resist honour when it comes to him' – cited in Thorpe, *Sunday Telegraph*, 15 October 1995.

27. *Sunday Times*, 20 October 1963; Fisher, *Macleod*, p. 237.

28. *Daily Telegraph*, 18 October 1963; Hailsham, *Sparrow's Flight*, p. 356. Brian Walden wrote that historians would puzzle over the Tory attitude of ' "anybody but Butler". I know about Munich, and arrogance, and "best Prime Minister we have" etc., but . . . he more than anybody built the post-war Tory Party' (Walden to Boyle, 22 June 1963, Boyle Papers, 660/5493).

29. 1978 interview with Anthony Howard, cited in Howard, *RAB*, p. 322.

30. Bevins, *Greasy Pole*, p. 145.

31. Butler, *Art of the Possible*, p. 250. He nevertheless reflected on what might have been, asking a former Cabinet colleague years later over drinks as Master of Trinity College: 'Do you think that if I had stood firm in 1963 I would have been Prime Minister?' On being told yes, Butler added, 'I think so too' (Boyd-Carpenter, *Way of Life*, pp. 178–9).

32. *Daily Telegraph*, 18 October 1963; *Guardian*, 19 October 1963.

33. Channon to Butler, 18 October 1963, Butler Papers, G40. Local party workers also complained that Home was 'not the man to face a newly virile opponent at a general election in 9 months' (R. W. Eades to Boyle, 22 October 1963, Boyle papers, 660/5588).

34. Benn, *Out of the Wilderness*: 14 and 18 October 1963, p. 70.

35. Sked and Cook, *Post-War Britain*, p. 214.

36. *The Economist*, 16 November and 28 December 1963.

37. Howard and West, *Making of the Prime Minister*, p. 120. Kinross and West Perthshire was the parliamentary seat won by Home in a by-election shortly after he succeeded Macmillan. Ramsden, *Winds of Change*, pp. 214–15, notes how friendly newspapers pointed out that Home was the only Prime Minister to have played first-class cricket, for Eton against Harrow; yet it was the type of elector who thought this was not really first-class cricket 'who was so hard for Sir Alec to reach'.

38. Lord Windlesham, *Communication and Political Power* (London, 1966), pp. 65–7 and 79.

39. Minute by Martin Redmayne, 20 December 1963, PRO PREM 11/5154.

40. James Margach, *The Abuse of Power: The War between Downing Street and the Media from Lloyd George to Callaghan* (London, 1978), p. 132.

41. Jay, *Change and Fortune*, p. 294. See also Campbell, *Heath*, pp. 150–7, which shows how MPs were especially perturbed by the lack of consultation, one asking why the first main example of modernisation aimed to antagonise the government's friends rather than its enemies.

42. *The Economist*, 18 April 1964.

43. Sir Burke Trend (Cabinet Secretary) to Home, 20 July 1964, PRO PREM 11/4778.

44. Brittan, *Steering the Economy*, pp. 282–3, where it is argued that if the Conservatives were not willing to consider devaluation in the event of re-election (and Maudling insisted it was never discussed while he was Chancellor) then criticism that electoral expediency was paramount carries more weight.

45. Michael Fraser memo to Butler, 28 August 1964, Butler Papers, H53, f. 45.

46. Pimlott, *Wilson*, pp. 308–11.

47. K. Young, *Sir Alec Douglas-Home* (London, 1970), p. 209.

48. 'Situation Report', memo by Fraser, 17 April 1964, Butler Papers, H51, f. 276. Fraser added that while there was no great difference between 1959 and 1964 in terms of policy or record, five years ago voters were moderately happy with the government and suspicious of Labour, whereas the real problem now was that they 'tend to give Labour the benefit of every doubt, while being rather bored and unreceptive towards us'.

49. Cited in Butler and King, *The British General Election of 1964*, p. 110.

50. 'Do Campaigns Win Votes?', the Third Programme, transcript of BBC Radio Broadcast, 4 December 1964: introduced by David Butler and featuring party organisers Lord Blakenham, Len Williams (Labour) and Frank Byers (Liberal).

51. Benn, *Out of the Wilderness*: 29 September–1 October 1964, pp. 147–8.

52. In order, with the most affluent first, the 15 seats (Labour-held unless stated) were: Bedfordshire South East (Con.) 4.0% swing; Bristol South East 4.0%; Hayes and Harlington 4.5%; Birmingham Perry Barr (Con. gain) −0.6%; Gosport and Fareham (Con.) 3.4%; Coventry East 4.1%; Enfield East 4.3%; Wellingborough (Lab. gain) 0.7%; Coventry South (Lab. gain) 3.3%; Bristol North East (Con.) 1.4%; Derbyshire South East (Lab. gain) 0.8%; Swindon 6.8%; Erith and Crayford 3.6%; Luton (Lab. gain) 5.9%; Gloucester 1.6%.

53. The six 'affluent-tenant seats outside Birmingham were Bristol North West (Con.) 0.9% swing; Dagenham 4.1%; Romford 4.9%; Thurrock 3.4%; Norwich North 0.7%; Plymouth Sutton (Con.) 5.5%.

54. 'Thoughts on a Close Election', CRD memorandum, 23 October 1964, p. 13: CRD 2/48/85.

55. M. Steed, 'An Analysis of the Results', in Butler and King, *1964*, pp. 357–8.
56. R. Rose, *The Times*, 19 October 1964; H. Berrington, 'The General Election of 1964', *Journal of the Royal Statistical Society*, 49: 1 (1965), pp. 29–32.
57. D. Butler and D. Stokes, *Political Change in Britain: The Evolution of Electoral Choice* (London, 1974 edn), pp. 369–88. Findings in this seminal work were based upon the British Election Survey.
58. Butler and Stokes, *Political Change*, pp. 296–9.
59. 'Voters and the 1964 General Election', report prepared by Market Analysis Ltd, spring 1964, CCO 180/11/2/1. This report was based on interviews with nearly 2000 voters carried out in January and February 1964.
60. S. Fielding, ' "White heat" and White Collars: the Evolution of "Wilsonism", in Coopey, Fielding and Tiratsoo (eds), *The Wilson Governments*, pp. 34–7.
61. *The Economist*, 20 June 1964.
62. Butler and Stokes, *Political Change*, pp. 351–64.
63. Home, *Way the Wind Blows*, pp. 214–15. Shortly before the election, six out of ten voters rated Wilson a good leader of his party, whereas those who wanted Home to remain in office were no greater in number than those who felt he should resign (Gallup, *The Gallup International Public Opinion Polls*, vol. 1, September–October 1964, pp. 762 and 773).
64. D. Howell, 'Wilson and History', *Twentieth-Century British History*, 4: 2 (1993), p. 182.
65. 'Thoughts on Election', CRD memo, 23 October 1964, p. 2.
66. Home, *Way the Wind Blows*, p. 215.
67. Margach, *Abuse of Power*, p. 131.
68. 'General Election 1964', Final Report by the General Secretary, NEC Minutes, 25 Nov. 1964.
69. Cited in J. Ramsden, *The Making of Conservative Party Policy: The Conservative Research Department since 1929* (London, 1980), pp. 225–6.
70. 'Voters and the Election', Market Analysis Ltd, CCO180/11/2/1.

Notes to the Conclusion

1. Richard Law MP, cited in Harriet Jones, 'Conservative Party and the Welfare State', p. 392.
2. Boyle to Butler, 15 November 1960: Boyle Papers, 660/22515.
3. 'Retreat from Politics', *Socialist Commentary*, March 1958, p. 3; 'British Electoral Behaviour', *Socialist Commentary*, May 1962, p. 10. See also R. Titmuss, *The Irresponsible Society* (London, 1960).
4. Archbishop Fisher to Macmillan, 28 January 1960; to Butler, 16 February 1960: Butler Papers, G35, ff. 39–43.
5. Davenport, *The Split Society*, p. 19.

Notes*

6. Williamson, *Temper of the Times*, p. 134.
7. Simmonds, 'Conservatives and the Housing Question', esp. pp. 3–6, 14 and 445–7.
8. *The Times*, 11 June 1963.
9. *Conservatism Lost? Conservatism Regained*, n.d. [1963]: copy in Butler Papers, G41.

Select Bibliography

Manuscript Sources

Private Papers

Edward Boyle (University of Leeds).
Patrick Buchan-Hepburn (Churchill College, Cambridge).
R. A. Butler (Trinity College, Cambridge).
Harry Crookshank diary (Bodleian Library, Oxford).
Anthony Crosland (London School of Economics).
Anthony Eden (Birmingham University Library).
Earl of Kilmuir (Churchill College, Cambridge).
Selwyn Lloyd (Churchill College, Cambridge).
Walter Monckton (Bodleian Library, Oxford).
Reginald Maudling (Churchill College, Cambridge).
*Harold Macmillan (Bodleian Library, Oxford).
Lord Swinton (Churchill College, Cambridge).
Lord Woolton diary (Bodleian Library, Oxford).

*Correspondence with Lady Ava Waverley only; diaries and papers not fully available.

Public Record Office, Kew

Cabinet (CAB).
Ministry of Education (ED).
Housing and Local Government (HLG).
Prime Minister's office (PREM).
Treasury (T).

Party Political Records

Conservative party
    Research Department.
    Central Office (Bodleian Library, Oxford)

Labour party
    NEC minutes.
    Shadow Cabinet minutes.

Parliamentary Committee minutes.
Parliamentary Party minutes.
Annual Conference proceedings.
(All held at the National Museum of Labour History, Manchester.)

See also party election manifestos and associated publications such as
Tribune, Socialist Commentary, New Left Review, Labour Organiser, The Spectator, Conservative Agents' Journal.

Official publications

Hansard, *Parliamentary Debates*, fifth series.
Cmd 8996, *Houses: The Next Step* (1953).
Cmd 9663, *Committee of Enquiry into the Cost of the National Health Service* (1956).
Cmd 1417, *The Economic Implications of Full Employment* (1956).
Cmnd 604, *Secondary Education For All: A New Drive* (1958).

Newspapers and Periodicals

Daily Mail.
Daily Mirror.
Daily Telegraph.
The Economist.
The Guardian.
Manchester Guardian.
News Chronicle.
New Statesman.
The Observer.
Private Eye.
Sunday Times.
The Times.
Yorkshire Post.

Memoirs, Diaries and Contemporary Writing

(Place of publication is London, unless otherwise stated).

Abrams, Mark and Rose, Richard, *Must Labour Lose?* (Harmondsworth, 1960).
Benn, Tony, *Out of the Wilderness: Diaries 1963–67* (1987).
Bevins, Reginald, *The Greasy Pole* (1965).
Boyd-Carpenter, John, *Way of Life* (1980).

Butler, Lord, *The Art of the Possible* (1971).

Cairncross, A. (ed.), *The Robert Hall Diaries, 1947–53* (1989).

Callaghan, James, *Time and Chance* (1987).

Castle, Barbara, *Fighting All the Way* (1993).

Chandos, Viscount, *The Memoirs of Lord Chandos* (1962).

Churchill, Randolph, *The Rise and Fall of Sir Anthony Eden* (1959).

——, *The Fight for the Tory Leadership* (1964).

Clark, William, *From Three Worlds: Memoirs* (1986).

Crosland, C. A. R., *The Future of Socialism* (1956).

Cockett, R. (ed.), *My Dear Max: The Letters of Brendan Bracken to Lord Beaverbrook, 1925–1958* (1990).

Colville, John, *The Fringes of Power: Downing Street Diaries 1939–1955* (1985).

Dalton, Hugh, *Memoirs, 1945–60: High Tide and After* (1962).

Davenport, Nicholas, *The Split Society* (1964).

Eden, Sir Anthony, *Full Circle* (1960).

Evans, Harold (ed.), *Downing Street Diary: The Macmillan Years 1957–63* (1981).

Fairlie, Henry, *The Life of Politics* (1968).

Hailsham, Lord, *The Door Wherein I Went* (1975).

——, *A Sparrow's Flight: Memoirs* (1990).

Healey, Denis, *The Time of My Life* (1989).

Hill, Lord, *Both Sides of the Hill* (1964).

Home, Lord, *The Way the Wind Blows* (1976).

Jay, Douglas, *Change and Fortune: A Political Record* (1980).

Jenkins, Roy, *A Life at the Centre* (1991).

Kilmuir, Lord, *Political Adventure: The Memoirs of the Earl of Kilmuir* (1964).

Koestler, Arthur (ed.), *Suicide of a Nation? An Enquiry into the State of Britain* (1964).

Macmillan, Harold, *Memoirs*, vol. III: *Tides of Fortune, 1945–55* (1969).

——, vol. IV: *Riding the Storm, 1956–59* (1971).

——, vol. V: *Pointing the Way, 1959–61* (1972).

——, vol. VI: *At the End of the Day, 1961–63* (1973).

Maudling, Reginald, *Memoirs* (1978).

Middleton, Drew, *The British* (1957).

Moorhouse, Geoffrey, *Britain in the Sixties: The Other England* (Harmondsworth, 1964).

Moran, Lord, *Winston Churchill: The Struggle for Survival, 1940–65* (1965).

Morgan, J. (ed.), *The Backbench Diaries of Richard Crossman, 1951–64* (1981).

Pimlott B. (ed.), *The Political Diary of Hugh Dalton, 1918–40, 1945–60* (1986).

Sampson, Anthony, *Anatomy of Britain* (1962).

Shanks, Michael, *The Stagnant Society* (Harmondsworth, 1961).

Shonfield, Andrew, *British Economic Policy since the War* (Harmondsworth, 1958).

Stacey, Margaret, *Tradition and Change: A Study of Banbury* (Oxford, 1960).

Swinton, Earl, *Sixty Years of Power: Some Memories of the Men who have Wielded It* (1966).

Thomas, Hugh (ed.), *The Establishment* (1959).

Watkinson, Harold, *Turning Points: A Record of our Times* (Salisbury, 1986).

Winstone, R. (ed.), *Tony Benn: Years of Hope. Diaries, Letters and Papers, 1940–62* (1994).
Woolton, Lord, *The Memoirs of the Rt Hon. Earl of Woolton* (1959).
Zweig, Ferdinand, *The Worker in an Affluent Society: Family Life and Industry* (1961).

Biographical Writing

Birkenhead, Lord, *The Prof in Two Worlds: The Official Life of Professor F. A. Lindemann, Viscount Cherwell* (1961).
——, *Walter Monckton: The Life of Viscount Monckton of Brenchley* (1969).
Campbell, J., *Nye Bevan and the Mirage of British Socialism* (1987).
——, *Edward Heath* (1993).
Carlton, D., *Anthony Eden: A Biography* (1981).
Cosgrave, P., *R. A. Butler* (1981).
Crosland, S., *Tony Crosland* (1982).
Fisher, N., *Iain Macleod* (1973).
——, *Harold Macmillan: A Biography* (1982).
Gold, A. (ed.), *Edward Boyle: His Life by His Friends* (1991).
Goodman, G., *The Awkward Warrior, Frank Cousins: His Life and Times* (1979).
Harris, K., *Attlee* (1982).
Horne, A., *Macmillan*, vol. I: *1894–1956* (1988).
——, *Macmillan*, vol. II: *1957–1986* (1989).
Howard, A., *RAB: The Life of R. A. Butler* (1987).
——, *Crossman: The Pursuit of Power* (1990).
Hutchinson, G., *The Last Edwardian at No. 10* (1980).
Pimlott, B., *Hugh Dalton* (1985).
——, *Harold Wilson* (1992).
Rhodes James, R., *Anthony Eden* (1986).
Roth, A., *Enoch Powell: Tory Tribune* (1970).
Rothwell, V., *Anthony Eden* (Manchester, 1992).
Sampson, A., *Macmillan: A Study in Ambiguity* (1967).
Shepherd, R., *Iain Macleod* (1994).
Thorpe, D. R., *The Uncrowned Prime Ministers* (1980).
——, *Selwyn Lloyd* (1989).
Turner, J., *Macmillan* (1994).
Williams, P., *Hugh Gaitskell* (Oxford, 1982 edn).
Young, K., *Sir Alec Douglas-Home* (1970).

Other Secondary Works

Baldwin, P., *The Politics of Social Solidarity: Class Bases of the European Welfare State, 1875–1975* (Cambridge, 1990).
Bogdanor, V. and Skidelsky, R. (eds), *The Age of Affluence 1951–64* (1970).

Brittan, S., *Steering the Economy: The Role of the Treasury* (Harmondsworth, 1971).

Burnett, J., *A Social History of Housing 1815–1985* (1986 edn).

Butler, D., *The British General Election of 1951* (1952).

——, *The British General Election of 1955* (1955).

Butler, D. and Rose, R., *The British General Election of 1959* (1960).

Butler, D. and King, A., *The British General Election of 1964* (1965).

Butler, D. and Stokes, D., *Political Change in Britain: The Evolution of Electoral Choice* (1974 edn).

Cockerell, M., *Live from Number Ten – Prime Ministers and Television* (1988).

Cockett, R., *Thinking the Unthinkable: Think Tanks and the Economic Counter Revolution, 1931–83* (1994).

Coopey, R., Fielding, S. and Tiratsoo, N. (eds), *The Wilson Governments, 1964–1970* (1993).

Crafts, N. F. R., Duckham B. and Woodward, N. (eds), *The British Economy since 1945* (Oxford, 1991).

Cronin, J., *The Politics of State Expansion: War, State and Society in Twentieth-Century Britain* (1991).

Dow, J. C. R., *The Management of the British Economy, 1945–60* (Cambridge, 1964).

Dutton, D., *British Politics since 1945: The Rise and Fall of Consensus* (Oxford, 1991).

Fenwick, I. G. K., *The Comprehensive School, 1944–70* (1976).

Gamble, A., *Britain in Decline: Economic Policy, Political Strategy and the British State* (1985 edn).

Gladstone, D. (ed.), *British Social Welfare: Past, Present and Future* (1995).

Glennerster, H., *British Social Policy since 1945* (Oxford, 1995).

Goldthorpe, J. H., Lockwood, D. *et al.*, *The Affluent Worker: Political Attitudes and Behaviour* (1968).

Gorst, T., Johnman, L. and Lucas, W. S. (eds), *Postwar Britain, 1945–64: Themes and Perspectives* (1989).

——, *Contemporary British History, 1931–1961: Politics and the Limits of Policy* (1991).

Harris, N., *Competition and the Corporate Society: British Conservatives, the State and Industry 1945–64* (1972).

Hennessy, P., and Seldon, A. (eds), *Ruling Performance: British Governments from Attlee to Thatcher* (Oxford, 1987).

Howard, A. and West, R., *The Making of the Prime Minister* (1965).

Howell, D., *British Social Democracy: A Study in Development and Decay* (1976).

Irving, C., Hall, R. and Wallington, J., *Scandal '63: A Study of the Profumo Affair* (1963).

Jenkins, M., *Bevanism: Labour's High Tide* (Nottingham, 1979).

Jones, Helen, *Health and Society in Twentieth-Century Britain* (1994).

Kavanagh, D. and Morris, P., *Consensus Politics from Attlee to Thatcher* (Oxford, 1989).

Knight, C., *The Making of Tory Education Policy in Post-War Britain* (Brighton, 1990).

Kogan, M., *The Politics of Education* (Harmondsworth, 1971).

Lamb, R., *The Failure of the Eden Government* (1987).
——, *The Macmillan Years, 1957–63: The Emerging Truth* (1995).
Lewis, P., *The Fifties* (1978).
Lowe, Rodney, *The Welfare State in Britain since 1945* (1993).
Lowe, Roy, *Education in the Post-War Years: A Social History* (1988).
McKenzie, R. T. and Silver, A., *Angels in Marble: Working-Class Conservatives in Urban England* (1968).
McKie, D. and Cook, C. (eds), *The Decade of Disillusionment: British Politics in the 1960s* (1972).
Margach, J., *The Abuse of Power: The War between Downing Street and the Media, from Lloyd George to Callaghan* (1978).
Middlemas, K., *Power, Competition and the State*, vols I and II (1986 and 1990).
Morgan, K. O., *The People's Peace: British History, 1945–1989* (Oxford, 1990).
Newton, S. and Porter, D., *Modernisation Frustrated: The Politics of Industrial Decline since 1900* (1988).
Nugent, N. and King, R. (eds), *The British Right: Conservative and Right-Wing Politics in Britain* (Farnborough, 1977).
Peden, G. C., *British Economic and Social Policy: From Lloyd George to Margaret Thatcher* (Hemel Hempstead, 1991 edn).
Pelling, H., *A History of British Trade Unionism* (1987 edn).
Pimlott, B. and Cook, C. (eds), *Trade Unions in British Politics* (1991 edn).
Pollard, S., *The Development of the British Economy, 1914–80* (1983).
Proudfoot, M., *British Politics and Government, 1951–1970: A Study of an Affluent Society* (1984).
Ramsden, J., *The Making of Conservative Party Policy: The Conservative Research Department since 1929* (1980).
——, *The Age of Churchill and Eden, 1940–1957* (1995).
——, *The Winds of Change: Macmillan to Heath, 1957–1975* (1996).
Ryder, J. and Silver, H., *Modern English Society: History and Structure, 1850–1970* (1970).
Seldon, A., *Churchill's Indian Summer: The Conservative Government, 1951–55* (1981).
Seldon, A. and Ball, S. (eds), *Conservative Century: The Conservative Party since 1900* (Oxford, 1994).
Short, J. R., *Housing in Britain: The Postwar Experience* (1982).
Simon, B., *Education and the Social Order, 1940–1990* (1991).
Sked, A. and Cook, C., *Post-War Britain: A Political History* (Harmondsworth, 1993 edn).
Taylor, R., *The Trade Union Question in British Politics: Government and Unions since 1945* (Oxford, 1993).
Thompson, A., *The Day Before Yesterday: An Illustrated History of Britain from Attlee to Macmillan* (1971).
Timmins, N., *The Five Giants: A Biography of the Welfare State* (1995).
Tiratsoo, N., *Reconstruction, Affluence and Labour Politics: Coventry 1945–60* (1990).
Webster, C., *The Health Services since the War*, vol. I (1988).
Williamson, B., *The Temper of the Times: British Society since World War II* (Oxford, 1990).

Worswick, G. D. N. and Ady, P. H., *The British Economy in the Nineteen-Fifties* (Oxford, 1962).
Young, W., *The Profumo Affair: Aspects of Conservatism* (1963).

Journal Articles

Alderman, K., 'Harold Macmillan's "Night of the Long Knives"', *Contemporary Record*, 6: 2 (1992).
Barnes, J. and Seldon, A., '1951–64: 13 Wasted Years?', *Contemporary Record*, 1: 2 (1987).
Crewe, I., 'The Politics of "Affluent" and "Traditional" Workers: An Aggregate Data Analysis', *British Journal of Political Science*, 3: 1 (1973).
Jefferys, K., 'British Politics and the Road to 1964', *Contemporary Record*, 9: 1 (1995).
Lowe, R., 'Resignation at the Treasury: the Social Services Committee and the Failure to Reform the Welfare State, 1955–57', *Journal of Social Policy*, 18: 4 (1989).
Potts, A., 'The Sunderland South By-Election of 13 May 1953 in the Context of Conservative Recovery', *Durham University Journal*, 84 (1992).
Rollings, N., '"Poor Mr Butskell: A Short Life, Wrecked by Schizophrenia"?', *Twentieth-Century British History*, 5: 2 (1994).
Symposium: '1961–64: Did the Conservatives Lose Direction?', *Contemporary Record*, 2: 5 (1989).

Unpublished Theses

B. Brivati, 'The Campaign for Democratic Socialism, 1959–64', London University PhD (1992).
M. Donnelly, 'Labour Politics and the Affluent Society, 1951–1964', Surrey University PhD (1994).
M. D. Kandiah, 'Lord Woolton's Chairmanship of the Conservative Party, 1946–51', Exeter University PhD (1992).
Harriet Jones, 'The Conservative Party and the Welfare State, 1942–55', London University PhD (1992).
A. Simmonds, 'Conservative Governments and the Housing Question, 1951–59', Leeds University PhD (1995).

Index

Index